THE BRITISH JOURNAL OF POLITICS & INTERNATIONAL RELATIONS

Volume 10   *Number 1*   *February 2008*

Economic Interests and European Integration
Edited by David Howarth and Tal Sadeh

INTRODUCTION

ARTICLES

doi: 10.1111/j.1467-856x.2007.00314.x

Economic Interests and the European Union: A Catalyst for European Integration or a Hindrance?

Tal Sadeh and David Howarth

Keywords: economic interests; European integration theory; European Union; interest groups

This special issue of *The British Journal of Politics & International Relations* focuses on the role of economic interests in European integration. Economic interest groups are defined as representative associations that pursue—as their overriding objective—the material economic interests of their members. They include peak and sectoral business associations, trade unions, professional associations, farmers' unions and associations representing small-scale businesses, shopkeepers and tradespeople. Economic interests can also include individual companies that lobby governments directly. Groups that represent political actors which do not focus explicitly on the material interests of their members and economic goals would be excluded from this definition: for example, women's groups as well as non-governmental associations that focus on environmental or human rights issues.

Existing studies of the role of economic interests in European integration fall into one or more of four camps, none of which has entered into a sustained analysis of the role of all major economic interests and European integration. First, there are studies where the role of economic interests is part of and is seen in terms of a particular theory or analytical approach that makes broader claims about European integration. Andrew Moravcsik (1998), notably, examines a limited range of economic interests in the context of his liberal intergovernmentalist study and understands national policy formation in terms of competing economic, and principally business, interests. Neo-functionalists emphasise the role of interests that operate supranationally and independently of the activities of national governments to shape EU-level policy developments. For neo-functionalists, economic interests proactively support the successive integration of various sectors of the economy in order to diminish the transaction costs created from the cross-border movement of goods, services, capital and people. Neo-Gramscians (van Apeldoorn 2002; Bieler 2001) focus upon the pro-integration role of transnational business and financial interests and the complex positioning of trade unions.

In the second camp, there are studies of a broad range of interest groups operating at the EU level but not economic interests per se. Justin Greenwood and Mark Aspinwall's (1998) edited volume explores EU-level policy-making as a collective action problem involving various interests. Greenwood (2007) has undertaken the most comprehensive study to date on interest representation and EU-level policy-making. In the third camp, there are studies that are focused upon a particular kind of economic interest (and principally with regard to EU-level policy-making)—notably there is a growing body of literature which focuses specifically on the lobbying activities of business groups at the EU level (Coen 2002 and 2004; Greenwood 2007). In the fourth camp, there are studies that explore preference formation and the role of one or more economic interests in national-level policy-making (in one or several countries) on EU policy developments. These studies almost always focus upon a single policy area. Numerous examples can be provided from the political studies literature on Economic and Monetary Union (EMU). Leila Talani (2000), Amy Verdun (2000) and Jeffrey Frieden (2002) examine the positions of a variety of economic interests in important EU member states on EMU. Daphné Josselin (2001) and Andreas Bieler (2006) centre their analyses more specifically on the policy positions on EMU of trade unions in a limited number of member states.

The objective of this special issue is to bring together recent analyses of the role of economic interests in various areas of EU policy and European integration more broadly (via national preference formation *and/or* EU-level policy-making). In their articles, the participating authors have been called upon to focus critically on the role of economic interests in the context of their analyses of specific EU-level policy and legal developments. The six articles take varying approaches to the direction of causality in the interest group–state–EU nexus. Economic interest groups shape the EU and the national interest of its member states but the EU and its member states also shape the opportunities facing economic interest groups. There is an inevitable risk involved in parsimoniously reducing economic interests (their preferences) to the independent variable (as in Frieden 2002) without treating the often crucial role of national and EU-level intervening variables. Thus the four articles of the special edition (by Quaglia, Leblond, Dür and Bieler) that treat the preferences of economic interests as an independent variable do so critically, while taking into account the relevance of other intervening variables. The articles by Bieler and Hennessy treat the preferences of economic interests on EU-level policy developments as an intervening variable, reflecting structural economic variables and national policy frameworks. Smith's article explores the influence of economic interests—*qua* concentrated interests—as a dependent variable determined by the structures of the EU policy-making process.

In light of the contributions to this special issue, the influence of economic interest groups on national policy-making seems to be case specific and circumstantial. Certain economic interests (for example, pension funds) are so influential that some of them become almost inseparable from the state. However, economic interests are less likely to become influential when broad institutional questions are negotiated, rather than specific rules with a clear cost–benefit balance. And it is especially when they feel challenged by the state that they turn their efforts to EU-level lobbying. The record of economic interest groups in EU policy-making appears also to be mixed. They are influential when they enjoy privileged institutionalised interactions with a policy-making node, such as European Parliament (EP) committees. However, access to the EP has recently become less privileged and institutional advocacy has become more contested, to the disadvantage of interest groups. Many economic interest groups actually obstruct the legislative process with seemingly inconsistent behaviour: they are in favour of European integration in general, but end up lobbying against concrete pieces of legislation if they are costly to them. However, when it comes to the EU's external trade policy, economic interest groups appear to call the shots.

In his article, Patrick Leblond argues that the behaviour of many economic interest groups appears inconsistent. They are in favour of European integration in general, but end up lobbying against concrete pieces of legislation if they are costly to them. Thus, economic interest groups may actually obstruct the EU legislative process. The preferences and activities of private economic interests explain progress as well as stagnation in European economic integration. When integration advances it is an alleged testimony to the hands of interests that press governments to harmonise laws, regulations and standards, in order to reduce the costs of cross-border transactions. When integration does not proceed it is presumably because governments yield to economic interests that expect to lose out because they face greater adjustment costs to the new rules. However, Leblond argues that the fate of European integration is not only decided by a struggle between competing interests, but is plagued by a seeming inconsistency in the behaviour of economic interests. In many instances these interests derail attempts to harmonise rules and standards across the EU which they initially supported.

Leblond asserts that this seeming inconsistency is a result of uncertainty on the part of economic interests with regard to the costs and benefits of integration. This uncertainty engulfs EU integration proposals at their preliminary stage, but once the Commission has tabled a draft piece of legislation this 'fog' lifts and the terms of integration become more concrete. At this point certain groups realise that the proposed legislation is not beneficial to them. Thus, they turn against it or lobby for amendments and exceptions, even if they initially supported integration in this particular policy area. If the adjustment costs outweigh the lobbying costs and enough of these interests mobilise and lobby against the proposal, then it is likely to fail.

Leblond defines two forms of integration failure. Direct integration failure occurs when a proposed piece of legislation is eliminated, such as the Software Patent Directive, which the EP rejected in July 2005. Indirect integration failure takes place when the adopted legislation contains so many loopholes that it ends up formalising the status quo, such as the Takeover Directive, which the EP adopted in December 2003 with some key amendments. Leblond expects direct failure when private economic interests polarise transnationally on a given policy issue, and indirect failure when interests polarise on a national basis.

Leblond's analysis raises a number of interesting implications. First, economic interests may support greater integration in principle but not promote it actively. Second, the actual impetus for integration may come more from a policy entrepreneur, such as the European Commission, than from interest groups. Finally, the potential for direct failure of integration suggests that in many policy areas where there exists European legislation, the degree of integration may be more formal than substantial.

© *2008 The Authors. Journal compilation* © *2008 Political Studies Association*
BJPIR, 2008, 10(1)

Andreas Dür argues that economic interest groups determine much of the EU's external trade policy. Several existing accounts of the making of EU trade policy stress the relatively large independence of decision-makers from societal interests. The argument is that the transfer of policy authority to the European level increases economic interests' uncertainty about who decides and what is being decided, and thus enhances the autonomy of public actors in shaping EU trade policies. This insulation, so the argument goes, was intended to strengthen the state *vis-à-vis* society (the collusive delegation argument), and explains the shift from protectionism to liberalisation witnessed since the 1960s. The autonomy that decision-makers gained as a result of delegation ostensibly allowed them to promote the interests of the general public against the resistance of protectionist forces.

However, Dür contests these assertions, maintaining that little empirical research has been undertaken to support them, and that the few studies of interest group involvement in EU trade policy-making report ambiguous results. Dür studies the EU's participation in two episodes of world trade talks—the Kennedy Round (1964–67) within the framework of the General Agreement on Tariffs and Trade (GATT), and the Doha Development Agenda (2001 onwards) of the World Trade Organisation (WTO). In both cases he expects that the preconditions were ideal for collusive delegation to work, and consequently, that on at least some issues public actors overrode opposition from societal interests when pushing for trade liberalisation. However, he finds that on the contrary, the EU's negotiating position was consistent with the demands voiced by both broad business associations and sectoral groups across a large number of issues. Even in situations in which EU governments have to find issue linkages to come to an agreement, the resulting trade policies tend to be tailor-made to avoid the imposition of concentrated costs on constituencies in any member country.

Dür confesses that his research cannot establish that economic interests actually determine EU trade policies, but he identifies a few factors that indicate the influence of domestic actors in shaping these policies. Economic interests enjoy excellent access to decision-makers in trade issues, and indeed consider themselves to be influential. Furthermore, it is difficult to explain the similarities between the EU's negotiation position and societal demands without recourse to economic interests-based explanations. All of this amounts to 'circumstantial evidence' against the collusive delegation argument and in favour of the importance of domestic input into European trade policies. Dür's conclusions suggest that the EU liberalised trade not because it is a 'good policy', but because exporters, importers and retailers pushed for openness. This raises concerns about the legitimacy of the EU's trade policy, if various interests are unequally represented.

Lucia Quaglia finds that interest groups have less influence when broad institutional questions are negotiated as opposed to specific legislation with a clearer cost–benefit balance. Regulation and supervision of financial services in the EU has become one of the most active areas of EU policy-making, undergoing significant change between 1999 and 2005. During this period the Lamfalussy framework was negotiated and implemented, the non-legally binding Basel 2 agreement was negotiated with non-EU member states and then the content of Basel 2 was incorporated into EU legislation through the Capital Requirement Directive (CRD).

Quaglia examines how the preferences of financial interest groups shaped the national input of the UK and Germany into EU and international policy-making processes and the final output in these three reforms. The UK and Germany are the two countries with the largest financial sectors in the EU, and have played crucial roles in the three reforms under consideration. Moreover, these two countries experienced important institutional and policy changes in financial service regulation and supervision in 1998 and 2002, respectively.

Quaglia finds that financial interests are more involved when specific rules are negotiated and are more influential when the domestic distribution of power gives them preferential access to policy-makers. In contrast, financial interests have little interest in broad institutional questions. Thus, whenever the policy discussions concern institutional issues, such as supranational delegation and scope of governance, bureaucratic preferences are more powerful in defining the national position in international and EU fora.

Quaglia admits that extrapolating these findings to other policies can be difficult, because the financial sector has traditionally been regarded as influential in policy-making, and because public authorities value the expertise, data gathering and first-hand experience provided by the industry, which strengthens its influence. Most financial interest groups are also at least partly foreign-owned and thus are not purely national. This distinguishes them from many other industries. However, Quaglia's findings support the notion that public authorities do not define the national interest and policy input independently of the preferences of financial interest groups.

Mitchell Smith finds that economic interest groups are influential in the EU legislative process when they enjoy privileged institutionalised interactions with a policy-making node, such as EP committees. The development of EU policy-making is often depicted as a favourable shift in opportunity structures for diffuse interests. The EU institutions, which seek to advance their own interests in deeper integration, are argued both to constitute effective access points and to stimulate the organisation of diffuse interests at the European level. The European Parliament's Environment Committee (ENVI) has been particularly consequential, delivering the institutional support of the full EP to legislative outcomes more favourable to environmental interests.

However, Smith argues that support from ENVI is no longer guaranteed for environmentalists seeking costly regulations for producers. ENVI helped sustain the EP's commitment to environmental interests in the case of the End-of-Life Vehicles (ELV) directive, which was adopted in September 2000, but not in the case of REACH, a regulatory framework for the chemicals sector adopted by the EP and Council in December 2006.

Smith argues that the value of an access point for organised interest groups depends on the extent to which they have privileged institutionalised interactions with a node in the policy-making apparatus (asymmetry) and on the extent to which institutional actors in the policy-making process defer to the particular institutional node (deference). Deference to EP committees (the acceptance by EP plenary of committee cues) is less likely when legislation involves a multitude of policy areas and cue givers, and conflict between committees.

ENVI members were able to frame the ELVs issue as a test for the Parliament's ability to serve as a voice of the public interest and to resist private interests. These appeals invoked the Parliament's collective interest and sustained deference to the ENVI position in plenary. In contrast, REACH was transformed from a piece of environmental legislation to a measure focused on the competitiveness of Europe's chemicals sector. In the course of the legislative process, other EP committees were granted enhanced status in generating the committee report for REACH. This opened up critical points of access for organised industrial interests to committees serving as cues to the full parliament, eliminating any asymmetry in favour of organised environmental interests.

Andreas Bieler argues that trade unions turn their efforts to EU-level lobbying when they feel challenged by the state. Trade unions have come under great pressure as a result of monetary integration in Europe, because differences in employment conditions within the EU have become more transparent, and interest rates and exchange rates can no longer be used to prevent lower wages, benefits and social standards. What Bieler sees as EMU's neo-liberal macroeconomic regime, which is committed to price stability, and the Lisbon strategy, which promotes employment through a deregulation of labour markets, further intensify the pressures on labour. Bieler analyses the position of trade unions on EMU, and the efforts that they direct at the European level to defend the interests of their members. Is it possible that unions in Europe may be part of a future counter-neo-liberal alliance within the EU?

Bieler introduces a neo-Gramscian, critical international political economy (IPE) perspective. He understands labour's role in the processes of transnational restructuring by conceptualising it as a potential international actor without neglecting specific national institutional set-ups. Applied to a comparative analysis of British and Swedish trade unions, he finds that labour employed in transnational business in both countries was in favour of EMU. By contrast, labour in national-oriented business opposed EMU because of its deflationary bias. However, the views of transnationally oriented labour diverged over the emphasis on European co-operation. British unions with a transnational focus continue to reject neo-liberalism and emphasise developments at the European level. In contrast, unions representing labour in transnationally focused economic sectors in Sweden have started to accept core neo-liberal concepts and rely on their co-operation with transnational capital and the national government. This is explained by the poor access of British trade unions to national decision-makers, and by the improved influence of Swedish unions on policy-making compared with what the EU institutional set-up offers. Thus, Swedish labour is unlikely to be a driving force in any future Euro-Keynesian project before the unions' influence at the European level develops further.

Alexandra Hennessy takes the approach that certain economic interests are so influential that it is difficult to separate them from the state. She examines the preferences of powerful pension funds as an intermediary variable that reflects national pension systems—Bismarckian and the Beveridgean. Due to unfavourable demographic developments, stretched budgets and swelling non-wage labour costs, the importance of employer-sponsored pensions is growing. Given that cutbacks of social security pensions tend to be politically toxic, most European governments face mounting pressure to improve access to second pillar pensions. However, labour unions tend to disapprove of the non-egalitarian properties of occupational plans since they do not extend the kind of inviolable social rights that state-sponsored pensions provide and may be too easily abused by the sponsoring firm. Legislative activity by the EU on pensions is mounting, and has a major domestic impact on economic interactions between governments, occupational pension plan sponsors and beneficiaries.

Hennessy argues that in 1991 uncertainty about the beliefs of each group of countries, and inability to distinguish Bismarckian states that were able to adjust to EU pension policies from those that did not, resulted in bargaining breakdown. However, EMU raised the costs for Bismarckian states of failure to agree on a single pension market. Thus, the Bismarckian states signalled their costs to their Beveridgean counterparts. As a result, the member states managed to adopt a politically efficient—albeit economically incomplete—pension fund directive in June 2003. Thus, her account shows how the power of labour unions, as reflected in national pension institutions, intervenes between financial globalisation and demographic change on the one hand and EU pension policy on the other.

In the conclusion to this special issue, Amy Verdun examines how the above six articles contribute to our understanding of economic interest groups in the context of European integration. She does this along four themes: (1) the role of economic interest groups in national preference formation; (2) the role of economic interest groups in EU policy-making; (3) the effect of the EU on the economic interest groups; and (4) the role of economic interest groups on the process of European integration.

Based on this examination, Verdun concludes that economic interest groups do not *a priori* act in favour of European integration, even if they have a general interest in integration. Economic interest groups seek to influence both national and EU-level actors and institutions, but their influence depends on the support that they receive from national governments, on the proximity of the draft legislation to their preferences and on the interest of EU institutions in consulting them on technical standards. Finally, an increasing amount of legislation is made at the EU level and economic interest groups can turn to this policy-making arena to secure their interests.

The articles of this special issue originated as papers submitted to a project of the Political Economy Interest Section of the European Union Studies Association (EUSA), launched at the EUSA's Ninth Biennial Conference which took place in Austin, Texas in Spring 2005. A workshop, organised by the editors of this special issue, followed in April 2006 at the University of Edinburgh. We are grateful to the British Academy, the University Association for Contemporary European Studies (UACES), the University of Edinburgh and the European Commission for supporting this workshop. Two panels, held at EUSA's Tenth Biennial Conference in Montreal, Canada in Spring 2007, presented work in progress. The work of several participants in this EUSA Interest Section project cannot be included in this special issue. We nonetheless wish to extend our gratitude for the vital intellectual contribution of these participants to the project over the past two years. Equally crucial has been the generous contribution of five paper referees who must remain anonymous. The seven contributors to this special issue are to be congratulated both for their thought-provoking articles and for their patient co-operation in what has been a lengthy review process. A final note of thanks must be extended to the managing editor of BJPIR, Chris Pierson, who was supportive of the idea of a special issue on economic interests and the European Union from the early months of our project.

About the Authors

Tal Sadeh, Department of Political Science, Tel Aviv University, PO Box 39040, Tel Aviv 69978, Israel, email: *talsadeh@post.tau.ac.il*

David Howarth, Politics, SPS, University of Edinburgh, Adam Ferguson Building, 40 George Square, Edinburgh EH8 9LL, email: *d.howarth@ed.ac.uk*

Note

The authors wish to thank Amy Verdun for helpful comments that contributed to the content of this introduction.

Bibliography

Bieler, A. (2001) 'Questioning cognitivism and constructivism in IR theory: Reflections on the material structure of ideas', *Politics*, 21:2, 93–100.

Bieler, A. (2006) *The Struggle for a Social Europe: Trade Unions and EMU in Times of Global Restructuring* (Manchester: Manchester University Press).

Coen, D. (2002) 'Business interests and integration', in R. Bulme, D. Chambre and V. Wright (eds), *Collective Action in the European Union* (Paris: Science-Po Press), 255–272.

Coen, D. (2004) 'Environmental and business lobbying alliances in Europe: Learning from Washington?', in D. Levy and P. Newell (eds), *The Business of Global Environmental Governance* (1st edn) (Cambridge: MIT Press), 197–220.

Frieden, J. A. (2002) 'Real sources of European currency policy: Sectoral interests and European Monetary Integration', *International Organization*, 56:4, 831–860.

Greenwood, J. (2007) *Interest Representation in the European Union* (2nd edn) (Basingstoke: Palgrave Macmillan).

Greenwood, J. and Aspinwall, M. (eds) (1998) *Collective Action in the European Union: Interests and the New Politics of Associability* (London: Routledge).

Josselin, D. (2001) 'Trade unions for EMU: Sectoral preferences and political opportunities', *West European Politics*, 24:1, 55–74.

Moravcsik, A. (1998) *The Choice for Europe: Social Purpose and State Power from Messina to Maastricht* (Ithaca NY: Cornell University Press).

Talani, L. S. (2000) *Betting For and Against EMU. Who Wins and Who Loses in Italy and in the UK from the Process of European Monetary Integration* (Aldershot: Ashgate).

Van Apeldoorn, B. (2002) *Transnational Capitalism and the Struggle over European Integration* (London: Routledge).

Verdun, A. (2000) *European Responses to Globalization and Financial Market Integration* (London: Macmillan).

doi: 10.1111/j.1467-856x.2007.00315.x   *BJPIR: 2008 VOL 10, 9–26*

The Fog of Integration: Reassessing the Role of Economic Interests in European Integration

Patrick Leblond

The main theories of European economic integration argue that private economic interests provide the impetus and pressures for integration to move forward. Public policy analyses of the European Union's legislative process, however, show that intense lobbying by such interests can prevent legislative proposals from being adopted, even if economic interests were initially in favour of supranational legislation. How do we explain this apparent contradiction? The answer is that economic interests initially face great uncertainty as to the precise costs and benefits of integrating a particular policy area; only once the 'fog of integration' lifts—as a result of concrete legislative proposals being tabled by the Commission—are economic interests able to calculate these costs and benefits and, consequently, decide whether to lobby for or against the proposal. To provide a first-run validation of the argument, the article examines the cases of the Software Patent and Takeover directives.

Keywords: economic interests; European integration; standards harmonisation; uncertainty

Introduction

There appears to be a common belief among scholars of European economic integration that the latter proceeds as a result of private economic interests asking for the harmonisation of laws, regulations and standards in order to reduce the transaction costs associated with the movement of goods, services, capital and people across borders. When integration does not proceed forward, it is because member state governments prevent it from doing so, often as a result of domestic private economic interests preferring to maintain existing obstacles to cross-border economic exchanges. The reality is, however, different. There are many instances where private economic interests are initially in favour of integration but where the attempt to create supranational legislation that would harmonise rules and standards across the EU ends up failing as a result of fierce lobbying by economic interests. It should be noted that integration failure takes place when the status quo remains. As such, it can take two forms: a direct and an indirect one. Direct integration failure occurs with the elimination of the proposed legislation.[1] Indirect integration failure takes place when the adopted legislation contains so many loopholes, opt-outs or acceptable standards that it formally recognises the status quo.

An example of the first case of integration failure is that of the Software Patent Directive. On 6 July 2005, the European Parliament (EP) rejected the Commission's

proposed directive on the patentability of computer-implemented inventions ('Software Patent Directive')[2] by an overwhelming majority. This vote effectively put an end to the proposed legislation. An example of the second case of integration failure is the Takeover Directive. On 16 December 2003, the EP adopted the Commission's proposed directive on takeover bids ('Takeover Directive')[3] but with a number of key amendments. The Council of Ministers finally approved the Takeover Directive along with the EP's amendments on 21 April 2004. The problem with this agreement, which was implemented into national law in May 2006, is that it contains many opt-outs that greatly reduce its usefulness in fostering European economic integration. As such, it is generally considered a failure.

What do these examples of legislative failures mean for European integration and the theories that explain it? How can they be possible when, after all, business interests were originally supportive of the intent to harmonise standards and regulations in these fields as a way to promote further European economic integration? Such questions find no answers in existing theoretical approaches to regional integration. One reason for this situation may be because these approaches always assume that economic interests know clearly the benefits and costs of integration beforehand. But what happens if in fact they do not? How does it affect our understanding of European integration, both practically and theoretically? These are the questions that this article seeks to answer.

It does so by examining the apparent paradoxical relationship between economic (especially business) interests and European integration, whereby supranational legislation in a given policy area can fail even though there is originally support from economic interests for integrating this policy area. If the EP and Council are responsive to the opinions of economic interests, this means that over time certain groups decide to oppose integration in the form of legislation proposed by the European Commission. What causes this change of heart? The answer, this article will argue, is to be found in the initial fog (i.e. uncertainty) that surrounds EU integration proposals in terms of their costs and benefits for economic interests. But as the fog lifts and the terms of integration become more explicit, certain economic agents may realise that the proposed legislation that is on the table is not beneficial to their interests. Thus, they turn against it or lobby for amendments and exceptions, even if they initially supported integration in this particular policy area. If enough of these interests mobilise and lobby against the proposal, then it is likely to fail (directly or indirectly) at the EP and/or the Council.

This phenomenon may be more prevalent in reality than is commonly presumed by scholars of European integration and lobbying, who usually assume that economic interests are fully cognisant of the net benefits or costs of integration in a given sector right from the start and, consequently, that they will readily share this information with uncertain policy-makers through lobbying activities. Although it is true that economic interests will share the information they possess in a given policy area, this does not mean that they know what the costs and benefits of integration are or will be. These depend on the form that integration will take, i.e. which rules, regulations and standards will be part of the new supranational legislation. As a result, economic interests may support greater integration in principle but not promote it actively. Consequently, the actual impetus for integration may come more from a policy entrepreneur like the European Commission (Nugent 1995).

The article is structured as follows. The next section discusses the weaknesses of the main theoretical approaches to the study of economic interests and regional integration. The subsequent section presents the argument regarding the relationship between economic interests and European integration under the assumption that there is initially a fair degree of uncertainty surrounding interests' cost–benefit calculations. The following two sections examine in detail the cases of the Software Patent and Takeover directives, which are both integration failures but with different characteristics. The first one is an example of direct integration failure (i.e. no supranational legislation) whereas the second case is representative of cases of indirect integration failure (i.e. the formalisation of the status quo).[4] Moreover, the Software Directive case is representative of situations where economic interests are organised on a transnational basis while the case of the Takeover Directive is an example of instances where interests are organised nationally. As such, these two cases allow us to assess the merit of the argument as well as draw certain hypotheses for future research on EU integration. The final section concludes on the need of existing theories of European integration to revise their understanding of the role played by economic interests in European integration.

Economic Interests and Regional Economic Integration

The main theories of European integration give a prominent place to the role that economic interests play in the process. For neo-functionalists, economic interests are proactively supportive of the successive integration of various sectors of the economy across borders (usually through the harmonisation of regulations and standards) as a way to overcome the increasing transaction costs that arise from the international exchange of goods, services, capital and people. For liberal intergovernmentalists, domestic economic interests determine the positions of the member states on a given policy issue, whose outcome is determined by states' bargaining among themselves.

In his study of regional economic integration, Walter Mattli (1999) argues that the demand for integration comes from business interests that wish to reduce the transaction costs associated with cross-border trade. Transaction costs arise because of such obstacles as tariffs, quotas, different standards and regulations, different languages and cultures, etc. (see Mattli 1999, 47). Consequently, firms lobby for a new governance structure that fosters market integration (Mattli 1999, 49). This new 'governance structure' may include (over time) such things as 'common trade rules, common industrial standards, tax harmonisation, macroeconomic policy co-ordination and common social policies' (ibid.).

Even if Mattli's 'transaction-cost' approach is based on new institutional economics (Williamson 1985; North 1990), it can easily be compared to neo-functionalism (Haas 1958; Lindberg 1963). One of the key building blocks of neo-functionalism is the concept of functional spillover, whereby the integration of particular economic sectors across countries creates pressures for integration in related sectors (so as to

© 2008 The Author. Journal compilation © 2008 Political Studies Association
BJPIR, 2008, 10(1)

reduce transaction costs and, thereby, increase economic exchanges across borders). These pressures originate from economic interests which are adapting and benefiting from policy areas that are already integrated. This process is complemented by another parallel one: political spillover. In the latter, socioeconomic interests transfer their loyalties and activities to the supranational level because they realise that this is where they can best achieve their objectives. In turn, this political spillover leads to greater functional spillover. In this ratcheting-up process, regional integration becomes almost irreversible, not to say teleological.

One important difference between Mattli's approach to regional integration and neo-functionalism is the role given to supranational institutions. According to neo-functionalism, such institutions (or higher authorities) are key drivers (sponsors and guides) of integration, as long as they have some degree of autonomy. As for Mattli, supranational institutions are much weaker drivers of integration; it is the regional leader (or hegemon) that is the key to the supply of integration. The implicit recognition here is that states are the suppliers of integration. As such, they also have the ability to slow down or stop integration (see also Hoffmann 1966). Andrew Moravcsik (1993 and 1998) argues that states' position *vis-à-vis* integration is a function of the pressures they face from domestic societal (mainly economic) interests. The outcome of integration then depends on the intergovernmental bargaining that takes place between states, which is itself a question of state power. This is why Geoffrey Garrett (1992) argues that focusing solely on the functional aspects of international integration is insufficient. Instead, analysts need to take into account 'the distributional conflicts between states and the impact of power asymmetries on conflict resolution' (ibid., 534). Daniel Drezner (2005) makes a similar point in his analysis of international policy convergence. For example, he indicates that co-ordination outcomes are dependent not only on the benefits of convergence but also on the adjustment costs that states would have to undertake if they were to switch to another country's standards.

> While governments may receive benefits from the development of a single global standard, this does not mean that states will prefer *any* global standard. For governments, any agreement to co-ordinate standards at a point that diverges from the domestic status quo comes with economic and political costs (Drezner 2005, 845, emphasis in original).

So, contrary to neo-functionalism, Moravcsik's liberal intergovernmentalist approach argues: (i) that economic interests exercise their influence at the domestic level, not at the supranational one; and (ii) that economic interests may not always be in favour of integration. In any case, both approaches give economic interests a prominent role in the integration process. This role requires, however, that economic interests be clearly aware of the costs and benefits of integration, which may not always be the case. Just as war does for armies, regional economic integration gives rise to a fair amount of uncertainty for its participants.

Following Clausewitz (1984 [1832]), we could indeed argue that there exists a 'fog of integration'. Governments as well as economic interests and supranational institutions are in fact most often unable to foresee all possible contingencies that can arise with respect to the integration of a given policy area. All sorts of unexpected 'frictions', to use Clausewitz's term, can arise to produce a less than optimal outcome. This uncertainty is readily recognised with regards to governments and supranational institutions but not in the case of economic interests. As the bearers of knowledge and information, the latter are generally seen as crucial elements in explaining regional economic integration. However, if economic interests are uncertain about their pay-offs regarding a certain integration policy outcome, they are unlikely to lobby actively in favour or against it, either at the national or supranational level. Only once there is a legislative proposal on the table will interest groups mobilise one way or the other. As a result, their role in giving integration's initial impetus may be less prominent than proponents of neo-functionalism and liberal intergovernmentalism would have us believe.

The case of Economic and Monetary Union (EMU) is illustrative. Although business interests and banks were generally in favour of a common currency, they did not lobby for it (McNamara 1998 and 1999; Grossman 2002; Leblond 2004). They supported it but did not actively push for it. In fact, although they could anticipate benefits from EMU, they could not assess their level (Verdun 2000). The same applied to the costs of EMU. Only once concrete legislative proposals were on the table could economic interests begin their calculations. Until then, the ambiguity caused them to act as mere 'cheerleaders' rather than robustly active players. This is why they were keen to obtain the political and legislative details of EMU from the Commission and the Council (Leblond 2004). The uncertainty regarding the net benefits of monetary integration made it difficult to lobby for or against it (McNamara 1999). Support was positive but only with respect to the principle of a single currency. The fact that policy issues are often not well understood from the start makes it difficult for economic interests to devise specific strategies and lines of action (Grossman 2004). It is only when the fog (uncertainty) recedes that economic interests can decide on a specific course of action (e.g. lobby for or against a proposed legislation).

The absence of lobbying or pressures by economic interests does not mean that integration cannot take place. It just leaves a greater role for states and supranational institutions to play in the process, especially as initiators of integration. In the case of EMU, for example, France, Italy and Germany put monetary union back on the European table (Gros and Thygesen 1992). However, the European Commission and a group of experts known as the Delors Committee also played a prominent role in moving European monetary integration forward towards the Maastricht Treaty (Jabko 1999; Verdun 1999). Then, the Commission and the European Monetary Institute ensured that EMU would indeed become a reality by completing the (incomplete) contract signed in Maastricht (Leblond 2004).

How does the fog or uncertainty that surrounds economic interests at the beginning of the integration process affect our understanding of the process of regional economic integration, especially if we continue to assume that economic interests have an important role in the process? For one, it highlights the importance that states and supranational institutions have in the process. This does not mean, however, that economic interests are not important players in the process. Without their support for integration (in principle) at the beginning of the process (in a given policy area), then it is doubtful that member states and/or the Commission would initiate it in the first place. Once they are able to calculate the costs and benefits of integration, economic interests will indeed play a determinant role in the outcome of the integration process (as defined by the existence of a body of supranational laws and regulations), as many analysts of the EU's policy-making process have now been arguing for over a decade (see *inter alia* Andersen and Eliassen 1991; Greenwood et al. 1992; Mazey and Richardson 1993; Coen 1997). In fact, the relationship between European integration and economic interests may be more dynamic than traditional theories of integration tend to argue. Such an approach would help rescue neo-functionalism in its inability to explain the absence or limited degree of integration in certain policy areas (Haas 1976). Economic interests may be rhetorically behind functional and political spillovers *in principle*—owing to the uncertainty of the costs and benefits of integration—but may end up backtracking *in practice* when an integrative piece of supranational legislation is tabled by the Commission if the net benefits of integration are negative.

The Argument: Uncertainty, Lobbying and the Roles the Economic Interests Play in the European Integration Process

So far, integration theories tell us that economic interests are often frustrated with the status quo of national rules, regulations and standards because they make international economic exchanges more costly than if borders did not exist. As a result, these interests are very supportive of any attempt to harmonise these rules, regulations and standards across borders (i.e. integration). It does not necessarily mean, however, that they will be proactive in their support, in terms of lobbying governments or supranational institutions to integrate a given policy area. This is because these economic interests may not be clear about the costs and benefits of integration. It is possible that the harmonised rules or standards may require a lot of adaptation (i.e. be costly). The proposed rules may also give a competitor a clear competitive advantage. So spending a lot of money and energy on lobbying for integration may be very costly while providing few or no net benefits. Furthermore, integration as a principle or general concept can be considered a sort of public good for economic interests, whereas lobbying by one firm or group allows other firms and groups to do nothing and free-ride. Consequently, no firm or group has any incentive actively to lobby in favour of integration. Claiming support for integration is sufficient. Public and private statements of support can be made, but little more. The burden of initiating the process of integration really lies with governments and/or supranational institutions.

Once the integration (harmonisation) process has been initiated and concrete proposals for legislation begin to emerge, then economic interests are in a better position to calculate the costs and benefits of harmonisation. This is because the initial fog or uncertainty of integration is being lifted by states and/or supranational institutions. In the case of the EU, the Commission is responsible for proposing legislation on a given policy issue, which has been accepted for integration by the member states. This does not mean, however, that the Commission drafts legislation in a *vacuum*. As many students of the EU have observed, the Commission does not hesitate to consult various organised interests to gather information and expertise at the drafting stage (Greenwood et al. 1992; Mazey and Richardson 1993;

© 2008 The Author. Journal compilation © 2008 Political Studies Association
BJPIR, 2008, 10(1)

Coen 1997; Bouwen 2002). But here economic interests are not lobbying in favour of a certain position but are rather providing information and expertise requested by the Commission. As Coen (1997) and Bouwen (2002) note, the Commission needs expert knowledge as a result of insufficient resources and expertise but it also requires that the advice it receives is not in the self-interest of those providing it; otherwise, it is likely to limit the access it grants to those information providers.

The Commission will not be successful in pushing through a given legislation at the EP and the Council if it does not have the support of economic interests. The challenge for the Commission is to maintain the original support from a large majority of economic interests as the uncertainty regarding the costs and benefits of integration disappears. Drezner (2005) indicates that the expected additional profit (i.e. the benefit) arising from integration (or harmonisation) is a function of the relative size of the market to which the firm (or economic interests) will now have an easier access. For its part, the adjustment cost is a function of the 'distance' between the pre-existing regulatory standards in various member states. This distance could be purely technical but it could also be more fundamental, i.e. based on different underlying philosophies. For example, accounting standards in the EU vary considerably: those of France and Germany are devised mainly for tax purposes while those in the United Kingdom and the Netherlands focus on the needs of investors. This reflects the different capitalist traditions in the various countries, with capital being traditionally provided by banks in France and Germany while it is mainly provided by securities markets in the Netherlands and the UK. One would expect that the adjustment cost would be higher when standards have different philosophies or underlying principles. A firm's adjustment cost could also be a function of some factor intrinsic to its business, such as its capacity to effect change within its organisation or products/services (e.g. a large firm with a bureaucratic culture).

If there is a conflict between various economic interests—e.g. one firm accepts the legislative proposal while the other rejects it, then the EP and the Council have to decide the final outcome. They will do so based on the amount of lobbying performed by the respective firms (or, more generally, interest groups). The firm (or group) that lobbies the most widely and intensely should in principle win. This can mean the rejection of the Commission's proposal or its amendment. There is also the possibility that the Commission withdraws its proposal beforehand in order to submit a new, maybe more diluted version.

If the Commission is strategic, then it should choose an appropriate proposal right from the beginning, in order to maximise its chances of getting the EP and Council to vote for it. It is not always possible, however, for the Commission to harmonise standards in ways that reconcile pre-existing standards or regulations. For example, in the case of accounting standards it was impossible for the Commission to come up with a new set of European standards that would make the cost of adjustment the same for everyone. The different philosophies underlying existing standards across the EU were simply not compatible. In such cases, the Commission has to choose one standard over another. This is likely to lead to intense lobbying on different sides of the debate: i.e. for and against the proposed supranational standard. If one group has too few resources to lobby effectively, then we can expect the other group to prevail (i.e. see the EP and the Council adopt its preferred position). However, as the case studies demonstrate in the next sections, such a situation is more likely when economic interests are organised on a transnational basis rather than on a national one, where it is cheaper to lobby. In the latter case, member state governments will oppose the legislation in the Council. If enough of them are against it, a sufficient minority will block the proposed legislation. In the former case (transnationally organised interests), opposition will come from the European Parliament.

Although a blocking minority in the Council could mean the end of the proposal, it could also push the Commission to introduce a new proposal that more or less codifies the status quo by recognising both standards as acceptable. This is what mutual recognition is all about. In most cases, though, it can be considered to be a case of non-integration because it does not remove the existing transaction costs in place as a result of the various rules, regulations and standards. For the Commission, such a situation may be preferable to outright legislative failure since it nevertheless affirms its jurisdiction in the given policy area and, as a result, allows it to build expertise, legitimacy and support for a renewed attempt at integration in the future.

This is the scenario that applies to the case of the harmonisation of accounting standards in the EU. From the late 1970s to the early 2000s, there were two accounting directives that harmonised only the rules for presenting financial accounts but not their measurement, which is the key issue in terms of being able to compare the accounts of companies located in different countries. This changed in January 2005 when the International Accounting Standards Board's reporting standards became the new harmonised rules for all firms quoted on an EU stock exchange. This integration of accounting standards in the EU became possible only as a result of changes in the international political economy (Leblond unpublished). As we will see below, the same thing happened in the case of the Takeover Directive.

In sum, it is possible for economic interests to support integration right from the beginning even though they do not know on what basis harmonisation would take place and there is a risk that the adopted standard strays too far from the standard under which they are currently operating, whereby they would face a net cost from integration. Firms can afford to take this risk because they know that they always have the possibility to lobby the EP and the Council down the road against a non-advantageous legislation being proposed by the Commission. For the latter, it is important to consult economic interests early in the process in order to assess their support for integration in a given policy area and obtain information regarding their potential pay-offs from standards harmonisation so that it may choose the most appropriate legislation to foster integration. If support is not forthcoming, then the Commission need not go any further with its intention to integrate a certain policy domain.

Even if economic interests are supportive of European integration, it does not necessarily mean that they will lobby in its favour. Some might not lobby at all. Others might lobby against integration. The present section has argued that there are situations where integration may fail as a result of lobbying by economic interests. This may seem paradoxical on the part of economic interests but, as the fog of integration lifts, the calculus of economic interests changes. The ability to determine more precisely the benefits and costs of harmonising standards, rules or regulations will lead economic interests to decide whether to lobby (for or against) or not with respect to a proposed legislation by the Commission. The structure and intensity of this lobbying will likely determine the integration outcome. The next sections examine two cases of failed European integration to assess the validity of the argument presented so far.

To Patent or Not to Patent: The Case of the Computer-Implemented Inventions Directive

The case of the Computer-Implemented Inventions Directive—better known as the so-called 'Software Patent Directive'—is indicative of the apparently paradoxical relationship between economic interests and European integration since it was rejected by the EP in early July 2006, following intense lobbying by developers and users of open-source software and small and medium-sized enterprises (SMEs). According to the Commission, however, there was clearly an initial demand for harmonising standards in this area. The objective was to remove the existing legal ambiguity regarding software patents. The problem was that 'a computer-implemented invention may be protected in one Member State but not in another, which has direct and negative effect on the proper functioning of the internal market' (Commission of the European Communities 2002a, 2–3). It was only once the Commission's proposal was published that the uncertainty (or fog of integration) lifted, which allowed various private economic interests to define their positions.

The Commission justified the need for harmonising national laws with respect to software patents on the grounds that the varying interpretations of patentability laws by national courts created nefarious legal uncertainty that limited innovation in Europe (Commission of the European Communities 2002a). This was despite the fact that there existed a supranational European Patent Office to grant European patents and a European Patent Convention to harmonise national laws regarding patentability. Divergence in court interpretations had the effect to render uncertain the scope of patent protection accorded to certain categories of software invention. The Commission argued that this situation had 'real and negative effect on investment decisions and free movement of goods within the internal market' (Commission of the European Communities 2002a, 9). This is because software companies would develop and sell their products only in jurisdictions where they found high patent protection from local courts.

At the time, the jurisprudence related to 'computer-implemented inventions' had been developed by courts in Germany and the United Kingdom only. In the UK, software (i.e. a computer programme) that corresponds to a method of doing business (e.g. e-commerce) or performing a mental act (e.g. some mathematical calculation) was considered unpatentable even if there was a 'technical contribution' (a term subject to interpretation and key to the Commission's proposed directive).[5] Instead, such programmes are protected by existing copyright laws, where the written code and instructions manual cannot be copied without autho-

© 2008 The Author. Journal compilation © 2008 Political Studies Association
BJPIR, 2008, 10(1)

risation from the copyright holder. In Germany, however, the jurisprudence did not exclude the possibility that business methods could be patentable. This means that the scope of patent protection in Germany was much larger than in the UK. The result was that a piece of software could be protected in Germany but not in the UK. Clearly, this contravened the EU's principle of the free movement of goods.

In October 2000, the Commission launched a wide (and final) public consultation on the issue. Two camps emerged (Commission of the European Communities 2002a, 4). On the one hand, there were developers and users of open-source software as well as SMEs, which argued against making software patentable. On the other hand, there were large software manufacturers, like Microsoft, and regional and sectoral organisations such as the Union of Industrial and Employers' Confederations (UNICE), the European Information and Communications Technology Industry Association[6] and the European IT Service Association. Intellectual property professionals, such as lawyers, were also supportive of patents for software. Another important group that supported the idea of a software patent directive was the Business Software Alliance (BSA). It represents members such as Adobe, Apple, Autodesk, Compaq, Dell, IBM, Intel, Microsoft and Symantec.

In February 2002, the Commission issued its proposed directive on the patentability of computer-implemented inventions (Commission of the European Communities 2002a).[7] The core element of the Software Patent Directive was the notion of 'technical contribution', which is defined as 'a contribution to the state of the art in a technical field which is not obvious to a person skilled in the art' (ibid., 13). This was the key concept in determining whether new software was patentable or not. The Commission saw it as a limit on the scope of patentability. Otherwise, the EU would have joined the United States, where the level of patent protection is very high since there is no requirement for a computer programme to provide a technical contribution in order to be patented. This means that patenting business methods is acceptable in the US. The fear with such an approach is that it stifles competition and innovation in information technology. It also limits the development of new business methods like e-commerce. 'By codifying the requirement for a technical contribution, the Directive should ensure that patents for "pure" business methods or more generally social processes will not be granted because they do not meet the strict criteria, including the need for technical contribution' (Commission of the European Communities 2002a, 11).

In September 2003, the EP, under the co-decision procedure, proposed an amended Software Patent Directive that further limited patentability. This followed strong lobbying by groups such as the Foundation for a Free Information Infrastructure (FFII)—which created *Nosoftwarepatents.com* to promote freeware and open-source software widely, the Free Software Foundation, the European Association of Craft, Small and Medium-sized Enterprises (UEAPME) as well as companies such as Red Hat, Novell and MySQL. These groups wished seriously to curtail the Commission's proposal regarding the patentability of software because they feared that it would prevent open-source software such as Linux—the alternative operating system to Windows—to emerge and compete against the products of larger software manufacturers, thereby stifling innovation and competition.

In the spring of 2004, the Council of Ministers made a counter-proposal to that offered by the EP. The 'compromised' document basically removed all the EP's amendments. After a year of wrangling between the member states, the Council finally adopted its 'common position' (i.e. the second reading that ratified the spring 2004 decision).[8] In early July 2005, the EP rejected the amended directive proposed by the Council (and the Commission). As a result, the Software Patent Directive failed to become law and the status quo with all its associated legal uncertainties and ambiguities remained.

In terms of the argument presented in the previous section, the Software Patent Directive case is akin to the situation where only two opposite standards are available: patents vs. no patents. Both groups initially supported the idea of harmonising EU standards in this area. They differed, however, as to how much harmonisation should take place. Large software firms and intellectual property professionals supported patents and the Europe-wide harmonisation of the rules applicable to them with respect to software. Small software developers and many individual users were in favour of harmonisation across the EU but saw an opportunity to limit the patentability of software programmes.

In the first case, large firms use patents defensively as bargaining chips when they collaborate in order to make their software programmes compatible with each other. Otherwise, they have to pay licensing fees to other manufacturers. So they argue that an absence of patent protection would reduce the incentive for innovation and new products. In the second case, SMEs claim that patents, which are costly to obtain, prevent them from competing against larger software manufacturers. Consequently, they are not in a position to negotiate with larger manufacturers. They lack bargaining chips. This is why they are fervent supporters of open-source software, which is made fully available to the public for interoperability at no cost. In such a world, there is no market protection. Any software developer is able successfully to enter the market simply by devising a programme that is compatible with other existing programmes and, therefore, can be marketed on its own merits. As such, copyright protection of the programme itself is sufficient.

The Commission proposed a directive favouring patents, which was accepted by large software manufacturers but rejected by small software developers and individual users. Because their competitive advantage was at stake one way or another, both groups lobbied forcefully for their position. Although financially less resourceful than the multinational firms, small software developers and users nevertheless managed to mount an effective lobbying campaign with the EP, framing the debate in terms of David against Goliath. Initially, the larger, multinational firms most probably thought that they could muster greater lobbying resources than the smaller firms, which is why they did not hesitate to lobby in favour of the Commission's proposal, especially with the member states to influence the Council's decision. As Peter Bouwen (2002 and 2004) argues, however, the EP has a greater demand for information about European encompassing interest than expert knowledge (which the Commission demands) or even domestic encompassing interest (which is more relevant to the Council).[9] As such, although the alliance of large software manufacturers was probably better at providing the Commission with expert knowledge and the Council with national encompassing interest (especially in countries where such firms have important operations), it found it much more difficult to provide the EP with high-quality information about European encompassing interest than small firms and the European association of consumers (BEUC) could.

In sum, the Software Patent Directive case is a good illustration of a situation where integration was clearly considered to be a good thing given the various national patent regulations in place across the EU, which represented an obstacle to the free movement of software programmes and the goods that use them. Not only did this limit competition, it also reduced innovation. Therefore, the Commission felt fully justified in proposing a directive that would harmonise the patentability of computer-implemented innovation across the entire EU. The reason why this attempt at integration failed is that private economic interests had different views as to what should be patentable or not. Large firms wanted more protection (i.e. wider applicability of patents) in order to maintain their existing competitive advantage, whereby patents were used as bargaining chips in making software programmes compatible across firms. For large multinational software manufacturers, it was important also to limit the gap between European patent rules for software and those of the United States, which had a permissible system of patenting software programmes. For their part, smaller firms and end users preferred a much more open system where the level of patent protection was very low. This would make it easier for them to compete with the large software manufacturers, especially in the key European market. In the end, the proponents of less protection won the day by gaining the EP's support, which caused the proposed directive to fail (i.e. be abandoned) and the status quo (i.e. national patent regulations) to remain.

Everything Goes: The Case of the Takeover Directive

At the end of 2003, the Council and the EP approved a Takeover Directive for the EU. This came after almost 15 years of wrangling on the issue, although all parties understood the need for harmonising company takeover rules across the Union.[10] Such harmonisation was seen as crucial for facilitating the cross-border mergers and acquisitions which in turn would facilitate the complete integration of EU economies. Many (including the Commission) complained, however, that the agreed (compromised) legislation did not improve economic integration in the EU but, instead, would increase protectionism. This is because the directive allows member states to opt out of key provisions limiting defensive measures that EU companies can adopt to fend off unwanted buyers: (i) multiple voting shares; and (ii) poison pill defences without shareholder approval.[11] The Commission had wanted to forbid such practices against takeovers unless they were approved by shareholders but it was forced by the EP and the Council to water down its proposal (Commission of the European Communities 2002b). As a result of these opt-outs, the Takeover Directive is now generally considered a failure because member states have taken full advantage of these opt-outs (*Financial Times*, 2 March 2006).

An earlier legislative proposal was rejected by the EP in July 2001,[12] following Germany's strong opposition as a result of intense lobbying by firms such as

Volkswagen, Porsche and BASF, which felt vulnerable to foreign predators without protection from takeovers (*Financial Times*, 24 November 2003). Many family-controlled German firms argued against the Commission's earlier proposal because it called for management to remain neutral in case of a takeover and, therefore, not undertake any defence against an acquisition attempt. For example, the German state of Lower Saxony owns approximately 20 per cent of Volkswagen (VW), which allows it to pressure the automaker to save local jobs rather than cut costs to maximise profits. As a result, it would want VW to fight any attempt by a foreign firm to take it over and force it to manage with the goal of maximising profits. VW was able to use its close links with the Social Democrats, which happened to be in power at the time, to influence the German government's position on the issue in its favour.[13] Many members of the EP (MEPs) agreed with the German position because they felt that the absence of a level playing field with the United States, which allows takeover defences such as poison pills, would open the door wide to US firms acquiring European ones while the reverse would be more difficult. Furthermore, many MEPs thought that the proposed directive did not sufficiently protect the employees of the targeted companies.

Given the fact that a directive on takeover bids was a key component of the Financial Services Action Plan that would integrate Europe's financial markets by 2010, the Commission submitted a new version of the Takeover Directive to the EP and the Council for approval at the end of 2002 (Commission of the European Communities 2002b). This move was welcomed by UNICE, the European employers' federation, which strongly favoured a common framework for cross-border takeover bids. The problem was that Germany and German MEPs opposed the Commission's new draft directive because it did not prohibit shares with multiple voting rights (Callaghan and Höpner 2005, 310–311). The draft directive proposed the so-called 'breakthrough rule' (article 11) to prevent the use of poison pills by suspending restrictions on voting rights as well as transfers of securities during the period for acceptance of the bid but did not, however, limit the existence of shares with multiple voting rights.[14] The German position was clear: either the Takeover Directive rules out all takeover defence mechanisms or it rules out none.

Given the fact that German opposition to the earlier proposed legislation had been successful, it was impossible for the Commission to ignore the German government's request for including multiple voting rights in article 11. Amending the draft directive in such a way, however, faced strong opposition from France and the Nordic countries (Denmark, Finland and Sweden), which had supported the previous version of the directive (Callaghan and Höpner 2005, 311). The reason is that these countries allow the issuance of shares with multiple voting rights. For example, the Wallenberg family in Sweden has been able to keep a significant degree of control over many Swedish industrial multinational firms (e.g. ABB, AstraZeneca, Ericsson, Electrolux, Saab, SKF) via its holdings of shares with multiple voting rights, even if it effectively owned a small percentage of these firms' capital stock. In Sweden, three quarters of the top firms are said to be deviating from the principle of 'one share, one vote' (*Financial Times*, 18 October 2005).[15] Faced with this imbroglio, the Commission tried to find a way to isolate the Nordic countries while keeping France's support for the draft directive by proposing that different classes of shares with multiple voting rights be prohibited but not France's double voting rights, which are allowed for certain shareholders if they meet certain conditions.[16] This strategy backfired when Germany maintained its position that all multiple voting rights be outlawed if other forms of takeover defences were to be restricted (Callaghan and Höpner 2005, 311).

After many months of wrangling, the Takeover Directive was adopted by the Council and the EP in a highly watered-down compromise that allowed member states to opt out of the neutrality (of management) rule (article 9) and the break-through rule (article 11). Everybody thought a deal was better than no deal at all given the amount of time that had passed since the Commission's first proposal in the late 1980s (*Financial Times*, 24 November 2003).[17] But the end result is pretty much the same as if the EU had not adopted the Takeover Directive given the number of member states that have taken advantage of the opt-outs (Sagayam 2006).

The case of the Takeover Directive is a good example of how the fog of integration causes private economic interests to be initially supportive of harmonising national regulations and standards in order to improve cross-border commercial exchanges. However, once the Commission tables a proposition, then interests tend to polarise. Contrary to the Software Patent Directive, where the division was between large firms and smaller ones (along with consumers) on a transnational basis, the Take-over Directive saw business interests divide themselves on the basis of nationality. As a result, lobbying was most intense at the national level. Even MEPs tended to vote on the basis of nationality rather than party affiliation (Callaghan and Höpner 2005). In the end, the Commission was faced with the choice of: (i) seeing its proposition—which aimed at truly harmonising the regulation of takeovers in the EU by restricting the use of defence mechanisms—defeated by the EP and the Council in favour of a compromised solution that more or less recognised the status quo; or (ii) withdrawing it in favour of the status quo. After so many years, it was considered that the cost of starting from scratch again would be too great. It was better to try to build on the existing directive, which had to be revised after five years.

Conclusion

Scholars of European integration in particular and regional economic integration in general have argued that private economic interests have an important role in the integration process. Usually, this role is a positive one. The argument is that such interests desire more cross-border economic exchanges but face important trans-action costs as a result of differentiated national laws, regulations and standards; consequently, they ask their respective governments to get together and harmonise these rules for conducting business (i.e. integrate various policy areas). Depending on the theoretical approach, this integration process can take either a transnational/ supranational form or a national/intergovernmental one.

In fact, private economic interests' initial support for integration does not always result in integration actually taking place, as the cases of the Software Patent and Takeover directives presented herein demonstrate. In any process to integrate a given policy area, there may be interests that are bound to lose out in terms of facing greater costs to adjust to the new harmonised rules or standards. Consequently, they are likely to lobby for amending the proposed rules, if not abandoning them altogether. This lobbying is likely to take place at the EP and the Council since the fog of integration lifts only once the Commission has tabled a draft piece of legislation. Only then can interest groups assess where they stand with respect to integration and how they will respond to integration efforts. Hence, the ultimate outcome depends on the adjustment and lobbying costs of both sides relative to the benefits they are likely to obtain from integration.

This means that the role of private economic interests in the integration process is not as straightforward as is traditionally understood by scholars of regional economic and European integration. Private economic interests can, under certain circumstances, slow down or prevent integration from progressing forward. This is something that students of European politics and public policy have long understood and was made clear by Simon Hix (1994) more than 10 years ago. The time has now come to try to combine these different approaches and foci into a more coherent theoretical framework for understanding regional integration in general and European integration in particular. Maybe theories of public policy-making in the EU can finally provide the missing link between neo-functionalism and liberal intergovernmentalism.

The two cases examined in this article show the way for the development of a fruitful research agenda. For instance, they help us derive two hypotheses: (i) we are likely to see no integration take place (i.e. no supranational legislation) when private economic interests polarise transnationally on a given policy issue; (ii) we are likely to see only the formalisation of the status quo in the form of supranational legislation that allows opt-outs or the mutual recognition of existing national rules and standards when interests polarise on a national basis. Another example lies with the Takeover Directive, which does not really push integration forward even if it is adopted. This suggests that in many policy areas where there exists European legislation the degree of integration may be more formal than substantial. Therefore, analysing and explaining the varying depth of European integration across policy areas should also be an important part of this new research agenda on regional integration. After all, maybe the EU is not as integrated as we think. In the same vein, maybe North America is more integrated than we think. If so, we need to know why and existing theories of regional economic integration are currently unable to offer us the answer.

About the Author

Patrick Leblond, HEC Montreal, Department of International Business, 3000 Cote-Ste-Catherine Road, Montreal, QC H3T 2A7, Canada, email: *patrick.leblond@hec.ca*

Notes

Previous versions of this article were presented at: a workshop on 'Economic Interests and European Integration' held at the University of Edinburgh on 8 April 2006; the annual meeting of the International Studies Association, Chicago, 28 February–3 March 2007; and the biennial meeting of the European Union Studies Association, Montreal, 17–19 May 2007. For comments and advice, I would like to express my gratitude to Andreas Bieler, David Howarth, Costanza Musu, Tal Sadeh, Anthony Zito and three anonymous referees. I would also like to acknowledge the advice received from the participants at the Edinburgh workshop. Finally, special thanks go to Jonathan Beauchesne for his able research assistance and HEC Montreal for providing financial support.

1. Either it is withdrawn by the Commission or it is rejected by the EP or the Council.

2. See Commission of the European Communities (2002a).

3. See Commission of the European Communities (2002b).

4. The integration concept of mutual recognition of standards generally falls into this category. The phenomenon of indirect integration failure has, curiously, received very little attention from EU scholars, even though many EU policy areas have experienced it.

5. The patent exists to protect the fundamental technical background of the software or computer programme. Thus, the automation of a technique, task or method already known does not represent a technical contribution worth patenting according to UK jurisprudence.

6. The EICTA merged with the European Association of Consumer Electronics Manufacturers (EACEM) in 2001 to form the European Information, Communications and Consumer Electronics Technology Industry Associations (EICEA). It combines 32 national digital technology associations from 24 European countries. It represents more than 10,000 enterprises with more than two million employees in total.

7. The directive defines computer-implemented invention as 'any invention implemented on a computer or similar apparatus which is realised by a computer program' (Commission of the European Communities 2002a, 13).

8. Poland, with some support from Hungary, Latvia and the Netherlands, opposed the directive.

9. Coen (1997, 103–104) indicates that large firms have been slower in transferring resources to lobbying the EP than the transfer of power to the EP as a result of the Maastricht Treaty would suggest.

10. In fact, the issue dates back to the early 1970s. For a history of the Takeover Directive, see Callaghan and Höpner (2005).

11. Multiple voting shares (shares that provide more than one vote) allow a minority of shareholders to block takeovers even if a majority of stockholders (with shares worth only one vote) are in favour of selling their shares to a (hostile) acquirer. Poison pill defences work to dilute the shareholdings of stockholders who might be interested in selling their shares to the acquirer. Obviously, if such defensive measures required the approval of a majority of existing shareholders, then it is likely that it would vote against such value-destroying measures.

12. The EP was split on the issue: 273 votes for and 273 votes against.

13. Chancellor Schröder was premier of Lower Saxony before becoming Germany's head of government.

14. Multiple voting rights are illegal in Germany.

15. A study conducted for the Association of British Insurers in March 2005 found that one third of the companies included in the FTSE Eurofirst 300 index (i.e. Europe's 300 largest firms) deviated from the one-share-one-vote principle, with about one fifth having classes of shares with multiple voting rights (*Financial Times*, 18 October 2005).

16. Double voting rights are often accompanied by caps on voting rights.

17. The only exception is Frits Bolkestein, the then Internal Market Commissioner, who threatened either to veto the agreement reached by the Council and the EP—such a move would have required a unanimous vote in the Council to pass the directive—or to retract the Commission's proposal altogether. In any case, his colleagues in the Commission did not support him (Callaghan and Höpner 2005, 311).

Bibliography

Andersen, S. and Eliassen, K. (1991) 'European community lobbying', *European Journal of Political Research*, 20:2, 173–187.

Bouwen, P. (2002) 'Corporate lobbying in the European Union: The logic of access', *Journal of European Public Policy*, 9:3, 365–390.

Bouwen, P. (2004) 'The logic of access to the European Parliament: Business lobbying in the Committee on Economic and Monetary Affairs', *Journal of Common Market Studies*, 42:3, 473–495.

Callaghan, H. and Höpner, M. (2005) 'European integration and the clash of capitalisms: Political cleavages over takeover liberalization', *Comparative European Politics*, 3:3, 307–332.

Clausewitz, C. (1984 [1832]) *On War* (indexed edition) (Princeton NJ: Princeton University Press).

Coen, D. (1997) 'The evolution of the large firm as a political actor in the European Union', *Journal of European Public Policy*, 4:1, 91–108.

Commission of the European Communities (2002a), 'Proposal for a directive of the European Parliament and of the Council on the patentability of computer-implemented inventions', COM (2002) 92 final, 2002/0047(COD), Brussels.

Commission of the European Communities (2002b), 'Proposal for a directive of the European Parliament and of the Council on takeover bids', COM (2002) 534 final, 20002/0240(COD), Brussels.

Drezner, D. W. (2005) 'Globalization, harmonization, and competition: The different pathways to policy convergence', *Journal of European Public Policy*, 12:5, 841–859.

Garrett, G. (1992) 'International cooperation and institutional choice: The European Community's internal market', *International Organization*, 46:2, 533–560.

Greenwood, J., Grote, J. and Ronit, K. (eds) (1992) *Organised Interests and the European Community* (London: Sage).

Gros, D. and Thygesen, N. (1992) *European Monetary Integration: From the European Monetary System to European Monetary Union* (New York: St Martin's Press).

Grossman, E. (2002) *Les groupes d'intérêts bancaires face à l'intégration européenne: une étude comparée de l'Allemagne, de la France et du Royaume-Uni* (Paris: Institut d'études politiques, Ph.D. Dissertation).

Grossman, E. (2004) 'Bringing politics back in: Rethinking the role of economic interest groups in European integration', *Journal of European Public Policy*, 11:4, 637–654.

Haas, E. B. (1958) *The Uniting of Europe: Political, Social, and Economic Forces, 1950–1957* (Stanford CA: Stanford University Press).

Haas, E. B. (1976) 'Turbulent fields and the theory of regional integration', *International Organization*, 30:2, 173–212.

Hix, S. (1994) 'The Study of European Community: The challenge to comparative politics', *West European Politics*, 17:1, 1–30.

Hoffmann, S. (1966) 'Obstinate or obsolete? The fate of the nation state and the case of Western Europe', *Daedalus*, 95, 892–908.

Jabko, N. (1999) 'In the name of the Market: How the European Commission paved the way for monetary union', *Journal of European Public Policy*, 6:3, 475–495.

Leblond, P. (2004) 'Completing the Maastricht contract: Institutional handicraft and the transition to European Monetary Union', *Journal of Common Market Studies*, 42:3, 553–572.

Lindberg, L. N. (1963) *The Political Dynamics of European Economic Integration* (Stanford CA: Stanford University Press).

McNamara, K. R. (1998) *The Currency of Ideas: Monetary Politics in the European Union* (Ithaca NY: Cornell University Press).

McNamara, K. R. (1999) 'Consensus and constraint: Ideas and capital mobility in European Monetary Integration', *Journal of Common Market Studies*, 37:3, 455–476.

Mattli, W. (1999) *The Logic of Regional Integration: Europe and Beyond* (New York: Cambridge University Press).

Mazey, S. and Richardson, J. (eds) (1993) *Lobbying in the European Community* (Oxford: Oxford University Press).

Moravcsik, A. (1993) 'Preferences and power in the European Community: A liberal intergovernmentalist approach', *Journal of Common Market Studies*, 31:4, 473–524.

Moravcsik, A. (1998) *The Choice for Europe: Social Purpose and State Power from Messina to Maastricht* (Ithaca NY: Cornell University Press).

North, D. C. (1990) *Institutions, Institutional Change, and Economic Performance* (New York: Cambridge University Press).

Nugent, N. (1995) 'The leadership capacity of the European Commission', *Journal of European Public Policy*, 2:4, 603–623.

Sagayam, S. (2006) 'Member states struggle to adopt Takeover Directive', *International Financial Law Review*, 25 (April, Mergers & Acquisitions Supplement). Available online at: http://www.iflr.com/?Page=17&ISS=21679&SID=624126

Verdun, A. (1999) 'The role of the Delors Committee in the creation of EMU: An epistemic community?', *Journal of European Public Policy*, 6:2, 308–328.

Verdun, A. (2000) *European Responses to Globalization and Financial Market Integration: Perceptions of Economic and Monetary Union in Britain, France and Germany* (New York: Palgrave Macmillan).

Williamson, O. E. (1985) *The Economic Institutions of Capitalism* (New York: The Free Press).

doi: 10.1111/j.1467-856x.2007.00316.x   *BJPIR: 2008 VOL 10, 27–45*

Bringing Economic Interests Back into the Study of EU Trade Policy-Making

Andreas Dür

Studies of EU trade policy-making often suggest that delegation of trade authority from the national to the European level strengthened the autonomy of public actors in formulating trade policies. Little empirical research, however, has been undertaken to corroborate this contention. To improve on this situation, I carry out two case studies of the EU's participation in the multilateral trade negotiations known as the Kennedy Round (1964–67) and the Doha Development Agenda (2001 onwards). The analysis reveals that in both cases the EU's negotiating position was largely in line with the demands voiced by economic interests. Although this finding is no proof of economic interests actually determining EU trade policies, it casts some doubt on the autonomy thesis. I also discuss some factors that indicate that interest group influence may be the most plausible explanation for the finding.

Keywords: interest groups; influence; trade policy; European Union

Introduction

What role do economic interests play in the making of European Union (EU) trade policy? Some current research dealing with this question suggests that policy-makers are relatively insulated from societal pressures and thus can implement trade policies in line with their economic beliefs or other preferences. The argument is that the transfer of policy authority to the European level, by increasing economic interests' uncertainty about who decides and what is decided, enhanced the autonomy of public actors in shaping EU trade policies. As many authors propose that this effect was intended to strengthen the state *vis-à-vis* society, this view is also known as the 'collusive delegation argument'. The autonomy that decision-makers gained as a result of delegation allowed them to implement trade policies that further the public good, that is, achieve trade liberalisation, against the resistance of protectionist forces.

Little empirical research, however, has been undertaken to back up this contention. In fact, the few studies that empirically tackle the question of interest group involvement in EU trade policy-making produce fairly ambiguous results. To improve on this state of the art, I carry out two case studies of the EU's participation in the Kennedy Round (1964–67) and the Doha Development Agenda (2001 onwards) of world trade talks. The choice of these two cases is based on the reasoning that in both of them the preconditions were ideal for collusive delegation to work. For the first case, this is so because domestic interests should have been particularly vulnerable immediately after the creation of a multi-level system, as

they should have found it difficult to adapt to the new institutional framework. For the second case, while societal actors may have become more familiar with the multi-level system, the extent of delegation of trade policy authority has increased as well (De Bièvre and Dür 2005), again creating a propitious situation for collusion by public actors. In both the 1960s and the early 2000s, consequently, on at least some issues one would expect to see that public actors overrode opposition from societal interests when pushing for trade liberalisation. This expectation is not borne out for either case, however; on the contrary, the EU's negotiation position was consistent with the demands voiced by both broad business associations and sectoral groups across a large number of issues.

While this research falls short of establishing that economic interests actually determine EU trade policies, I suggest that some factors indicate that domestic actors may indeed be influential in shaping them. In particular, economic interests enjoy excellent access to decision-makers in this policy field, which provides them with opportunities to influence outcomes. Economic interests active on trade policy issues also consider themselves to be influential. Finally, explanations not based on the lobbying efforts by economic interests find it quite difficult to explain the close parallels between the EU's negotiation position and societal demands. Together, these factors make it plausible that interest groups indeed have a substantial impact on EU trade policies.

The Collusive Delegation Argument

Studies on EU trade policy often maintain that the distribution of power between societal and public actors in this policy field is skewed in favour of the state. The delegation of trade policy authority to the EU level, which was agreed upon in the Rome Treaty (1957), supposedly insulated policy-makers from protectionist pressures (Nicolaïdis and Meunier 2002, 175; Meunier 2005, 8–9; Woolcock 2005, 247; Zimmermann 2007, 163). The insulating effect of delegation, according to this view, was not unintended. On the contrary, the collusive delegation argument postulates that politicians consciously designed the EU's institutional framework to minimise the influence of societal interests. After gaining independence from specific economic interests, politicians used their autonomy to cut tariffs in international trade negotiations, a policy that is in the public interest but runs counter to the policies demanded by sectoral pressure groups. Illustratively, Sophie Meunier (2005, 8) posits that European policy-makers 'chose to centralize trade policymaking in order to insulate the process from protectionist pressures and, as a result, promote trade liberalization'.

The causal argument, which originated in studies of United States (US) trade policy-making (Destler 1986; for a critique see Bailey et al. 1997), starts with the assumption that protectionist trade interests dominate policy-making processes because collective action problems inhibit political action by consumers, the main winners from free trade. In this situation, politicians have an incentive to limit the influence of import-competing interests if they either are concerned about the negative consequences of protectionism for economic growth or have a pro-trade preference for other reasons. They may hope that by delegating trade policy authority to another level of government or from the legislative to the executive they can combat the extraction of rents by particular firms or sectors.

Several arguments exist for how delegation reduces societal actors' control over trade policies, most of which explicitly or implicitly allude to an increase in uncertainty resulting from delegation for domestic interests. In one view, delegation to a higher level of government may increase the free-rider problems of societal interests. The larger number of actors benefiting from specific policies in a larger geographical district could exacerbate collective action problems, and thus keep societal interests from influencing policy outcomes. Another prominent explanation draws attention to the size of electoral districts. It suggests that in political systems with small districts, the negative effects of pork barrel policies (that is, policies that provide targeted benefits to constituencies) can be externalised to other constituencies (Weingast et al. 1981). In political systems with large districts, by contrast, the constituency that receives the benefits of specific policies also has to carry their costs (Rogowski 1987). A move from small to large districts consequently makes sure that the losers from protectionist policies are to be found in the same districts as the winners. Such a situation may enhance decision-makers' ability to find alternative support coalitions, making it easier for them to ignore protectionist special interests (McKeown 1999, 30, fn. 10).

Delegation to an intergovernmental forum as happened in the EU may have other important effects. It provides governments with control over the agenda, alters decision-making procedures, creates more pronounced information asymmetries that favour the government and provides governments with additional ways to justify their policy choices (Moravcsik 1994). All of these factors can strengthen the state *vis-à-vis* societal interests. In addition, intergovernmental co-operation in a policy field may enhance governments' bargaining power in domestic negotiations by allowing them to refer to international constraints that impede their giving in to societal demands (Grande 1996). Whatever the specific causal chain suggested in a study, all of these explanations concur in the prediction of greater autonomy by public actors in the aftermath of delegation of trade authority from the national to the European level.

Given the prominence of the state autonomy claim in the literature, it is astonishing to see how little empirical research has been carried out actually to test the hypothesis for the case of EU trade policies. A few case studies provide the only empirical evidence of interest group influence on EU trade policy choices currently available. One such analysis shows that the EU decided to start a dispute settlement case in the World Trade Organisation (WTO) against American tax refunds for exporters based on only casual business consultation. It concludes that the 'relative autonomy enjoyed by states on deciding which cases to bring and pursue does not support the more extreme arguments that governments are mere messengers at the WTO for corporate preferences' (Hocking and McGuire 2002, 466). The study, however, does not provide (and in fact does not claim to provide) evidence in support of the collusive delegation hypothesis. There is little to indicate that business interests actually pushed the European Commission to become active in this case (although Airbus Industries most likely did exert some pressure). Neither, however, was there strong opposition to the launching of the case, which member states would have had to overcome by way of collusive delegation.

© 2008 The Author. Journal compilation © 2008 Political Studies Association
BJPIR, 2008, 10(1)

For the case of the Uruguay Round (1986–93) of multilateral trade negotiations, some evidence suggests that the French government may not have been particularly responsive to the interests of French industry (Cowles 2001, 167). Again, however, the collusive delegation argument is hardly useful in explaining this finding. Rather, it seems that the French government's position was heavily influenced by other domestic interests, in particular farmers and audiovisual services providers (Devuyst 1995; Keeler 1996). Once French industry became more insistent on the need for a successful conclusion of the Uruguay Round, moreover, the French government changed course. Still other studies actually stress the influence that economic interests can have on EU trade policy-making (van den Hoven 2002; Dür 2004; Coen and Grant 2005; De Bièvre and Dür 2005). Empirical support for the collusive delegation hypothesis is hence limited.

What is more, a series of theoretical shortcomings also casts doubt on the collusive delegation hypothesis, at least as applied to the case of EU trade policies. For one, this line of reasoning is built on the assumption that politicians have a short-term incentive to provide protection and are relatively unconcerned with the long-term gains from freer trade. Why then would they move to insulate trade policy-making to achieve long-term welfare gains that are close to irrelevant for their short-term electoral success? Even if politicians, in a moment of autonomy, should manage to move decision-making to a larger geographical area, it is not obvious why politicians should consistently have more liberal preferences than domestic interests. This is particularly so because societal actors can also influence the selection of policy-makers (Fordham and McKeown 2003). Moreover, for the case of supranational actors, it might actually be in the bureaucratic self-interest of an agent to be more protectionist than its principals (Frey and Buhofer 1986). The reason for this is that the agent's standing should increase as it becomes the addressee of demands for protection.

More importantly still, the EU's institutional framework for trade policy-making runs counter to the collusive delegation argument. Following article 113 of the Treaty of Rome (1958), which governed trade policy-making in the EU until the revisions in the Treaties of Amsterdam (1999) and Nice (2003), the Council of Ministers was to decide on international trade agreements unanimously for an initial period of eight years. The treaty stipulated that after this period trade agreements should be ratified by a qualified majority. Yet, just before this provision was to come into force, France insisted on the need to maintain unanimous decisions on issues concerning important national interests, a demand that was accepted by the other member states in the Luxembourg compromise of 1966.

Later, when the Luxembourg compromise started to be whittled away in other policy fields, the extension of the scope of trade negotiations to new issues such as intellectual property rights, investments and services, made sure that unanimity persisted in the trade policy field. For these issues, the original treaty provisions did not assign exclusive competences to the EU and thus required unanimous decisions (see also the discussion in Young 2002). Although the Treaty of Nice extended qualified majority voting to services and intellectual property rights, the situation has not changed fundamentally. With governments continuing to defend their right to veto trade agreements, it is not plausible that the current Doha Development

Agenda could be concluded against the opposition of a member state. As a result, throughout these decades decisions concerning trade negotiations have had to be taken unanimously.[1]

The unanimity requirement makes sure that the European Commission, although endowed with the sole right to make proposals on trade policy matters, is tightly constrained (De Bièvre and Dür 2005). Interest groups, consequently, may concentrate their lobbying effort on their national governments (Feld 1967, 34), and push them to block trade agreements that run counter to their interests. Aware of this, the European Commission has an incentive to listen to economic interests, rather than having its proposals rejected by the Council of Ministers. The resulting 'symbiotic' relationship between the Commission and interest groups (Mazey and Richardson 2003, 209, 212) can lead to a situation in which 'companies and the Commission present the member states with a negotiating strategy "pre-approved" by European industry' (Cowles 2001, 171).

Delegation may even enhance governments' ability to give in to special interests. Loosely applying a principal-agent framework, the more informed the electorate is, the more difficult the government will find it to engage in actions that run counter to the preferences of voters. The loss in transparency resulting from delegation should inhibit voters' monitoring of policy decisions more than any other interests. Less scrutiny by voters should allow politicians to impose policies that are even more in line with special interest group demands than before. Delegation may hence boost the power of economic interests by giving politicians more leeway from electoral demands. The resulting expectation is an 'increasing prevalence of special interests over the general public interest' in the EU (Petersmann 1991, 167). In short, neither existing empirical studies nor theoretical reasoning supports the collusive delegation argument.

Economic Interests and Trade Policy-Making in the EU

To scrutinise further the collusive delegation argument, I compare European trade policy choices and interest group demands in two periods, namely the 1960s and the years from 1998 until 2006. In these two periods, the EU engaged in the Kennedy Round of world trade talks and the Doha Development Agenda, respectively.[2] The collusive delegation argument suggests that the EU's position in these trade negotiations should have been shaped by the preferences of decision-makers. These preferences, in turn, are expected to be less protectionist than those of domestic interests, leading to the prediction that at least on some issues the EU's position should have diverged from the demands voiced by domestic interests. A close reflection of societal demands in the EU's negotiating position, by contrast, will cast doubt on the collusive delegation hypothesis.

The EU and Trade Liberalisation in the Kennedy Round

Shortly after the creation of the European Economic Community in 1958, the US asked this new entity to engage in international trade negotiations with the aim of substantially liberalising trade flows. In particular, the US administration proposed linear tariff cuts by 50 per cent of the tariffs of developed countries. The trade liberalisation that resulted from the ensuing Kennedy Round sharply contrasts with protectionist European trade policies in the 1950s. Was this liberalisation a result of the increased autonomy of public actors from societal demands, as postulated by advocates of the collusive delegation hypothesis?

I suggest that the answer to this question is no. In fact, the available evidence shows that economic interests supported the EU's trade policy stance. Exporting firms became politically active (*Washington Post*, 28 February 1963, C23), and pushed for reciprocal trade liberalisation, which should lead to improved market access in other countries. They accepted linear tariff cuts, but insisted on the elimination of tariff disparities between the US and the EEC (*Washington Post*, 4 June 1964, B5).[3] In practice, this meant that for goods on which the US had substantially higher tariffs than the EEC, the former should make more far-reaching concessions than the latter to achieve a harmonisation of tariff levels. In line with these demands, European governments called for the reduction of high American tariffs to achieve tariff harmonisation.[4] Throughout the negotiations, the EEC insisted on this point, which finally also found its way into the Kennedy Round agreement.

In addition, European exporters pushed for an extension of the scope of negotiations to non-tariff barriers such as the American Selling Price, a method used in the US to evaluate the price of imported chemicals that inflated the tariffs that had to be paid.[5] French and German economic interests also demanded that the US accept international rules for the use of its anti-dumping instrument.[6] The Paris section of the French Chamber of Commerce, moreover, asked for American concessions on issues such as internal taxes and the Agricultural Adjustment Act, which allowed the US president to impose quotas for agricultural products.[7] The French Federation of Mechanical Industries, moreover, complained about the Buy America Act, which disadvantaged European producers in American public procurement.[8]

Again, the positions of European governments and the European Commission were in line with these demands. All of them pushed for an expansion of the agenda to non-tariff barriers (*Economist*, 13 April 1963, 171). For example, the French Foreign Ministry suggested that parallel negotiations concerning non-tariff barriers would be necessary.[9] Since Germany also pushed for negotiations on at least the abolition of the American Selling Price system, it is no wonder that in its recommendations to the Council of Ministers the European Commission insisted that '[p]ara-tariff barriers should also be considered' in the negotiations.[10]

Not only exporting interests, however, were active in lobbying. Sectors suffering from import competition, such as the aluminium, ceramics, coal, electrical and glass industries in Germany, and the car industry in France, were demanding exceptions from the linear tariff cuts agreed upon.[11] Throughout the EEC, the textile industry and the agricultural sector (Neunreither 1968, 371–373) were vocal in rejecting trade liberalisation. In accordance with these demands, the EEC pushed for the exclusion of some 19 per cent of industrial goods from the linear tariff cuts (*Wall Street Journal*, 16 November 1964, 30). On the exception list were most of those goods for which producers had lobbied for continued protection, such as commercial vehicles and cotton textiles. In addition, the EEC made clear that the agricultural sector would have to be largely exempted from trade liberalisation. In the

© 2008 The Author. Journal compilation © 2008 Political Studies Association
BJPIR, 2008, 10(1)

Kennedy Round, consequently, the EEC's negotiating position was essentially in line with the demands voiced by economic interests.

The EU's Push for the Doha Development Agenda

The EU currently engages in a new round of global trade negotiations in the framework of the WTO, known as the Doha Development Agenda. Preparations for this round started in the mid-1990s, with the EU in the forefront of the countries supporting the commencement of new multilateral negotiations. After a first attempt at starting this trade round failed during the WTO ministerial conference in Seattle in 1999, WTO members finally launched the Doha Development Agenda in November 2001. After the start of the round, however, the negotiations made only slow progress. The WTO ministerial meeting in Cancún in 2003, which was supposed to signal the mid-term of the negotiations, broke down in failure, and the negotiations could only be brought back on track in July 2004, with an agreement on the future negotiating agenda. The Hong Kong ministerial meeting in December 2005, which should have decided upon the further negotiating modalities, again did not manage to achieve this aim. The negotiations were suspended for half a year in July 2006, and re-launched at the end of January 2007, but at the time of writing there is still no agreement in sight.

In the negotiations, the EU asked for substantial reductions of tariffs and the elimination of tariff peaks in industrial goods. All WTO members other than least-developed countries should agree to the binding of 100 per cent of tariff lines to impede future increases. High on the EU's agenda was also a further liberalisation of trade in services, but excluding audiovisual ones. With regard to international rules, the EU insisted on the need for agreements on the so-called 'Singapore issues', namely trade facilitation, public procurement, competition policy and investment rules (EU Council 1999). Finally, with respect to agriculture, the EU was willing to make some concessions, but without completely abandoning the use of quotas or of domestic supports. In late 2005, it suggested cuts of agricultural tariffs of between 35 and 60 per cent, a widening of existing quotas and the complete elimination of export subsidies. While far-reaching, these proposals would still leave most EU producers of agricultural goods with ample protection against foreign competition.

How does this EU position compare with societal demands? An analysis reveals that it is surprisingly close to the positions voiced by economic interests, often managing to bridge conflicting interests among societal groups. For one, most European business interests have supported the EU's push for new, wide-ranging negotiations. The Union of Industrial and Employers' Confederations of Europe (UNICE, now BusinessEurope), for example, hoped for 'comprehensive [negotiations]', to be 'concluded by a single agreement' (Unice 1999), a position that was echoed by the European Roundtable of Industrialists. At the national level, practically all broad employers' associations, such as the Federation of German Industry, the Confederation of British Industry, the Movement of French Enterprises, the General Federation of Italian Industry and the Spanish Employers' Confederation have been sympathetic to the EU's position (see, for example, CBI 2000; BDI 2002;

© 2008 The Author. Journal compilation © 2008 Political Studies Association
BJPIR, 2008, 10(1)

CEOE 2003; MEDEF 2004; Confindustria 2005). Backing has also come from importers, retailers and traders, represented by EuroCommerce and the Foreign Trade Association at the European level.

Particularly strong has been the pressure for negotiations in the services sector (van den Hoven 2002, 20–21; Böhmer and Glania 2003, 29–32). Service providers in several member states, especially Great Britain, Ireland and the Nordic states, have been adamant in demanding a further liberalisation of trade in services. In 1999, these providers established a specific organisation at the European level, the European Services Forum, with the sole purpose of defending the industry's interests in the new WTO negotiations (interview, Brussels, 10 January 2006). Ever since, the European Services Forum has spoken out in favour of a strengthening of the General Agreement on Trade in Services that currently governs international trade in services (European Services Forum 2003 and 2005). The services negotiations were also pushed by industrial producers, who increasingly sell hardware together with complementary services. Given these societal demands, it is no wonder that the EU was the main advocate of a services agreement in the WTO.

Business also supported an international agreement on investments, which should protect foreign investments against expropriation and increase the transparency of national investment policies (UNICE 1999; Foreign Trade Association 2003). Only when witnessing the problems of the negotiators in making progress, some groups became sceptical about the utility of investment negotiations, arguing that an overburdened agenda could protract the negotiations for too long. At the same time, the negotiations on trade facilitation received increasing support. Trade facilitation should reduce the costs of trade by streamlining customs procedures and harmonising data and documentation requirements. An agreement on trade facilitation is a major aim of such groups as the Foreign Trade Association (interview, Brussels, 13 January 2006), the European Round Table of Industrialists (ERT 2005), the chemical industry (CEFIC 2003b) and the European Information and Communication Technology Industry Association (EICTA 2005). Several of these organisations joined forces in the form of the informal European Business Trade Facilitation Network, which was created in 2001 to push for a WTO agreement on trade facilitation.

Again, these demands are reflected in the EU's position. Initially, the EU asked to have the negotiations on the four Singapore issues concluded in the form of a 'single undertaking', meaning that all countries would have to accept or reject the negotiation results as a package. The EU's hope for wide-ranging negotiations, however, was disappointed at the Doha ministerial meeting in 2001, when developing countries, especially, opposed its demand for the inclusion of the Singapore issues. In the WTO ministerial meeting in Cancún (2003), the EU once more failed to receive a commitment by the other negotiating parties to extend the scope of the trade round. The agenda of the round was only finalised in July 2004, when the EU was successful in salvaging the negotiations on trade facilitation, the issue which also seems dearest to European economic interests.

Protectionist interests have become less vocal over time. Nevertheless, some sectors still lobby for exceptions from trade liberalisation. Prominent among them is the audiovisual part of the services sector. The European Broadcasting Union (1999) stresses the 'democratic, cultural and social specificity of audio-visual services'. Similarly, the European Film Industry GATS Steering Group (2002) points out that the EU should safeguard its current system and should not negotiate in this area. In line with these demands, the EU defends an exception for the cultural and audio-visual sectors to preserve 'cultural diversity' (EU Council 1999). A further group with an essentially protectionist position are the European automobile producers. They advocate the maintenance of a tariff of 6.6 per cent against foreign imports, meaning a reduction of the tariff by no more than one third. Once more, the EU's position echoes industry demands (*Financial Times*, 8 March 2003, 9). Finally, the EU's defence of less extensive tariff cuts in the textile sector mirrors demands for protection by producers in this industry.

Farmers also clearly oppose trade liberalisation, arguing that such liberalisation would undermine the viability of European small-scale farming (COPA-COGECA 2005). They signal some willingness to accept cuts of trade-distorting supports, but only if all developed countries accept the same disciplines, and if the result is fair rather than free trade. Recognising the fact that the EU will have to make concessions on agriculture to achieve its objectives in other areas of the negotiations, several broad business groups try to counter the lobbying effort of farmers, arguing that meaningful concessions in this area are necessary (CEFIC 2003a; MEDEF 2004; see also Böhmer and Glania 2003, 32–33). Others mainly see agriculture as a bargaining chip in the negotiations, which can be used to gain better foreign market access on other issues. As put by the European Services Forum (2004), if the EU does not get a substantial agreement on services, 'WTO members cannot expect the EU to give much on agriculture'.

The EU's position on agriculture largely bridges these various demands. It stresses the need to establish a 'fair and market-oriented agricultural trading system' (EU Council 1999). By conceding just enough on agriculture, it hopes to induce other countries to accept an agreement on the issues where the EU wants to achieve foreign market openings. For the outward-oriented agricultural interests, it managed to push the issue of protecting geographical indications on to the negotiating agenda of the round. The internal reform of the Common Agricultural Policy in 2003, which was made necessary by financial constraints, allowed the EU to offer some concessions on agriculture in the Doha round, without fearing major opposition from European farm groups. In 2006, however, the EU's decision not to make further concessions with respect to agriculture, which was in accordance with a strong lobbying effort by European agricultural interests (COPA-COGECA 2006), contributed to the suspension of the negotiations.

Overall, therefore, the EU's negotiating position is closely in line with the demands of concentrated business and agricultural interests. Table 1 subdivides the EU's negotiating position into 19 issues, and shows that on all of them the EU could build on support from concentrated economic interests. What is more, there is little opposition to the EU's negotiating position from concentrated interests: among the few exceptions are the questions of the extent of agricultural liberalisation and whether or not to open the trade-related intellectual property rights package.

The same cannot be said about non-governmental organisations, which defend such diverse objectives as environmental protection, more focus on development

© 2008 The Author. Journal compilation © 2008 Political Studies Association
BJPIR, 2008, 10(1)

Table 1: EU Negotiating Position and Sectoral Demands in the Doha Development Agenda

EU position	Supporters	Opponents
Tariffs on non-agricultural products: far-reaching cuts, elimination of peaks, sectoral zero-tariff agreements	Chemicals; food and drink industry; information and communication technologies; iron and steel industries; mechanical, electrical, electronic and metalworking industries; non-ferrous metals; spirits	
Lower tariff cuts for some products	Automobile manufacturers; textiles	Retailers
Reduction of non-tariff barriers	Automobile manufacturers; chemicals; information and communication technologies; mechanical, electrical, electronic and metalworking industries; non-ferrous metals; spirits	
Services: far-reaching liberalisation	Mechanical, electrical, electronic and metalworking industries; services sector	Labour unions, development groups
Exception for audiovisual services	Audiovisual services providers	
Trade facilitation	Chemicals; iron and steel industries; mechanical, electrical, electronic and metalworking industries; retailers	
Multilateral investment rules	Construction sector; electricity sector; iron and steel industries; mechanical, electrical, electronic and metalworking industries; services sector	Non-governmental organisations

© 2008 The Author. Journal compilation © 2008 Political Studies Association
BJPIR, 2008, 10(1)

Table 1: *Continued*

EU position	Supporters	Opponents
Competition policy: transparency, non-discrimination	Construction sector	
Public procurement	Iron and steel industries	
Strengthening of intellectual property rules	Mechanical, electrical, electronic and metalworking industries; services sector; textiles	Pharmaceutical industry (protect the *acquis*)
Protection of geographical indications	Agricultural sector; food and drink industry; spirits producers	
Revision of anti-dumping rules (both offensive and defensive demands)	Iron and steel industries; non-ferrous metals	
Defend the Common Agricultural Policy	Agriculture	Some industrial interests; some development groups
Cut agricultural subsidies	Most industrial interests	Agricultural sector; food and drink industry
(Nearly) tariff-free treatment for least developed countries	Practically everybody	
Reciprocity from 'more advanced' developing countries	All economic interests	Development groups
Clarification of relationship between WTO rules and multilateral environmental agreements	Environmental groups; most industrial sectors	Some environmental groups (not far-reaching enough)
Strengthening of precautionary principle	Agricultural sector; some non-governmental organisations	Biotechnology industries
Labour standards, but not linked to trade sanctions	Most industrial interests	Some labour unions (would like to see trade sanctions)

Source: own compilation based on the position papers of 16 EU-level sectoral trade associations and a few non-governmental organisations

© 2008 The Author. Journal compilation © 2008 Political Studies Association
BJPIR, 2008, 10(1)

and regard for human and labour rights. Development groups, for example, want a profound reform of the EU's agricultural policies, which should lead to the elimination of all export subsidies and all trade-distorting domestic subsidies (CIDSE and Caritas Internationalis 2005). Environmental groups push for the inclusion of environmental standards in trade agreements. At the level of rhetoric, the demands of these groups have been taken up in the EU's negotiating position, which refers to the importance of development and the need to protect the environment. Nevertheless, on issues of key concern to concentrated interests, whether these are farmers or business groups, the EU's position is most often in line with the latter. Illustratively, while non-governmental organisations make a strong call for unilateral concessions by developed countries, the EU's position is in accordance with economic interests that argue that larger developing countries such as Brazil and India should 'have a responsibility to commit to ambitious market opening for goods and services' (UNICE and ESF 2005; see also CEFIC 2003a, 2; MEDEF 2004). This finding does not run counter to the argument made in this article. It simply supports the view that European trade policies are more in line with the preferences of concentrated interests than those of diffuse interests (see also Dür and De Bièvre 2007).

Luck or Influence?

Both cases have shown close parallels between the demands voiced by concentrated economic interests and the positions defended by the EU in international trade negotiations, a finding that casts substantial doubt on the collusive delegation argument. Nevertheless, the evidence presented so far does not allow for conclusions about the influence of economic interests over trade policy outcomes. Societal preferences could coincide with policy outcomes by chance only (Barry 1980), although the probability of this being so in this case is very low given that trade policy choices have a series of dimensions. I will shed some more light on this issue when discussing three factors that support the influence rather than the luck conjecture: economic interests' excellent access to decision-makers, their self-evaluation as being influential and the lack of a plausible alternative explanation for the finding of close parallels between the EU's negotiating position and interest group demands. Even though in this process I cannot present a 'smoking gun' that establishes interest group influence beyond doubt, I still propose that the interest group influence hypothesis accounts rather well for the available evidence.

Access to Decision-Makers

In the EU, economic interests have the benefit of first-rate access to decision-makers on trade policy issues (Gerlach 2006, 178–179). In the case of the Kennedy Round, archival records in France and Germany reveal close consultation between governments and economic interests. In both countries, the governments even informally surveyed all economic sectors to prepare an informed negotiating position. As a result, decision-makers' level of information about the preferences of economic interests was high. In the French case, for example, officials in the foreign ministry knew that the paper sector, which faced competition from Scandinavia, wanted to preserve trade barriers. They also noted, however, that producers of 'thin paper', which is used for cigarettes and condensers, were export oriented and thus requested trade liberalisation.[12]

Similarly, in the case of the Doha Development Agenda, business enjoyed excellent access to decision-makers (interviews, Brussels, 10–13 January 2006). For example, the British government, and here particularly the Department of Trade and Industry, has held regular meetings with all actors concerned with trade policy within the Trade Policy Consultative Forum. In Denmark, societal actors have had access to decision-makers on trade policy matters through the so-called 'Beach Club process' since 1998 (OECD 2001, 37–38). In addition, the European Commission directly approached trade associations to get information on their preferences before drawing up its own position paper on the new round in early 1999. Illustratively, to get business input for the investment negotiations, the European Commission initiated an informal 'Investment Network' in 1998 (European Commission 1998). In the framework of this network, the Commission repeatedly met representatives of major companies in the run-up to the Seattle ministerial conference in 1999. The EU also commissioned a survey of 10,000 large companies to get to know their position on the investment talks in the WTO (Taylor Nelson Sofres Consulting 2000). In the document setting out the EU's position on this part of the world trade round, therefore, the European Commission could cite support by European business as a reason for its insistence on an investment agreement: 'The European business community has made clear its position in favour of multilateral rules on investment' (European Commission, DG I 1999).

Later, DG Trade upgraded these initial informal meetings into the Civil Society Dialogue, which regularly brings together Commission officials and representatives of non-governmental organisations and economic interests. Similarly, DG Agriculture organised general hearings with societal organisations before the start of the Doha Development Agenda (European Commission, DG VI 1999). It also has regular contact with societal interests through a series of advisory groups that are composed of representatives of agricultural producers, traders and consumers. Both DGs continue having less formal meetings with the peak agricultural and business associations (see for example COPA-COGECA 2006). Overall, therefore, both in the Kennedy Round and in the Doha Development Agenda, economic interests enjoyed privileged access to decision-makers, a condition that should have facilitated their attempts at influencing outcomes.

Self-Assessment of Influence

A small survey of business and farm groups with an interest in trade policy provides further evidence that economic interests actually manage to influence European trade policies (De Bièvre and Dür unpublished). We approached 100 groups, chosen randomly among all groups registered in the Civil Society Dialogue database of the European Commission (excluding those which have their base in third countries).[13] Our response rate was 47 per cent, with about half of the respondents filling in the online questionnaire only after being called by phone. The respondents fall into two

© 2008 The Author. Journal compilation © 2008 Political Studies Association
BJPIR, 2008, 10(1)

categories: non-governmental organisations (26); and business and agricultural constituencies (21). One of the questions posed was how these groups themselves evaluate the extent to which their activities affect European trade policy, with the possible responses being: to a large extent, to some extent, not really and not at all. Of the 21 organisations representing economic interests, 20 responded with 'to a large extent' or 'to some extent'. Qualitative evidence also points in the same direction. Representatives of some trade associations even suggest that they perceive the European Commission as a service institution, with the task of representing European business interests in international trade negotiations (interviews with EU business organisations, Brussels, January 2006).

Given this self-assessment of influence, it is no wonder that economic interests generally tend to be quite satisfied with the EU's negotiating position. Illustratively, the German Chambers of Industry and Commerce strongly welcomed the results of the Kennedy Round (*Frankfurter Allgemeine Zeitung*, 17 May 1967, 1, 4). More recently, economic interests explicitly praised the EU's efforts to push for progress in the services sector in the Doha Development Agenda (UNICE and ESF 2005). The European Services Forum (2004) lauded the efforts of the 'Commission's hardworking negotiating team'. Even agricultural interests, although concerned about possible concessions to foreign countries, are mostly satisfied with the negotiating position of the EU (COPA-COGECA 2000).

Alternative Explanations of the Observed Pattern

It is difficult to find an alternative explanation, not based on interest group lobbying, for the observation of a close reflection of the demands voiced by economic interests in the EU's negotiation position. One argument suggests that economic interests often adopt rather than influence the position of decision-makers (Yoffie and Bergenstein 1985; Woll and Artigas 2005). If firms realise that they have to interact with government repeatedly, their rational response may be to establish a special relationship with decision-makers (Woll and Artigas 2005). By supporting the latter on some issues, societal actors may gain access to policy-makers for issues that are more important to them (Yoffie and Bergenstein 1985, 131). Alternatively, groups' need for public funding (Mahoney 2004) may provide them with an incentive to assume positions that are welcome to decision-makers.

While these arguments may capture a part of reality, they have to assume that decision-makers have specific preferences concerning trade policy, independent from societal demands. But this just raises the question of where these preferences come from. A possible response is that economic efficiency and an attempt to boost the competitiveness of the European economy were the actual driving forces behind the EU's trade policy stance in both negotiations. This argument, however, is put in doubt by the EU's defence of exceptions for import-sensitive sectors in both negotiations. Import-competing sectors were politically more active in the 1960s than they are now, but the EU still stands up for the interests of audiovisual services providers, automobile producers and the textile and agricultural sectors. In particular, the EU defends the Common Agricultural Policy although cheaper imports of food and an alternative usage of the funds used to support agricultural production in Europe would most likely boost the competitiveness of the European economy. The argument positing that economic interests adopt a position that pleases public actors is also put in doubt by the fact that the positions defended by different firms and sectors are easily explained by their competitive position, that is, whether they are struggling with imports or able to compete in world markets. In short, alternative arguments fall short of fully accounting for the parallels between the EU's negotiating position and interest group demands. Interest group influence remains as the most plausible explanation for the available evidence.

Conclusion

Several existing accounts of the making of EU trade policy stress the relatively large independence of decision-makers from societal interests. The argument is that delegation of trade authority from the national to the European level insulated policy-makers from protectionist interests. This insulation, so the argument goes, explains the shift from protectionism to liberalisation witnessed since the 1960s, as policy-makers could implement 'good' economic policies in the absence of societal pressures. I have countered this interpretation with empirical evidence on the coincidence between societal demands and the EU's position in trade negotiations in the Kennedy Round and the Doha Development Agenda. The two case studies show striking parallels between the positions defended by economic interests and public actors. Even in situations in which EU governments have to find issue linkages to come to an agreement, the resulting trade policies tend to be tailor-made to avoid the imposition of concentrated costs on constituencies in any member country. Although this correlation between demands and the EU's negotiating position by itself does not allow for the conclusion of interest group influence, several factors suggest that reference to influence is needed to explain trade policy outcomes.

'Collusive delegation', consequently, may not be as forceful as is sometimes claimed. Little evidence supports the view that the EU acted against the demands of economic interests when liberalising trade after the creation of this customs union. Moreover, it seems that domestic input into European trade policies remains important. In this view, the EU did not choose trade liberalisation because it is a 'good policy', but because societal interests, initially mainly exporters and later also importers and retailers, pushed for it. This is not to say that the system of interest group input into EU trade policies is unbiased. The policy-making process actually seems to favour concentrated over diffuse interests (see also Dür and De Bièvre 2007). The latter, although increasingly vocal on European trade policy through a variety of non-governmental organisations, generally tend to have little impact on policy formulation. Criticisms of the legitimacy of the EU's trade policy-making process, which recently have become more pronounced (see Meunier 2005, ch. 7), should therefore be directed at the unequal representation of concentrated and diffuse interests rather than at the autonomy of state actors from economic interests. To deal with these questions, research needs to bring economic interests back into the study of EU trade politics.

© 2008 The Author. Journal compilation © 2008 Political Studies Association
BJPIR, 2008, 10(1)

About the Author

Andreas Dür, School of Politics and International Relations, University College Dublin, Belfield, Dublin 4, Ireland, email: *andreas.duer@ucd.ie*

Notes

Earlier versions of this article were presented at the workshop on 'Economic Interests and the Construction of Europe' at the University of Edinburgh, at the 2006 Annual Conference of the Political Studies Association of Ireland in Cork, and the 2007 meeting of the European Union Studies Association in Montreal. I gratefully acknowledge helpful comments from the participants in these conferences, in particular Andreas Bieler, John Peterson, Cornelia Woll and Alasdair Young, and from two anonymous reviewers.

1. The situation is different for administrative trade instruments such as anti-dumping duties and for the use of the WTO dispute settlement mechanism. The main features of trade policy are, however, decided in international trade negotiations.

2. By selecting these two cases, which are temporally relatively far apart, I can show that essentially the same dynamics were at play at the beginning of the process of European integration and now, although the issues covered by the negotiations have changed substantially. I see no reason to believe that an analysis of the Tokyo Round (1973–79) or the Uruguay Round (1986–94) would result in a different finding.

3. 'Note. Préparation de la Conférence Kennedy. Opinions des producteurs français.' 5 February 1963. Archives Diplomatiques, Paris (henceforth AD), Service de Coopération Economique, No. 931. 'Stellungnahme der deutschen Landesgruppe der Internationalen Handelskammer zu den Dokumenten der IHK Nr. 102/20 betr. Zolldisparitäten und Nr. 102/21 betr. Nichttarifäre Handelshemmnisse', January 1964. PA, B53-III-A2, No. 276.

4. 'Aide-Mémoire à l'attention de M. le Secrétaire Général', Bruxelles, 22 October 1962. AD, Service de Coopération Economique, No. 930.

5. Verband der chemischen Industrie, E. V., to Ministerialdirigent D. W. Keller, Foreign Office, 'Wirtschaftspolitik im Chemiebereich 1962/63', 29 August 1963. Politisches Archiv, Berlin (henceforth PA), B53-III-A2, No. 283.

6. CNPF, 'Note. Préparation de la Conférence Kennedy. Opinions des producteurs français', 5 February 1964. AD, Service de Coopération Economique, No. 931.

7. Chambre de Commerce & d'Industrie de Paris, 'Futures négociations commerciales en application du Trade Expansion Act', 9 May 1963. AD, Service de Coopération Economique, No. 930.

8. F.I.M.T.M. 'Négociations tarifaires C.E.E./Etats-Unis au sein du G.A.T.T.: Note complémentaire de la Fédération des Industries Mécaniques', August 1963. AD, Service de Coopération Economique, No. 949.

9. Ministère des Affaires Etrangères, Direction des Affaires Economiques et Financières, Service de Coopération Economique, 'Note', 19 November 1962. AD, Service de Coopération Economique, No. 930.

10. Communauté Economique Européenne, 'Négociations a la suite du Trade Expansion Act. Autorisation de négociations tarifaires dans le cadre du G.A.T.T.', 26 March 1963. AD, Service de Coopération Economique, No. 930.

11. Internal paper in the German economics ministry, February 1964. PA, B53-III-A2, No. 290. Chambre Syndicale des Constructeurs d'Automobiles à Monsieur le Ministre des Affaires Etrangères Paris, 7 July 1964. AD, Service de Coopération Economique, No. 932.

12. 'Note. Préparation de la Conférence Kennedy. Opinions des producteurs français', 5 February 1964. AD, Service de Coopération Economique, No. 931.

13. See http://trade.ec.europa.eu/civilsoc/search.cfm?action=form, accessed 18 July 2007.

Bibliography

Bailey, M. A., Goldstein, J. and Weingast, B. R. (1997) 'The institutional roots of American trade policy: Politics, coalitions, and international trade', *World Politics*, 49:3, 309–338.

Barry, B. (1980) 'Is it better to be powerful or lucky? Part 1', *Political Studies*, 28:2, 183–194.

BDI (2002) 'Die Doha Development Agenda zum Erfolg führen', Position Paper.

Böhmer, A. and Glania, G. (2003) 'The Doha development round: Reintegrating business interests into the agenda. WTO negotiations from a German industry perspective', *Beiträge zum internationalen Wirtschaftsrecht*, Heft 15.

CBI (2000) 'Global trade, global gain: The CBI's international trade policy', International Brief.

CEFIC (2003a) 'CEFIC's views on EU trade policy post-Cancún', November. Available online at: http:// www.cefic.org/Files/Publications/PostCancun_final.doc (accessed 6 February 2007).

CEFIC (2003b) 'Trade facilitation in the DDA', presentation at the WTO Public Symposium 'Beyond agriculture: Business perspectives on the DDA', 18 June 2003.

CEOE (2003) 'Las noticias de CEOE', No. 275, November.

CIDSE and Caritas Internationalis (2005) 'Make a difference for poverty reduction at the Sixth WTO Ministerial Conference in Hong Kong', Position Paper.

Coen, D. and Grant, W. (2005) 'Business and government in international policymaking: The transatlantic business dialogue as an emerging business style?', in D. Kelly and W. Grant (eds), *The Politics of International Trade in the Twenty-First Century: Actors, Issues and Regional Dynamics* (Basingstoke: Palgrave Macmillan), 47–67.

Confindustria (2005) 'Posizione dell'industria italiana sulla preparazione della conferenza ministeriale WTO di Hong Kong'. Available online at: http://www.confindustria.it (accessed 28 September 2006).

COPA-COGECA (2000) 'COPA and COGECA's comments on the EC comprehensive negotiating position proposal to be submitted to the WTO', Brussels, 10 November. Available online at: http:// www.cogeca.be/pdf/pr_02_60f_1e.pdf (accessed 28 September 2006).

COPA-COGECA (2005) 'COPA and COGECA's expectations in the WTO negotiations on agriculture: Coming to a fair and balanced agreement', 2 December. Available online at: http://www.cogeca.be/ pdf/wto_05_199s_2e.pdf (accessed 28 September 2006).

COPA-COGECA (2006) 'European farm leaders meet with Commissioner Mandelson to demand: No more EU concessions in WTO', 19 July. Available online at: http://www.copa-cogeca.be/pdf/ cdp_06_38_1e.pdf (accessed 28 September 2006).

Cowles, M. G. (2001) 'The transatlantic business dialogue and domestic business–government relations', in M. G. Cowles, J. Caporaso and T. Risse (eds), *Transforming Europe: Europeanization and Domestic Political Change* (Ithaca NY: Cornell University Press), 159–179.

De Bièvre, D. and Dür, A. (2005) 'Constituency interests and delegation in European and American trade policy', *Comparative Political Studies*, 38:10, 1271–1296.

Destler, I. M. (1986) 'Protecting Congress or protecting trade?', *Foreign Policy*, 62:Spring, 96–107.

Devuyst, Y. (1995) 'The European Community and the Conclusion of the Uruguay Round', in C. Rhodes and S. Mazey (eds), *The State of the European Community, Vol. 3: Building a European Polity?* (Boulder CO: Lynne Rienner), 449–467.

Dür, A. (2004) *Protecting Exporters: Discrimination and Liberalization in Transatlantic Trade Relations, 1932–2003* (European University Institute, Ph.D. Dissertation).

Dür, A. and De Bièvre, D. (2007) 'Inclusion without influence? NGOs in European trade policy', *Journal of Public Policy*, 27:1, 79–101.

EICTA (2005) 'The World Trade Organisation Doha Development Agenda', 9 September. Available online at: http://www.wto.org/english/forums_e/ngo_e/posp57_eicta_e.pdf (accessed 6 February 2007).

ERT (2005) 'ERT survey on trade facilitation', Available online at: http://www.ert.be/doc/0135.pdf (accessed 6 February 2007).

EU Council (1999) 'Preparation of the Third WTO Ministerial Conference: Council conclusions', 25 October. Available online at: http://www.thunderlake.com/ministerials/EC_Oct26decision.pdf (accessed 6 February 2007).

European Broadcasting Union (1999) 'GATS 2000/WTO Round: Preliminary EBU reply to the questionnaire on audio-visual services', 10 February. Available online at: http://www.ebu.ch/CMSimages/en/ leg_gats_tcm6-4286.pdf (accessed 6 February 2007).

European Commission (1998) 'Civil society consultation on trade and investment: Report. Minutes of the First Meeting of the Investment Network', Brussels, 27 November.

European Commission, DG I (1999) 'International rules for investment and the WTO', Brussels.

European Commission, DG VI (1999) 'Informal hearings with NGOs on WTO negotiations and agricultural aspects', 22 October. Available online at: http://ec.europa.eu/agiculture/external/wto/archive/ index_en.htm (accessed 28 September 2006).

European Film Industry GATS Steering Group (2002) 'The GATS and the European film industry', submission to the 133 Committee, 14 November.

European Services Forum (2003) 'ESF call for progress on reaching a WTO agreement on trade facilitation', 25 June. Available online at: http://www.esf.be (accessed 28 September 2006).

European Services Forum (2004) 'Briefing paper for ESF meeting with Peter Mandelson, incoming EU Trade Commissioner', 20 October.

European Services Forum (2005) 'The importance of the services negotiations in the WTO ministerial in Hong Kong', Letter to the prime ministers of all EU member states, 21 November. Available online at: www.esf.be (accessed 28 September 2006).

Feld, W. (1967) *The European Common Market and the World* (Englewood Cliffs NJ: Prentice-Hall).

Fordham, B. O. and McKeown, T. J. (2003) 'Selection and influence: Interest groups and congressional voting on trade policy', *International Organization*, 57:3, 519–549.

Foreign Trade Association (2003) 'FTA position regarding the WTO investment agreement', Position Paper.

Frey, B. S. and Buhofer, H. (1986) 'Integration and protectionism: A comparative institutional analysis', in H. Hauser (ed.), *Protectionism and Structural Adjustment* (Grüsch: Verlag Rüegger), 167–188.

Gerlach, C. (2006) 'Does business really run EU trade policy? Observations about EU trade policy lobbying', *Politics*, 26:3, 176–183.

Grande, E. (1996) 'The state and interest groups in a framework of multi-level decision making: The case of the European Union', *Journal of European Public Policy*, 3:3, 318–338.

Hocking, B. and McGuire, S. (2002) 'Government–business strategies in EU–US economic relations: The lessons of the foreign sales corporations issue', *Journal of Common Market Studies*, 40:3, 449–470.

Keeler, J. (1996) 'Agricultural power in the European Community: Explaining the fate of CAP and GATT negotiations', *Comparative Politics*, 28:2, 127–149.

McKeown, T. (1999) 'The global economy, post-Fordism, and trade policy in advanced capitalist states', in H. Kitschelt, P. Lange, G. Marks and J. D. Stephens (eds), *Continuity and Change in Contemporary Capitalism* (Cambridge: Cambridge University Press), 11–35.

Mahoney, C. (2004) 'The power of institutions: State and interest group activity in the European Union', *European Union Politics*, 5:4, 441–466.

Mazey, S. and Richardson, J. (2003) 'Interest groups and the Brussels bureaucracy', in J. Hayward and A. Menon (eds), *Governing Europe* (Oxford: Oxford University Press), 208–229.

MEDEF (2004) 'Une organisation mondiale du commerce: Pour quoi faire? Les entreprises françaises et l'avenir du système commercial multilatéral', Available online at: http://www.medef.fr/staging/medias/upload/73116_FICHIER.pdf (accessed 28 September 2006].

Meunier, S. (2005) *Trading Voices: The European Union in International Commercial Negotiations* (Princeton NJ: Princeton University Press).

Moravcsik, A. (1994) 'Why the European Community strengthens the state: Domestic politics and international institutions', Center for European Studies Working Paper Series No. 52.

Neunreither, K. (1968) 'Wirtschaftsverbände im Prozeß der europäischen Integration', in C. J. Friedrich (ed.), *Politische Dimensionen der europäischen Gemeinschaftsbildung* (Köln: Westdeutscher Verlag), 358–445.

Nicolaïdis, K. and Meunier, S. (2002) 'Revisiting trade competence in the European Union: Amsterdam, Nice, and beyond', in M. Hosli, A. van Deemen and M. Widgrén (eds), *Institutional Challenges in the European Union* (London: Routledge), 173–201.

OECD (2001) *Government–Citizen Relations: Country Profile Denmark* (Paris: OECD).

Petersmann, E.-U. (1991) *Constitutional Functions and Constitutional Problems of International Economic Law: International and Domestic Foreign Trade Law and Foreign Trade Policy in the United States, the European Community and Switzerland* (Boulder CO: Westview Press).

Rogowski, R. (1987) 'Trade and the variety of democratic institutions', *International Organization*, 41:2, 203–223.

Taylor Nelson Sofres Consulting (2000) 'Survey of the attitudes of the European business community to international investment rules', Brussels.

UNICE (1999) 'UNICE and the WTO Millennium Round', WTO Ministerial Conference, Seattle WA, 30 November–3 December 1999.

UNICE and ESF (2005) 'European business backs Commissioner Mandelson', Hong Kong, 16 December.

Van den Hoven, A. (2002) 'Interest group influence on trade policy in a multilevel polity: Analysing the EU position at the Doha WTO Ministerial Conference', EUI Working Paper, RSC No. 2002/67.

Weingast, B. R., Shepsle, K. A. and Johnsen, C. (1981) 'The political economy of benefits and costs: A neoclassical approach to distributive politics', *Journal of Political Economy*, 89:4, 642–664.

Woll, C. and Artigas, A. (2005) *Trade Liberalization as Regulatory Reform: On the Transformation of Business–Government Relations in International Trade Politics*. Paper presented at the ECPR General Conference, Budapest, 8–10 September.

Woolcock, S. (2005) 'European Union trade policy: Domestic institutions and systemic factors', in D. Kelly and W. Grant (eds), *The Politics of International Trade in the Twenty-First Century: Actors, Issues and Regional Dynamics* (Basingstoke: Palgrave Macmillan), 234–251.

Yoffie, D. and Bergenstein, S. (1985) 'Creating political advantage: The rise of the corporate political entrepreneur', *California Management Review*, 28:1, 124–139.

Young, A. R. (2002) *Extending European Cooperation: The European Union and the 'New' International Trade Agenda* (Manchester: Manchester University Press).

Zimmermann, H. (2007) *Drachenzähmung: Die EU und die USA in den Verhandlungen um die Integration Chinas in den Welthandel* (Baden-Baden: Nomos).

doi: 10.1111/j.1467-856x.2007.00317.x   *BJPIR: 2008 VOL 10, 46–63*

Setting the Pace? Private Financial Interests and European Financial Market Integration

Lucia Quaglia

The regulation and supervision of financial services in the EU has undergone significant change between 2000 and 2005, when the so-called Lamfalussy framework, the Basel 2 agreement and its transposition into the Capital Requirements Directive were agreed. This research examines the preferences of national financial interest groups in Germany and the UK (the independent variable) in shaping national input and, more precisely, the contributions given by the relevant public authorities to EU and international policy-making processes (the dependent variable). The impact, if any, on the final outputs (the relevant international and EU agreements) is also discussed. It is argued that the level of involvement of each interest group depends on the policy content, namely, whether the policy concerns a broad institutional issue or specific rules, while the degree of interest group influence in policy-making processes depends on domestic institutions, namely state structure, interest representation and political economy institutions.

Keywords: European Union; financial interests; financial market integration; Lamfalussy framework

Introduction

Financial services regulation and supervision in the European Union (EU) has become one of the most active areas of EU policy-making, undergoing significant change between 1999 and 2004, when the so-called Lamfalussy framework was devised, negotiated and implemented. Moreover, the EU and its member states were active in regulatory and supervisory fora at the international level, for the negotiations of the Basel 2 agreement were initiated by the Basel Committee of Banking Supervisors (BCBS) in 1999, and concluded in 2004. The content of this non-legally binding international agreement was incorporated into legally binding EU legislation, through the Capital Requirements Directive (CRD) adopted in 2005. The CRD was discussed in the EU almost in parallel with the Basel 2 negotiations, though the most intensive phase of EU negotiations took place after the agreement had been reached in Basel in 2004.

As Tal Sadeh and David Howarth (2008) note, there is an ongoing debate in EU studies as to whether socially constructed elements or economic interests drive the 'construction of Europe' (see Moravcsik 1998, 1999 and 2001; Checkel 1999 and 2001), and it is therefore important to examine the influence of economic interest groups across a variety of policy areas. The literature on lobbying in the EU has mostly focused on the activities of interest groups at the EU level (Knill

2001; Bouwen 2002 and 2004), whereas limited attention has been paid to the role of interest groups in shaping national input into EU policy-making (for some exceptions see Beyers 2002; Eising 2004). The national lobbying activity of interest groups is important not only in order to explain national preference formation, but also because in certain policy areas domestic interest groups have preferred to use national channels to articulate their interests, rather than engaging in EU-level lobbying, at least under certain circumstances (i.e. in the short term and when faced with a new or uncertain situation (Grossman 2004)).

This research, which focuses on financial regulation, has both theoretical and empirical rationales. The theoretical rationale contributes to the academic debate on the construction of Europe by evaluating the role of national economic interests and interest groups in the policy-making process in one specific policy area. This involves an investigation of the process of national preference formation and articulation, which is a core component of the main interest-based integration theory, liberal intergovernmentalism. It also contributes to the literature on lobbying in the EU. The empirical rationale is to explain the reform of financial regulation and supervision both within the EU and internationally, by adopting a 'bottom-up' approach from the perspective of domestic interest groups.

This work examines the preferences of financial interest groups (the independent variable) in shaping the national input (more precisely, the contributions made by the relevant public authorities) into EU and international policy-making processes (the dependent variable). The impact, if any, on the final output (the international and EU agreements) is also discussed. The null hypothesis is that the public authorities (national central banks, supervisory agencies, treasuries) defined the 'national interest' and thus the national input into EU and international policy-making processes independently of the preferences of the interest groups in the financial sector; in other words, they articulated their own preferences (Peters 2001). This is likely to come to the forefront whenever national bureaucratic preferences differ from the preferences of interest groups and, where this is the case, it is important to understand under what conditions one set of preferences will prevail over the others.

A complementary explanation that is not considered here is that financial groups used channels at the EU level such as lobbying of the Commission or European Parliament, either directly or through European umbrella associations (see Knill 2001; Beyers 2002; Bouwen 2002 and 2004; Greenwood 2003; Eising 2004). Certain interest groups (for example, the main national banking associations) and individual companies—generally those with considerable economic resources and/or established international and European contacts—engaged in lobbying and consultation activities at the EU level, thus bypassing the national authorities. However, EU lobbying activities are bracketed within this study, which focuses on the national arenas, because the specific question that informs this research concerns the influence of interest groups in national preferences formation and their articulation in the EU. This choice is also justified by the fact that empirical investigation suggests that financial interest groups mainly (but by no means exclusively) used national channels to promote their policy preferences in the policy issues under scrutiny. This finding adds to previous evidence put forward (Josselin 1997; Story and Walter 1997; Grossman 2004).

The proceeding empirical analysis focuses on two country studies: the UK and Germany, which, as well as being two of the largest countries in the EU, have played crucial roles in the three reforms under consideration, not least because they have the two largest financial sectors across the EU. Moreover, these two countries experienced important institutional and policy changes in financial service regulation and supervision in 1998 and 2002, respectively. The interest groups studied within this article are those in the banking sector, with a particular focus on national banking associations, and a number of individual banks and investment firms. Other non-financial groups, such as consumer groups, are not considered because their involvement in the policy discussions on these financial matters was marginal, as they lacked the economic resources, technical expertise and specific incentives (the policy cases discussed do not have direct immediate repercussions for consumers) to contribute to the policy debate. The three policy decisions selected, besides being among the most significant in financial regulation in the last decade, range from a high level of generality (the Lamfalussy process) to a high level of specificity (the CRD). As explained below, this variation is important for the argument put forward in this article.

Most of the empirical data reported in this article were gathered through semi-structured interviews with public authorities, interest groups and individual firms in Germany and the UK. Other useful sources of information were the policy papers and consultation documents produced by the Treasury (or Finance Ministry), the central bank and the supervisory authority in Germany, Britain, the Commission, the European Central Bank (ECB), the BCBS, the European Parliament (EP) and by national and European peak associations and individual firms. A systematic survey of press coverage was also conducted.

Three complementary caveats are needed at this stage. First, it is slightly problematic to consider some financial interest groups or individual companies as purely 'national'. For example, the majority of financial companies in the City are non-British owned and approximately 75 per cent of members of the British Bankers Association (BBA) are non-British (i.e. foreign-owned banks). Deutsche Bank, one of the main German banks, conducts most of its investment activities in London. Further, Allianz, a leading German insurance company that recently acquired the Drezner Bank, is one of the main insurance companies in other EU countries, such as Ireland.

Second, the Allianz-Drezner case highlights another important caveat, namely, the increasingly blurred boundaries between different segments of the financial sector, a trend that is well under way in Britain and has more recently gained momentum in Germany. For this reason, this discussion will utilise the term 'financial' interest groups rather than 'banking' interest groups, unless reference is made to specific banking associations.

Third, it is not argued that the sole influence on national positions is the preference of interest groups. Rather, the research aims to elucidate better the role of interest groups in national preference formation and articulation, explaining under what conditions their influence is likely to be paramount (or otherwise).

© 2008 The Author. Journal compilation © 2008 Political Studies Association
BJPIR, 2008, 10(1)

The article is organised as follows. Section 2 provides an overview of the main features of the financial (banking) sector and mode of interest representation in Germany and the UK. Sections 3, 4 and 5 deal with the contents and policy-making processes of the Lamfalussy framework, the Basel 2 agreement and the CRD. Each section discusses the policy preferences of the main financial interest groups in Germany and Britain and the involvement of these groups in the policy-making process at the national level, especially their interactions with the public authorities. Section 6 conducts an overall assessment, before Section 7 discusses whether the findings can be extrapolated to apply to other EU policies.

By investigating three case studies in the same policy area and by considering two countries, the research design permits the identification of intervening variables that explain different degrees of interest groups' involvement and influence in financial sector policy-making. These two intervening variables also determine the conditions under which the bureaucratic preferences of the national authorities are likely to prevail when shaping national contributions to the EU and international policy-making processes.

Financial Interests Configuration in Germany and the UK

This section outlines the structural features of the financial system in Germany and the UK, with a particular focus on the banking system, the mode of interest representation and the channels of access to policy-making at the national level. A reference is also made to the national framework for regulation and supervision. This domestic political economy analysis assists in the identification of German and UK interest groups' preferences with respect to the policy issues discussed in the following sections.[1]

Germany

The banking and insurance markets in Germany are among the largest in Europe, with a number of significant European market players located in the country. Until the late 1990s, the financial system tended to be mainly bank based, in that use of credit facilities was among the highest in Europe, with the use of debt securities among the lowest (Allen and Gale 2000). However, since the late 1990s, the financial system has become more market oriented, though the universal banks maintain an important role due to their prominence as leading traders of securities.

In Germany, the universal bank model is widespread, even though there has recently been a kind of increasing specialisation of universal banks (cf. the strategy chosen by Deutsche Bank and Drezner Bank, *Financial Times Deutschland*, 22 November 2002). The universal banks in Germany can be divided into three main sectors: private commercial banks, savings banks and co-operatives, and there are also a number of specialised banks (e.g. *bausparkassen*) that are often part of universal banking groups. It is important to note, however, that group competition (*gruppenwettwerb*) has been widespread in Germany, leading to a lack of individual competition and rather a tendency towards collaboration within the three groups, each of which has powerful peak associations (Deeg 1999).

© 2008 The Author. Journal compilation © 2008 Political Studies Association
BJPIR, 2008, 10(1)

The private bank sector is mainly composed of the four big banks: Deutsche Bank, Dresdner Bank, Commerzbank and Bayerische Hypo und Vereinsbank, with a number of other smaller (often regional and local) banks; and foreign banks. The common features of such private commercial banks are that they are active abroad, they privilege short-term credit and have a high degree of capitalisation. The 'big four' detailed above possess a market share of 16 per cent when measured against the total aggregate balance sheet of all banks in Germany, with all private commercial banks having a share of 28 per cent. Public sector banks, which include savings banks and publicly owned regional banks (*Landesbanken*), have a larger market share of 36 per cent when measured against the aggregate balance sheet total of all banks in Germany, with co-operatives possessing a share of 20 per cent (*Financial Times Deutschland*, 12 June 2002).

Foreign banks have only penetrated the German market to a relatively low degree, though their limited activity in retail banking contrasts with the more significant activity in the wholesale market (mergers and acquisitions and investment banking). The retail market is dominated by savings banks and co-operatives, whereas private commercial banks currently face difficulties in expanding their market quotas; this is one of the reasons why the big German banks have expanded abroad by acquiring European or US banks. This is especially so in the case of investment banking (*Financial Times Deutschland*, 22 November 2002).

In recent times, there has been a general trend towards consolidation (or concentration) in the banking sectors, under the stimuli of EU and domestically inspired competition. Between 1999 and 2005, the number of banks fell by 40 per cent, but bank density (the number of banks in relation to the population) in Germany remains twice as high as the EU average (excluding Germany), due to the presence of so many savings banks (Deutsche Bank 2004).

Small and medium enterprises (SMEs) or *mittlestand*, account for approximately three quarters of German output, and have a large political voice (*The Banker*, 4 April 2005). All banks, but in particular public banks, used to make extensive loans to *mittlestand*, at low margins (*Financial Times Deutschland*, 22 August 2002), even though this practice was challenged by the pressure exerted by EU and domestic reforms (Grossman 2006).

In Germany, interest groups are highly integrated within the policy-making process, and public authorities often consult with the peak associations (Coleman 1994, 282), albeit this is primarily true for the savings and co-operative banks. Moreover, regulatory duties are shared between the public authorities and peak associations of the three banking groups (Busch 2004). There are three main peak associations in the banking sector representing the three main categories of banks, all of which are members of comparable European umbrella associations.

The regulation and supervision of financial services in Germany underwent an important reform in 2002, which was designed to streamline the existing framework. Following this reform, which also coincided with a reshaping of the governance structure of the central bank, a single supervisory authority, the BAFIN, was established for all segments of the financial sector. However, banking supervision remained a shared task between the single authority, BAFIN, which has a specific division dealing with banking supervision, and the Bundesbank, whose regional offices are responsible for operational supervision, the collection of data and information and their transmission to BAFIN, which, like its forerunner BAKRED, does not have units based in the Länder.

Both the Bundesbank and BAFIN were involved in the negotiations of Basel 2 and, though the central bank remained an important player, BAFIN displayed more institutional clout than its predecessor, the BAKRED, which had taken part in the negotiations of Basel 1 in 1988. In contrast, in the EU negotiations on the CRD and the Lamfalussy process, the Federal Finance Ministry was in the driving seat, albeit with significant input from BAFIN and the Bundesbank.

The federal state structure in Germany created repercussions not only on power sharing between the public authorities, but also on interest representation, thus strengthening the voice of the public banks (saving banks and *Landesbanken*) and SMEs, which have excellent access to policy-makers in the Länder (cf. Deeg and Lutz 2000). Given the federal structure of the Bundesbank before the 2002 reform, Länder-based interest groups were also given a sympathetic audience in Frankfurt. Big private banks, however, have instead tended to have better access to both federal policy-makers and policy-makers at the EU level.

The UK

The financial system in Britain is highly developed, with the traditional distinction between the three segments of the financial market receding earlier than in the rest of Europe. This led to the creation of powerful financial conglomerates, with the UK now hosting the largest securities market in Europe, one that competes directly with the financial centres of the US.

As a result of both the impact that EU legislation has made and the largely domestically driven reforms of the banking system that took place in the 1980s, there are two 'bank circuits' in the UK: retail banking (mainly large domestic banks dealing with consumer credit and loans to SMEs), and investment banks (dealing with corporate finance, mergers and acquisitions and international banking), many of which are foreigners. There are, however, no public banks in the UK, in stark contrast to Germany.

Investment banking is closely related to securities, the main source of corporate finance (Allen and Gale 2000). Investment banks and, more generally, investment firms that perform some banking tasks, tend to be concentrated in the City, which hosts the largest number of foreign banks in Europe. In domestic retail banking, there are only a few providers, creating a status quo that was criticised by the British competition commission (cf. Cruickshank 2000), with reference to the banking services offered to consumers, and specifically with reference to the provision of funding to SMEs. Further, the concentration of banks in London is among the highest in Europe, leading to a greater concentration also of profitability and efficiency (*Financial Times*, 22 August 2002).

The British Bankers Association is the principal professional association for banks in the UK, with members holding 90 per cent of UK banking sector assets and 95 per

© 2008 The Author. Journal compilation © 2008 Political Studies Association
BJPIR, 2008, 10(1)

cent of all banking employment. Eighty-five per cent of the members are involved in wholesale banking and 75 per cent of members are of non-UK origin, from 60 different countries. Further, the London Investment Banking Association (LIBA) represents investment banks and firms, many of which are foreign owned. It should also be noted that in addition to this are the various associations of building societies and mortgage lenders.

The main business associations in Britain are not 'peak associations' as they are referred to in Germany, but 'umbrella associations'; the structure of 'peak associations' is more hierarchical, thus creating coherent positions and the enforcement of internal discipline. However, previous studies on British policy-making in the financial sector portray the mode of interest intermediation as 'meso-corporative' (Moran 1991) with substantial input from the sector in shaping policy. Others, taking a policy network approach, portray the system of financial interest representation and interaction with the public authorities as one that is, in contrast, open and horizontal (Josselin 1997).

Financial services regulation and supervision in Britain underwent a watershed reform in 1998, in conjunction with the restructuring of the Bank of England, which, though losing its responsibility for banking supervision, was given operational independence in monetary policy. The governance structure of the bank was also changed with the creation of the Monetary Policy Committee; the Financial Services Authority (FSA) was established, with responsibility for the whole financial sector, including banking supervision, though it should be noted that the Bank of England remained responsible for overall financial stability together with the Treasury and the Financial Services Authority.

Until the creation of the FSA in 1998, the Bank of England had been the only negotiator for Britain in Basel 1. In Basel 2, however, both the Bank of England and the FSA were involved in the negotiations. Most of the implementation studies concerning Basel 2 and the CRD were conducted or co-ordinated by the FSA, whereas the Treasury was in charge of co-ordinating the consultation on the CRD in order to define the British negotiating position. With regards to the Lamfalussy process, the Treasury and FSA were mostly involved in EU negotiations.

The Lamfalussy Framework

In July 2000, the Economic and Financial Affairs Council (ECOFIN) appointed an *ad hoc* 'Committee of Wise Men', led by the former central banker Alexandre Lamfalussy, to discuss the best means of adopting the Commission's Financial Services Action Plan (FSAP) (Commission of the European Communities 1999) and adapt EU regulations to an ever-changing financial marketplace. The Committee invited the member states, regulatory authorities and the industry itself to submit contributions and take part in confidential hearings (Committee of Wise Men 2001, 32–35) before the Report was completed in December 2000. It proposed the framework described at the end of this section, though initially only with reference to securities. After the question of parliamentary scrutiny was resolved in February 2002 on the basis of a compromise between the EP and the Commission, the Lamfalussy framework was endorsed by the Stockholm European Council.

In May 2002 ECOFIN, following the proposal of the German Finance Minister Hans Eichel and the British Chancellor Gordon Brown, decided in favour of extending the fast track procedure of reporting to banking and insurance (*Financial Times*, 15 April 2002). The issue was negotiated throughout 2002, and in December of that year, ECOFIN approved a proposal of the Economic and Financial Committee for the extension of the Lamfalussy framework to other sectors, taking into account the ECB's request for involvement (Economic and Financial Committee 2002). The new framework was then implemented during 2003 and 2004.

Since 2004, the governance of the financial service sector has been based on a complex multi-level system of EU rule making and enhanced co-operation between national supervisory authorities, underpinned by newly created EU committees (such as the Securities Committee, set up in 2001) and reformed committees (such as the Banking Advisory Committee and the Insurance Committee, which date back to 1977 and 1992, respectively). The functional division between banking, securities and insurance remains and specific arrangements for the supervision of financial conglomerates have been set in place. Further, as the Lamfalussy report recommended, the EU institutions established an inter-institutional monitoring group, which consists of Council, Commission and EP representatives.

If the British and German governments were among the main players in the establishment of the Lamfalussy framework (for a more detailed account see Quaglia 2007), this does not mean that domestic interest groups in those countries were formally consulted or de facto involved in the policy-making process at the national level. To be sure, the BBA expressed full support for the Lamfalussy model with reference to securities and subsequently for the extension of the model to banking and, similarly, the main players in the City (some of which had been consulted by the Committee of Wise Men) were supportive of the new regulatory architecture.

The association of German private banks expressed support for the Lamfalussy framework, as did a number of big market players, some of which had been consulted by the Committee of Wise Men, or had senior executives sitting on it, albeit serving in their personal capacity and not representing their companies' interest. It should also be noted that in Germany, whereas the big private banks expressed clear views in favour of the revised regulatory framework, the public banks, traditionally more inward oriented and less keen on market integration, omitted to take a position on it.

Overall, the most competitive and outwards-oriented part of the banking industry in both Germany and the UK endorsed the Lamfalussy framework in such a way as to promote further market integration and co-operation among supervisors, possibly leading to a convergence of supervisory standards. Moreover, the European Banking Federation, to which the two main banking associations in Germany and the UK belong, also endorsed the Lamfalussy architecture. However, the intensive and extensive consultations that took place with reference to Basel 2, and especially on CRD, did not take place in relation to the Lamfalussy process either in Germany or the UK, and only some of the big companies volunteered to provide their opinions on it. Some of the main market players even put forward innovative proposals that went beyond what was eventually agreed upon: for example the

© 2008 The Author. Journal compilation © 2008 Political Studies Association
BJPIR, 2008, 10(1)

Deutsche Bank proposed the creation of a European System of Supervisory Authorities (similar to the European System of Central Banks (ESCB)), which would include but not be limited to a European Financial Service Authority.

The public authorities (primarily the Treasury Ministries, and to some extent the supervisory authorities, namely, the FSA for the UK and the BAFIN and Bundesbank for Germany) largely defined national preference in accordance with their own priorities, opposing any extension of the ECB's supervisory competences as well as the creation of a single European regulator, two options which were instead welcomed by parts of the banking sector that had contributed to the debate. Furthermore, it is certainly true that the industry's drive for the establishment of a fully integrated and more stringently regulated single market in financial services provided the trigger for the reform, but it is also the case that this goal was supported by both the British and German authorities possessing the two largest (and possibly expanding) financial centres and financial markets in Europe. The British authorities have always been quite outspoken regarding their objective of maintaining the City's position as the leading financial centre in Europe (Moran 1991; interview, London, December 2005) and towards the end of the 1990s, the German government has also taken a similar approach to the Frankfurt *finanzplatz* (interview, Frankfurt, January 2006).

The Basel 2 Accord

International standards for capital requirements had been established by the Basel 1 agreement signed in 1988, which was then revised and integrated by the Basel 2 Accord signed in 2004. The rationale for the revision was to tailor the capital requirements of banks more closely to the actual economic risk that they faced, while also taking account of innovations in financial markets and risk management strategies.

The Basel 2 Accord based capital requirements on three pillars (BCBS 2005a).[2] Pillar One was concerned with the minimum capital requirements, covering three types of risk: credit risk, market risk and, innovatively, operational risk. Innovations were also introduced with reference to risk measurement. Pillar Two was the supervisory review process aimed at covering external factors that were not fully taken into account when computing the minimum capital requirements. Supervisors were therefore enabled to take measures which, if necessary, could go beyond the minimum capital requirements. Finally, Pillar Three was the discipline imposed by the market, facilitated by transparency requirements.

The Basel Committee of Banking Supervisors, where the Basel 2 Accord was proposed, negotiated and eventually agreed, is composed of the central banks and supervisory authorities of 13 countries (9 EU member states, in addition to Canada, Japan, Switzerland and the US). Further, the European Commission and ECB participate as observers, both in the general Committee and in the various task-forces (for example, on risk management, capital ratios, etc.) that report to the Committee.

The negotiations on Basel 2 gained momentum in June 1999, with the publication of the first consultative paper (CP) by the BCBS, followed by a second consultative

© 2008 The Author. Journal compilation © 2008 Political Studies Association
BJPIR, 2008, 10(1)

paper in January 2001 and a third in May 2003. Further, the BCBS conducted four quantitative impact studies (QIS) in 2001 (QIS1), 2002 (QIS2), 2004 (QIS3) and 2005 (QIS5) concerning the implementation of the new rules and such assessments were conducted in aggregate terms, that is, they were not country or sector specific. For example, for QIS5, the BCBS requested that banks in 90 different countries carry out a series of data studies to strengthen the models for the Basel 2 Accord, three years after the conclusion of the QIS3, which included data from 350 banks and 43 countries. However, since not all countries were satisfied by the results of the QIS3, the US, Japan, South Africa and Germany decided to conduct national impact studies, which became the QIS4.

The following account, though incomplete, focuses on the main issues that were raised during the negotiations of the Basel 2 Accord and were of direct relevance to industry. Some of these issues, such as the use of internal rather than external rating, the need to counteract the pro-cyclical effects of the Accord and the potential negative effects for SMEs and mortgage lenders, were partly addressed throughout the negotiations in Basel (see Wood 2005). Other issues, such as the 'solo' or 'consolidated' model of supervision, the role of the leading or consolidating supervisor and the risk weighting for intra-group exposure, featured more prominently during the discussions regarding the transposition of the Accord into the CRD (see below).[3]

An important issue, settled early on in the negotiations, concerned the initial US-led proposal to use *external rating* in order to assess the credit risk that is part of the first pillar (Lütz 2004). The public authorities and banking sectors in Britain and Germany instead suggested the use of *internal rating*, which was regarded as more reliable. This proposal was endorsed by the BCBS, and it was thus included in the Second Consultative Paper (CP2).

A key issue in shaping Basel 2 concerned the implications of the new capital rules relating to the terms of, and access to, bank credit for *small and medium-sized enterprises*. During the negotiations towards the proposed Accord, a concern was voiced that risk weights for SMEs would remain the same as when lending to large unrated corporates due to the fact that most SME borrowers do not have external credit ratings (Bundesverband Deutscher Banken 2003; European Savings Banks Group 2003). This issue was prominent for the SMEs in Germany, the *mittlestand*, which largely rely on bank loans for their funding (Lütz 2004) and the German authorities were so concerned about the domestic impact of Basel 2 that they decided to conduct a QIS of their own accord (QIS4). The changes that were subsequently made to the rules of Basel 2 regarding these issues can largely be ascribed to the activity of the German representatives, which joined forces with the Italian authorities, also worried about the implications for SMEs. As a result, the process of lending to SMEs under the proposed Accord is seen by many observers to be attracting more favourable treatment than is the case under existing arrangements.

If the UK authorities (namely the FSA and the Bank of England) were not concerned about SMEs and small-sized banks, one of their main priorities was the *trading book review*, a measure agreed by the Basel Committee and the International Organisation of Securities Commissions (IOSCO) in July 2005. Essentially, the trading book (BCBS 2005b) introduced advanced rules for trading activities in which several investment firms in the City are involved, and is to be incorporated into EU legislation.

With regards to Basel 2, the preferences of financial interest groups were more intense than those presented during the Lamfalussy framework. In the UK, direct policy input was mainly provided by a few internationally active banks, those to which Basel 2 applies. However, if anything this proved a hindrance for the national public authorities involved in the negotiations, as they would have welcomed more information from industry. In contrast to the low domestic political salience that Basel 2 had in the UK, it was high in Germany, with interest groups mobilising intensively and extensively, in particular with regard to the issue of the implications for SMEs. Not only did the national public authorities in Germany engage in an in-depth consultation process, they also received a great number of position papers from the public.[4] While the Bundesbank engaged in several hearings before the federal parliament, political pressure was exerted upon it, along with the BAFIN, both at the Länder and federal levels, accompanied by the lobbying activities of various sectors of society (interview, Frankfurt, January 2006).

It should also be noted that during the Basel 2 negotiations, several national delegations, including the German and British ones, were composed of senior officials from the central banks and the (banking) supervisory authority. With regards to co-operation between the Bank of England and the FSA, the former was in ultimate control during the Basel 2 negotiations, primarily due to its technical capacity: for example, as a result of previous experience, the Bank boasted staff with experience in the field of 'calibration' (large international banks are actively present in London). Further, while the FSA maintained a greater degree of involvement with regards to the drafting of the language of the Accord, all the QIS conducted in Basel were led by senior officials from the Bank of England (interview, London, January 2006).

Similarly, the Bundesbank and the BAKRED/BAFIN had different foci at the working level: while BAFIN dealt with regulatory issues, the Bundesbank maintained a focus on economic studies. Overall, the Bundesbank proved more responsive than the BAKRED/BAFIN with regard to the policy preferences of the banks, especially the small ones, due to the close and frequent contact that they maintained at the local level (interview, Frankfurt, January 2006).

The EU Capital Requirements Directive

Capital requirements were already regulated by existing EU legislation that was issued throughout the 1990s and largely implemented the Basel 1 Accord. When negotiations began on the Basel 2 agreement, the member states agreed that the new capital requirements framework agreed in Basel 2 would be incorporated into EU legislation by the amendment of the existing directives, the Codified Banking Directive 2000/12/EC and the CAD 93/6/EC, through the re-casting procedure. In late 2004, ECOFIN reached an agreement, under the Dutch presidency, on the draft of the CRD. After the text was transmitted to the EP for co-decision, the directive was approved by a plenary vote in September 2005 during the British presidency.

The CRD came into force in 2007, with the most sophisticated approaches available from 2008, in line with the introduction of Basel 2 rules. The Committee of European Banking Supervisors (CEBS), created as part of the Lamfalussy framework, is responsible for ensuring consistency and convergence in the application of this new framework.

Although it possessed the same rationale as Basel 2, the CRD had a wider scope of application. The intention of the directive was to ensure a level playing field between firms competing within the same EU markets and thus it applied to all credit institutions and investment firms as defined by the Investment Services Directive (ISD). In common with the Basel 2 agreement, the CRD is articulated on three pillars: requirements for an internal capital assessment by financial institutions (exposure to credit, market and operational risks); a supervisory review process conducted by supervisors to evaluate the risk profile of each institution; and market discipline.

However, there are three main differences between Basel 2 and the CRD. Basel 2 is an international agreement, signed by 13 countries, including the US, Japan and Switzerland, and de facto extending worldwide (for example, Basel 1 was applied by most banks in 100 countries). In contrast, the CRD applies to only the 27 EU member states. Second, Basel 1 and 2 are so-called 'gentleman's agreements', that is, they are not legally binding, whereas the CRD is a legally binding and directly enforceable instrument. Third, Basel 2 applies only to credit institutions (banks), whereas the CRD also applies to investment firms. The first applies only to internationally active banks (for example it is estimated that in the US only up to 10 internationally active banks will be affected by Basel 2 (*Financial Times*, 8 October 2004)), whereas the CRD applies to all banks and investment firms, even if their activities are purely domestic.

On some more specific points, the CRD made a number of adaptations of the Basel 2 rules.[5] Further, in addition to the issues raised in the context of the Basel process, a number of concerns directly relevant to industry were raised over the EU's implementation of Basel through the CRD. The following account is by no means exhaustive.

The CRD enhanced the role of the *consolidating supervisor* for the supervision of EU cross-border groups, namely, the national supervisor in the member state where the group's parent firm is authorised. The consolidating supervisor is in charge of co-ordinating the treatment of an application that such a group may make for the approval necessary to use the more sophisticated capital calculation rules. All supervisors concerned are expected to reach an agreed decision on the application within six months, and in the event of a failure to do so, the consolidating supervisor is empowered to make a decision in order not to impose extra burdens on firms dealing with multiple supervisors. Banks with cross-border activities (mainly British-based banks and large private German banks) were largely in favour of the establishment of a fully consolidated supervision, though this was ultimately successfully opposed by the national supervisors.

For the BBA/LIBA, a specific concern related to the initial Commission proposal requiring the calculation of capital requirements at a 'solo' and 'sub-consolidated'

© *2008 The Author. Journal compilation* © *2008 Political Studies Association*
BJPIR, 2008, 10(1)

level, as well as at the 'aggregate' holding company level. Fundamentally, the 'solo' model insulates the principal regulated entity from other members of its group, whereas the 'consolidated' model allows regulation and supervision to be applied to the top tier (i.e. parent or holding companies) of the group covering all members that provide financial services (British Bankers Association 2004). British banks, in conjunction with the British authorities, wanted the application of the 'solo' model to remain a possibility in the UK by virtue of the EU legislation, and after an intensive period of lobbying aimed at both the Commission and the EP, this was achieved.

Another relatively minor yet extremely controversial issue was the *treatment of intra-group exposure*, as the German savings and co-operative banks wanted zero-risk weighting for this within their sub-sector, and directed intense lobbying at the EP in order to achieve this objective. This provision lowers the capital requirements of savings and co-operative banks, giving them a competitive advantage, and thus it was challenged by private banks in the UK and especially in Germany. However, a compromise solution of zero-risk weighting was achieved in the event that certain conditions were met.[6]

The British Treasury and the FSA undertook extensive consultations with industry on the CRD (HM Treasury 2003 and 2005), with the former focusing on issues relating to the overall cost and benefits of the new regulation in order to inform the position and strategy to be taken by the UK in EU fora, and the latter focusing on domestic implementation issues. Between December 2003 and April 2004, the Treasury engaged in a formal consultation exercise on the Commission's proposal for the implementation of the Basel 2 Accord through the CRD Directive. Approximately 100 firms and organisations responded, with representations coming from banks, building societies, consumer groups, investment firms, venture capitalists, small business, private investment managers, stockbrokers, academics and trade associations. The Treasury also held several industry round-table meetings and small drafting groups in order to consult the market on the government's negotiating stance in Brussels.[7] The FSA established two groups, the credit risk standing group and operational risk standing group, in order to facilitate discussion with industry regarding implementation, the minutes of which were posted on the Internet in order to promote transparency and facilitate the flow of information.

The German authorities also engaged in a formal consultation exercise on the Commission's proposal for the implementation of the Basel 2 Accord through the CRD. In order to prepare for the national implementation of Basel 2 and the CRD, the Bundesbank and BAFIN established the 'Implementation of Basel 2' Working Group as well as a number of specialist sub-committees to consider the issues of: the Internal Ratings-Based Approach; operational risk; credit protection techniques; securitisation; the Supervisory Review Process; and disclosure requirements. Composed of experts from the banking industry, BAFIN and the Bundesbank, the sub-committees' proposals were discussed and examined in a wider context, which included representatives of the banking industry's peak associations. In common with the British model, minutes of the meetings were posted on the Internet, thus promoting transparency and information exchange.

© 2008 The Author. Journal compilation © 2008 Political Studies Association
BJPIR, 2008, 10(1)

An Overall Assessment

The case studies examined above highlight the importance of distinguishing between the degree of involvement and the degree of influence of interest groups in the policy-making process. The *degree of involvement* primarily depends on the *policy content*; that is whether broader *institutional issues* (such as the decision to delegate competences and the creation of a regulatory framework) or *specific rules* are negotiated in international or EU fora. In the case of the first, the involvement of interest groups is likely to be low due to the high degree of *uncertainty* usually concerning the effects of broader institutional issues on the activities of interest groups (cf. Grossman 2004). In addition, such issues tend to have the character of *public goods*, thus removing the incentive for interest groups to engage in lobbying. By contrast, when specific rules are decided, the involvement of interest groups is likely to be higher, and informed by *costs–benefits calculations*.

However, the reverse is true for public authorities. Since institutional issues tend to exhibit a substantial effect on national authorities' competences, they are likely to possess strong preferences that shape national input into international and EU policy-making processes on these matters. Instead, when specific rules are negotiated, the national authorities are generally willing to incorporate the preferences of domestic interest groups in defining the national position that will be externally articulated.

The *degree of influence* that interest groups hold in shaping the national input is dependent on *domestic institutions*, first and foremost the state structure (federal or unitary), which in turn affects the structure of interest representation and political economy institutions, such as the linked bank-SMEs in Germany (cf. Deeg 1999; Deeg and Lutz 2000). The distribution of power at the national level is very important whenever there are competing domestic preferences, or more precisely, where there are interest groups with different preferences competing for influence with regard to the definition of the national position in EU and international fora.

The Lamfalussy process, which established a broad regulatory framework for financial services in the EU, did not elicit a high degree of involvement by interest groups. To a degree, it had the characteristics of a public good, which meant that financial associations and private companies had limited direct interest to engage in lobbying activities on this issue; the specific costs of doing so outweighed the diffuse potential benefits. Moreover, the implications of the new framework for the activity of interest groups were highly uncertain. Broadly speaking, the most internationally active large banks supported it (as did their governments) because it was seen as instrumental to further market integration and they were in favour of streamlining the framework for financial service regulation and supervision in the EU. International financial groups also favoured a further transfer of competence to the EU level. By contrast, the national authorities vehemently opposed this institutional change, and the national input into EU fora represented a reflection of their bureaucratic preferences.

With regards to Basel 2, which contains detailed rules on capital requirement and supervisory implementation, the preferences of financial interest groups were less uncertain and more intense than in respect of the Lamfalussy framework. There was therefore a higher level of lobbying activity, though this varied across countries. In the UK, direct policy input was mainly provided by a few internationally active banks, whereas in Germany interest groups mobilised intensively and extensively, primarily on the issue of the implications for SMEs, one that was politically salient in the domestic arena. It should be noted that both the federal state structure and the federal organisational structure of the Bundesbank (until 2002) and of interest representation in Germany, including the banking sector (cf. Deeg 1999), account for the influence of Länder-based interest groups (savings and co-operative banks) in shaping Germany's negotiating position.

The preferences of interest groups were more intense and widespread in relation to the CRD and its implementation than the Basel 2 negotiations, because the directive contained specific rules that applied to all credit firms (banks) and investment firms in the EU. The fact that these rules applied to investment firms, which have a stronghold in the City, increased the mobilisation of economic interest groups in Britain. Further, national public authorities in Germany and the UK engaged in extensive consultation processes and were willing to articulate and promote the preferences of the domestic banking sector in international and EU policy-making arenas, also because they did not have alternative bureaucratic preferences.

In the second and third case studies (Basel 2 and CRD), central banks, supervisory authorities and treasuries have generally acted as country representatives, defending the national interests, or more precisely, the interests of powerful domestic groups. By contrast, in the case of Lamfalussy, and on specific issues of the CRD, such as the consolidating supervisor, the public authorities involved in the negotiations partly acted as self-interest bureaucracies, trying to pursue their institutional preferences, successfully safeguarding their competences in this area.

The case study that is more surprising is Basel 2, particularly when compared with the negotiations towards Basel 1 (cf. Speyer 2006), which took place among national supervisors behind closed doors, with minimal involvement of the interest groups. In the case of Basel 2, it was clear to all the participants that it was not simply an international agreement concerning banking regulation, but rather financial diplomacy and a very political game in which the national authorities tried to achieve competitive advantages through banking regulation (interview, Frankfurt, January 2006). The Bank of England has always been keen to promote London as a leading financial centre in Europe, and after Economic and Monetary Union (EMU), the Bundesbank has become sympathetic to the goal of promoting *finanzplatz Deutschland*.

The drafting of the technical and detailed content of Basel 2 and the CRD also required close co-operation between the public authorities (central banks and supervisory agencies) and the banking sector, which was involved in intensive and extensive consultations, and the provision of data, information and expertise, with information exchange operating in both directions. For example, after each important meeting in Basel, the Bundesbank and BAFIN organised a debriefing session for the German banks, either in Frankfurt or Bonn (interview, Frankfurt, January

2006). Before important EU meetings, the national authorities in Germany and the UK also engaged in extensive consultation with the industry.

Conclusion

The aim of this article was to evaluate the role of national economic interest groups in shaping national contributions (or 'input') to EU and international policy-making processes, and more generally, to the process of European integration. The explanation that considers financial interest groups as active policy-makers, rather than passive policy takers, is broadly confirmed by the empirical record. It has, however, to be qualified, in that it depends on the policy content (interest groups' involvement is higher when specific rules are negotiated) and domestic institutions (interest groups are likely to be more influential when the domestic distribution of power gives them preferential access to policy-makers). The null hypothesis concerning the power of bureaucratic preferences in defining the national position in international and EU fora holds in specific circumstances, that is, whenever the policy discussions concern institutional issues (such as supranational delegation and scope of governance), whereas interest groups have little interest in broad institutional questions.

These findings extend existing understandings of economic interests and European integration. Whereas the literature on lobbying at EU level is by now extensive, national lobbying concerning EU issues has mainly been explored as step one[8]—national preference formation—of liberal intergovernmentalism, not always receiving sufficient attention. This research explains under what conditions national economic interests are more likely to engage in lobbying activity on EU issues and under what conditions they are more likely to be successful in doing so. Whereas the role of domestic institutions in accounting for the influence of certain interest groups has been pointed out in other bodies of political economy literature (with specific reference to financial issues see Deeg and Perez 2000; Lütz 2004), the importance of the 'types' of policy content in activating interest groups or not is a relatively novel finding.

It is difficult to say to what extent these findings can be extrapolated to other policies, because the financial service sector has traditionally been regarded as influential in domestic policy-making. It should however be noted that in the case studies of EU and international policy-making considered here, the public authorities also valued the expertise, data gathering and first-hand experience provided by the industry, a move that ultimately strengthened its policy input.

About the Author

Lucia Quaglia, Senior Lecturer in Politics and Contemporary European Studies, Department of Politics and Contemporary European Studies, University of Sussex, Falmer, Brighton BN1 9RG, UK, email: *l.quaglia@sussex.ac.uk*

Notes

I wish to thank Roman Walega for valuable research assistance and the Department of Politics, University of Bristol, for the financial support necessary to collect empirical research material. I also wish to thank all the practitioners who generously gave me their time, allowing me to benefit from their first-hand experience in the policy process. Any errors and omissions are mine. I am grateful to Anna Maria Johansson, Yang Lin, Huw Macartney, Machiko Miyakoshi, Bernhard Speyer and Ken Takeda for their perceptive comments on an earlier draft of this article. I would also wish to thank all participants at the UACES conference in Limerick, at the SEI research seminar and at the workshop of EUSA political economy section, in particular, John Peterson, who acted as a discussant, and Emiliano Grossman, David Howarth, Patrick Leblond, Tal Sadeh and two anonymous referees.

1. Some of the points highlighted in this section are also discussed in the literature on varieties of capitalism (see Hall and Soskice 2001).

2. See also http://www.bis.org/publ/bcbs118.htm, accessed December 2005.

3. For industry's comments received by the BCBS on the Third Consultative Paper (CP3) see http://www.bis.org/bcbs/cp3comments.htm, accessed December 2005.

4. The Bunsdesbank received more than 200 letters and policy documents from the public, including, among others, churches.

5. For an overview, see http://europa.eu.int/rapid/pressReleasesAction.do?reference=MEMO/04/178&language=en&guiLanguage=en, accessed December 2005.

6. Finally, there was the concern that if the *implementation* of Basel 2 and the CRD was not *simultaneous*, compliance and operation costs for international banks would increase, particularly if they had to run different systems for their EU and non-EU operations. The UK banking sector feared it could be placed at a competitive disadvantage.

7. At the end of the consultation process, the Treasury produced a document called 'Capital Requirement Directives: Regulatory impact assessment' (2004).

8. The other two steps being intergovernmental bargain and EU institution building.

Bibliography

Allen, F. and Gale, D. (2000) *Comparing Financial Systems* (Cambridge: MIT).

Basel Committee of Banking Supervision (BCBS) (2005a) *Basel II: International Convergence of Capital Measurement and Capital Standards: A Revised Framework* (Basel: Basel Committee of Banking Supervision).

BCBS (2005b) *The Application of Basel II to Trading Activities and the Treatment of Double Default Effects* (Basel: Basel Committee of Banking Supervision).

Beyers, J. (2002) 'Gaining and seeking access: The European adaptation of domestic interest associations', *European Journal of Political Research*, 41:5, 585–612.

Bouwen, P. (2002) 'Corporate lobbying in the European Union: The logic of access', *Journal of European Public Policy*, 9:3, 365–390.

Bouwen, P. (2004) 'Exchanging access goods for access: A comparative study of business lobbying in the European Union institutions', *European Journal of Political Research*, 43:3, 337–369.

British Bankers Association (2004) *Letter to the Rapporteur of the EP concerning the Capital Requirement Directive* (London).

Bundesverband Deutscher Banken (2003) *Response to the Consultative Paper 3 on the Basel 2 Accord*.

Busch, A. (2004) 'National filters: Europeanisation, institutions, and discourse in the case of banking regulation', *West European Politics*, 27:2, 310–333.

Checkel, J. (1999) 'Social construction and integration', *Journal of European Public Policy*, 6:4, Special Issue, 545–560.

Checkel, J. (2001) 'A constructivist research program in EU studies?', *European Union Politics*, 2:2, 219–226.

Coleman, W. (1994) 'Policy convergence in banking: A comparative study', *Political Studies*, 42:2, 274–292.

Commission of the European Communities (1999) *Financial Services: Implementing the Framework for Financial Markets: Action Plan*. Communication of the Commission, COM(1999)232, 11 May.

Committee of Wise Men (2001) *Final Report of the Committee of Wise Men on the Regulation of Securities Markets* (Brussels: Committee of Wise Men).

Cruickshank, D. (2000) 'Cruickshank report', *Competition and Regulation in Financial Services: Striking the Right Balance* (London).

Deeg, R. (1999) *Finance Capitalism Unveiled. Banks and the German Political Economy* (Ann Arbor MI: University of Michigan Press).

Deeg, R. and Lutz, S. (2000) 'Internationalization and financial federalism—The United States and Germany at the crossroads?', *Comparative Political Studies*, 33:3, 374–405.

Deeg, R. and Perez, S. (2000) 'International capital mobility and domestic institutions: Corporate finance and governance in four European cases', *Governance*, 13:2, 119–153.

Deutshe Bank (2004) 'Bank Performance in Europe', *EU Moniter 13*, 28 June, Frankfurt.

Economic and Financial Committee (2002) 'Report on Financial Regulation, Supervision and Stability', revised to reflect the discussion at the 8 October meeting of the ECOFIN Council, 9 October, Brussels.

Eising, R. (2004) 'Multilevel governance and business interests in the European Union', *Governance*, 17:2, 211–245.

European Savings Banks Group (2003) *Response to the Consultative Paper 3 on the Basel 2 Accord.*

Grossman, E. (2004) 'Bringing politics back in: Rethinking the role of economic interest groups in European integration', *Journal of European Public policy*, 11:4, 637–654.

Grossman, E. (2006) 'Europeanization as an interactive process: German public banks meet EU state aid policy', *Journal of Common Market Studies*, 44:2, 325–348.

Hall, P. and Soskice, D. (eds) (2001) *Varieties of Capitalism: The Institutional Foundations of Comparative Advantage* (Oxford: Oxford University Press).

HM Treasury (2003) *The New Capital Adequacy Directive, CAD 3: The Transposition of the New Basel Accord into EU Legislation*. London, Consultation Document.

HM Treasury (2005) *Capital Requirements Directive—Regulatory Impact Assessment* (London).

Josselin, D. (1997) *Money Politics in the New Europe: Britain, France and the Single Financial Market* (Basingstoke: Macmillan).

Knill, C. (2001) 'Private governance across multiple arenas: European interest associations as interface actors', *Journal of European Public Policy*, 8:2, 227–246.

Lütz, S. (2004) 'Convergence within national diversity: The regulatory state in finance', *Journal of Public Policy*, 24:2, 169–197.

Moran, M. (1991) *The Politics of the Financial Services Revolution: The USA, UK and Japan* (London: Macmillan).

Moravcsik, A. (1998) *The Choice For Europe* (London: UCL Press).

Moravcsik, A. (1999) 'Is something rotten in the state of Denmark? Constructivism and European integration', *Journal of European Public Policy*, 6:4, Special Issue, 669–682.

Moravcsik, A. (2001) 'A constructivist research program in EU studies?', *European Union Politics*, 2:2, 226–249.

Peters, B. G. (2001) *The Politics of Bureaucracy* (London: Routledge).

Quaglia, L. (2007) 'The politics of financial service regulation and supervision reform in the European Union', *European Journal of Political Research*, 46:2, 269–290.

Sadeh, T. and Howarth, D. (2008) 'Economic interests and the European Union: A catalyst for European integration or a hindrance?', The *British Journal of Politics & International Relations*, 10:1, 1–8.

Speyer, B. (2006) 'Governing global financial markets—Basel I and II: The role of non-state actors', in G. F. Schuppert (ed.), *Global Governance and the Role of Non State Actors* (Baden-Baden: Nomos), 101–116.

Story, J. and Walter, I. (1997) *Political Economy of Financial Integration in Europe: The Battle of the System* (Manchester: Manchester University Press).

Wood, D. (2005) *Governing Global Banking* (Aldershot: Ashgate).

© 2008 The Author. Journal compilation © 2008 Political Studies Association
BJPIR, 2008, 10(1)

doi: 10.1111/j.1467-856x.2007.00318.x   *BJPIR: 2008 VOL 10, 64–83*

All Access Points are Not Created Equal: Explaining the Fate of Diffuse Interests in the EU

Mitchell P. Smith

According to literature on organised interests in the European Union, the European Parliament's Environment Committee (ENVI) gives environmental interests a potent point of legislative access. Yet while ENVI helped sustain the EP's commitment to environmental interests in the case of the End-of-Life Vehicles Directive adopted in September 2000, it did not do so for REACH, a regulatory framework for the chemicals sector adopted by the EP and Council in December 2006. Ultimately, the value of legislative access for organised interest groups depends on the extent to which they have privileged interactions with a node in the policy-making apparatus and the degree to which actors in the policy-making process defer to the particular institutional node. For environmental interests, both privileged interactions between environmentalists and ENVI and deference to the committee decline when environmentalists seek regulations that impose concentrated costs on producers. Such instances invoke calls to protect industrial competitiveness and intensify conflict between EP committees.

Keywords: European Parliament; parliamentary committees; environmental interests; REACH directive

The literature on diffuse interests in the EU, including environmental and women's rights movements, depicts the development of EU policy-making as a favourable shift in opportunity structures for these interests (Marks and McAdam 1996; Pollack 1997; Pollack and Hafner-Burton 2000).[1] The essence of the argument is that EU institutions seeking to advance their own interests in deeper integration both constitute effective access points and stimulate the organisation of diffuse interests at the European level. For environmentalists, for example, the Council of Environment Ministers, the European Commission's DG Environment and the European Parliament's Committee on Environment, Public Health and Consumer Policy represent sympathetic institutional venues.[2] Case-study evidence suggests that the last of these institutions has been particularly consequential; on a range of environmental and health issues, from auto emissions (Hubschmid and Moser 1997; Warleigh 2000; Pedler 2002; Würzel 2002) to tobacco control (Judge and Earnshaw 2003, 271–276), the Environment Committee has not only been favourably inclined towards interest associations organised on behalf of public goods, but has delivered the institutional support of the full European Parliament. This in turn has fostered legislative outcomes more favourable to environmental interests.

The European Parliament's Environment Committee (ENVI) has been a critical component of the EP's institutional influence, accounting for 29 per cent of all

co-decision procedures concluded during the fifth Parliament (1999–2004), more than any other committee (European Parliament 2004a). Yet environmental movements seeking regulation in the public interest that may impose high regulatory costs on producers are not always able to parlay access to ENVI into satisfaction of their preferences. This article considers two recent cases with contrasting outcomes: first, the directive on end-of-life vehicles (ELVs), which was proposed by the European Commission in 1997 and reached its legislative conclusion in September 2000, and, second, the development of REACH, a regulatory framework for the chemicals sector launched by a 2001 European Commission White Paper (Commission of the European Communities 2001) and adopted by the European Parliament and Council in December 2006. In the case of ELVs, the European Parliament's Environment Committee helped sustain the EP's commitment to the 'producer pays' principle critical to environmental interests. In contrast, ENVI became internally divided and did not defend the vital principle of compulsory substitution for dangerous chemicals during the REACH legislative process.

How might we account for this difference in outcomes? Under what conditions does the Parliament's Environment Committee serve as an effective access point for public interest associations? More generally, what explains the effectiveness of any institutional access point—that is, the degree to which the articulation of organised interests significantly affects policy outcomes? I argue that the value of an access point depends upon two dimensions: asymmetry and functional differentiation. Asymmetry refers to the extent to which a particular organised interest—whether diffuse or concentrated—has privileged, institutionalised interactions with a node in the policy-making apparatus. Considering this from the vantage point of diffuse interests, to the extent that there is a shift from privileged access to an institutional node for interests organised in pursuit of public goods (such as environmental protection) towards greater symmetry between interests organised on behalf of public goods and private goods or producer interests, the value of the access point to public interest advocates diminishes. This is so for reasons revealed in studies of lobbying in the US Congress. First, lobbying affects legislators' interpretations of the relationship between their objectives and policy actions (Smith 1984). The presentation of alternative interpretations is likely to cause legislators to reconsider or moderate their support for a piece of legislation. Second, influence on legislative committees is a product both of lobbying and of the degree of conflict between competing interests (Evans 1996). Consequently, influence of public interest advocates will be greatest where access is highly asymmetrical and conflict limited.

Differentiation refers to the extent to which institutional actors in the policy-making process (members of the legislature, for example) defer to the particular institutional node (such as a parliamentary committee) in areas of its functional expertise. Asymmetrical access to the Environment Committee will be most effective to the extent that the full European Parliament and other EP committees defer to the Environment Committee on critical environmental issues, limiting their efforts to amend ENVI positions. Drawing again on studies of the US Congress, deference implies that committee members act as 'cue givers' to other members of the legislative body with less information and less-intense preferences (Smith 1984, 46); where there is little such deference or functional differentiation, the number

© 2008 The Author. Journal compilation © 2008 Political Studies Association
BJPIR, 2008, 10(1)

and diversity of cue givers multiplies, rendering lead committee positions more vulnerable to amendment on the floor.

I argue that deference to committees—the acceptance by plenary of committee cues—is most likely when legislation does not involve conflict between policy areas. Where policy objectives intersect, there is likely to be greater conflict between committees, a multiplication of cue givers and a less direct relationship between the recommendations of a lead committee and the ultimate position of the full parliament. Furthermore, the reinvigoration during the past few years of the EU's Lisbon process, with its focus on the competitive standing of European industry, has penetrated the European Parliament; the intersection of heightened competitiveness concerns with environmental regulation has drawn in more actors to debates over environmental regulation. This includes intensified industry lobbying, more extensive EP dialogue with the Council during the first reading of proposed legislation and the active involvement of additional EP committees.

In general, the number and complexity of issues confronting the EP puts a premium on technical expertise. But while members of the Internal Market Committee, for example, may defer to ENVI members on technical environmental issues, they do not make the same concessions on questions of economic impact of environmental measures. The intersection of environmental and competitiveness concerns therefore multiplies and diversifies information resources. This reduces deference to the Environment Committee, rendering ENVI reports less likely to carry convincing majorities in plenary without concessions to the competitiveness concerns of MEPs outside ENVI. Beginning from the period of the fifth Parliament (1999–2004) and continuing into the sixth (2004–09), both asymmetrical access of environmental interests to the Environment Committee and deference to ENVI by the full European Parliament have diminished.

I illustrate these elements of the argument in a comparison of the legislative processes of the End-of-Life Vehicles Directive and REACH, two areas of regulation in which environmental concerns contend with competitiveness concerns. The defining issue in deliberations over recycling end-of-life vehicles was the tension between exclusive producer responsibility for their products and an approach to recycling based on cost sharing between producers, dealers and car owners. Representatives of the auto industry initially pursued their preference for cost sharing through national channels; German auto producers called upon members of Germany's Christian Democratic party to win the support of its party group in the European Parliament, the European People's party and European Democrats (EPP-ED), and also sought backing from the Social Democrats, the senior partner in Germany's coalition government. While some of these MEPs worked from inside the Parliament's Environment Committee to induce the Committee to advocate cost sharing for environmentally-friendly disposal of ELVs, the Environment Committee as a whole remained committed to 'producer pays' as a core principle of environmental policy for manufactured products reaching the end of their useful lives. In plenary debate, members of the Environment Committee cautioned that any departure from this concept would weaken the Parliament's ability to produce rigorous regulation in product areas scheduled for future regulation, such as electrical and electronic waste. Invoking the Parliament's collective interest, ENVI members framed the issue as a test of whether the Parliament would continue to serve as a distinctive voice of the public interest, or would capitulate to private interests and become a less committed protector of the environment than the Council of Environment Ministers. These appeals sustained deference to the ENVI position in plenary.

At the outset of the legislative process for the new chemicals sector regulation in 2000–01, national environment ministers from several member states as well as the EU Environment Commissioner firmly backed rigorous protection of public health and the environment. In the European Parliament, the Environment Committee assumed responsibility for the institution's response, with a Green party rapporteur. A dramatic shift in favour of environmental protection appeared likely. Yet, following the European Parliament's first reading on REACH in November 2005, and continuing with the announcement of a Council common position in November and the EP's second reading in December 2006, the regulation was transformed from a piece of environmental legislation to a measure focused on the competitiveness of Europe's chemicals sector. In the course of the legislative process, the Internal Market and Consumer Affairs (IMCO) and Industry, Research and Energy (ITRE) Committees were, in accordance with internal EP rules, granted enhanced status in generating the committee report for REACH. This opened up for organised industry interests critical points of access to committees serving as 'cues' to the full parliament, eliminating any asymmetry in favour of organised environmental interests. Given its position as a participant in producing the committee report, the Internal Market Committee's advocacy for competitiveness concerns neutralised deference to the Environment Committee.

In short, asymmetrical access in favour of environmental interests and a high level of differentiation made the EP's Environment Committee a productive access point in the case of end-of-life vehicles regulation. However, the rise of competitiveness concerns and the granting to EP committees with close industry links shared competence for REACH undermined both asymmetry and differentiation in the instance of chemicals regulation.

The following section elaborates on the concepts of asymmetry and functional differentiation. The article then turns to a comparative evaluation of these determinants of the value of access in the cases of end-of-life vehicles and chemicals regulation. The concluding section considers the implications of reduced asymmetry of access for interests organised on behalf of public goods and diminished committee deference for the ability of the European Parliament to serve as a distinctive voice of the European public interest.

Evaluating Access Points: Asymmetry of Access and Functional Differentiation

The existing literature suggests that interests organised on behalf of public goods have advantages in EU policy-making relative to national policy-making, largely because the geographically decentralised and institutionally fragmented EU political system multiplies access points, adding to the national level of policy-making the participation of the European Commission, European Parliament and European

Court of Justice (Pollack 1997). Where interest associations are not deeply embedded in domestic policy networks, and EU institutions are receptive to their issues of concern, these groups can mobilise to influence the agenda at the European level (Marks and McAdam 1996; Fairbrass and Jordan 2001).

EU institutions, in turn, can reap institutional benefits by encouraging the aggregation and intermediation of interests at the European level. A European Commission that seeks to advance the cause of integration and to generate support for European-level solutions to policy problems and an increasingly powerful European Parliament that provides direct representation of the people of the EU constitute sympathetic venues for the advancement of diffuse interests. The existence of EU-level institutions with their own preferences for further integration stimulates the mobilisation of societal interests at the European level.

This argument focuses on the relationship between opportunities for the pursuit of preferences at the national level and opportunities created by institutional evolution at the European level. Much of the debate about the impact of EU policy-making on interest articulation concerns the relative balance of political activity between national and European levels (Marks and McAdam 1996; Imig and Tarrow 2001, 47; Beyers 2002) and the motives for activity at the European (as opposed to national) level (Fairbrass and Jordan 2001).[3] While the focus on political opportunity structures differentiates between national and European levels, it does not distinguish between nodes of access at the European level. Environmental interests have benefited from the sectoral autonomy of EU policy-making across policy areas, in which horizontal policy co-ordination has been weak. Individual Commission Director-Generals (DGs), for example, have been able to operate as policy entrepreneurs, cultivating constituencies and expanding their policy competence to the extent that they could gain qualified majority support in Council for their proposals. With the supranational institutions of the EU—the European Commission, European Court of Justice and European Parliament—motivated by the meta-objective of deeper integration, each sought advancement of institutional interests through policy entrepreneurship and functional autonomy. However, the recent invigoration of the Lisbon agenda, with its objective of competitiveness of European industry rather than integration per se, has increased horizontal policy co-ordination. This in turn has strengthened hierarchy within the European Commission. Similarly, where European Parliament committees in the past have been able substantially to represent interests and advance legislation corresponding to their substantive domains, the ascendance of competitiveness concerns within the Commission, Council and industry interests highly mobilised and organised at European level has created more overlap between the policy realms of EP committees, limiting autonomy to realms in which committee goals do not conflict. One effect has been to reduce differentiation and deference to ENVI as a lead committee on issues of environmental regulation.

There is an extensive literature on the relationship between lobbying and legislative outcomes in the US Congress. Three elements of this literature are relevant here. The first concerns how lobbying affects the positions of legislators. Does lobbying ensure the support of legislators favourably inclined towards a piece of legislation, does it counteract the efforts of opponents or does it in fact have little effect? Setting aside the long-standing debate about whether lobbying simply reinforces legislators' existing positions on issues or counteracts the impact of lobbying on the other side of an issue, Richard A. Smith argues that the significance of lobbying is its ability to alter legislators' interpretations of the relationship between policy objectives and outcomes (Smith 1984 and 1995). Lobbying does not necessarily alter legislators' goals, but rather their understandings of the link between policy measures and goal attainment. The essential implication of this mode of influence is that lobbying can have a highly significant impact on legislators' behaviour, but also that this influence can be very tenuous, and can disintegrate as competing groups present legislators with plausible alternative interpretations of the connection between legislative actions and members' policy objectives.[4]

A second informative component of studies of lobbying in the US Congress addresses the impact of lobbying in the committee stage of the legislative process. Diana Evans focuses her study of lobbying influence in the House of Representatives on committee reports rather than roll call votes. She examines cases of a highway reauthorisation bill before the Public Works and Transportation Committee and the Nutrition Labelling and Education Act of 1990 considered by the Energy and Commerce Committee. Evidence indicates that in the latter case committee members were motivated by policy commitments rather than constituency concerns (Evans 1996, 292). Nonetheless, Evans finds that conflict between public interest groups and producer group lobbying sharply reduced the success of citizen groups in realising their preferences (Evans 1996, 300).[5] Symmetry between public and private interest groups precluded the translation of access into influence.

A third strand of the literature on the US Congress considers the sources of committee power. Under what conditions do members of the legislature defer to committee positions in areas of their jurisdiction? Kenneth Shepsle and Barry Weingast reject arguments based on the agenda-setting role of committees or norms of reciprocal deference between committees. They demonstrate that the power of legislative committees derives from the sequencing of the legislative process and, in particular, from their ability to wield final veto authority (Shepsle and Weingast 1987). Shepsle and Weingast argue that reciprocal deference cannot by itself explain the power of committees, since often there are high incentives for members of the legislature to defect from this arrangement (Shepsle and Weingast 1987, 88). However, the incentive of representatives to introduce amendments not supported by committee members diminishes when committees have the authority to control outcomes at the conference stage of legislation. In other words, final veto authority 'influences the antecedent actions of others by conditioning their beliefs and expectations' (ibid., 91).

So what does this tell us about the power of committees in the EP? To begin with, in their discussion of the incentives to observe reciprocal deference, Shepsle and Weingast do not consider a factor that, while perhaps irrelevant to the US House of Representatives, has had critical consequences for behaviour in the EP: collective institutional interests. For decades members of the EP were engaged in an effort to advance the collective influence of the institution, an objective best served by responsiveness to constituencies newly aggregating and articulating interests at the European level. Violations of reciprocal deference would occur only when the gains

© *2008 The Author. Journal compilation* © *2008 Political Studies Association*
BJPIR, 2008, 10(1)

members could attain from amendments to committee reports according with their policy preferences—gains measured by the satisfaction of members' policy commitments, advancement of political party objectives and support of private interests— exceed the harm to institutional interests resulting from weakening of the incentives for public interest advocates to mobilise and seek interest intermediation through the European Parliament. However, we would expect a reduction in deference to lead committees as commitment to collective institutional interests diminishes. Specifically, we would expect that the European Parliament's attainment of long-sought co-decision powers would be followed by reduced emphasis on collective institutional interests and an elevation of the policy preferences of individual members or political groups (McElroy 2006).

In addition, agreements reached in the EU's conciliation process cannot be amended on the floor of the EP, only accepted or rejected. Since the Parliament's conciliation delegation is composed of members of the committee responsible for reporting on the legislation in the EP, committees in fact wield the ex post veto authority required to deter floor amendments not supported by the lead committee. At the same time, any impact on the behaviour of MEPs associated with anticipation of the exercise of this authority depends upon members' convictions that the legislation may go to conciliation. To the extent that committee members express at an early stage of the legislative process a determination to avoid conciliation, the value of its ex post veto authority is eliminated. In fact, as the volume of legislation and the number of co-decision procedures in which EP committees are involved has increased during the fifth and sixth Parliaments, committees such as Environment have expressed a preference for earlier resolution of legislation (Corbett et al. 2003, 186). As Richard Corbett et al. suggest, with the advent of the revised co-decision procedure codified in the Amsterdam Treaty, 'all three institutions accepted as a behavioral norm that early conclusion of legislative procedures should be sought' (Corbett et al. 2003, 173).[6] The increasing aversion to conciliation on behalf of EP committees may in fact contribute to reduced deference to committees.

In sum, literature on both the US Congress and the European Parliament suggests that committee members are likely to have policy commitments that favour creation of public goods in areas of the committee's substantive responsibility (Collins et al. 1998; Kaeding 2004). However, support for specific legislative measures is contingent on interpretations of the legislation's impact that accord with members' policy goals. Lobbying can be effective in shaping these interpretations. Accordingly, committees whose members are exposed asymmetrically to the arguments of environmental interest associations concerning the consequences of legislative measures are more likely to endorse robust environmental provisions in legislation. If members are more evenly exposed to counter-interpretations by industry groups, the access enjoyed by environmental groups is unlikely to determine the committee's position on proposed legislation. Meanwhile, the committee's report to plenary is more likely to be treated with deference when: (i) members of the legislature are motivated less by partisan policy positions and more by a desire to advance the role of the institution in the legislative process; and (ii) committee members have expressed a determination to pursue their policy position to the ultimate stage of the legislative process.

The following discussion tests this argument by examining two pieces of legislation and a single point of access to the legislative process—the European Parliament's Environment Committee. The activities of environmental interest associations advanced both issues—EU regulation of end-of-life vehicles and of chemicals—on the EU legislative agenda. Both pieces of legislation came under consideration of the Environment Committee, whose members initially endorsed a position of rigorous environmental protection. And both legislative proposals faced producer interests powerfully organised at national and European levels.

For the end-of-life vehicles regulation, producer interests gained de facto access to the Environment Committee via the German delegations of the European People's party (EPP) and the Party of European Socialists (PSE). Nonetheless, Committee members from other party groups and countries resisted the compromise on the 'producer pays' principle desired by industry interests, and the Environment Committee was able to sustain support in plenary, ultimately gaining the approval of the full EP for 'producer pays' in the conciliation stage of the legislation.

In the instance of REACH, producer interests were able to overcome access advantages enjoyed by environmental interest associations because the Internal Market and Industry, Research and Energy Committees were granted a more prominent role on the bill under the EP's internal rules of procedure. The 'enhanced Hughes' procedure amplified the weight of amendments to the ENVI position desired by members of these committees, and thereby augmented the influence of producer interests with links to these committees. Furthermore, in response to the enormous complexity and onslaught of lobbying on the bill, Environment Committee members expressed at an early stage a desire to reach agreement with the Council of Ministers on the bill without resort to conciliation.[7]

In several recent instances in which a legislative proposal has both environmental and competitiveness implications, the EP's Conference of Presidents has responded by invoking the enhanced Hughes procedure, which grants a second committee enhanced status in report drafting. Under internal rules of the EP, a committee responsible for a piece of legislation must consider the positions of committees assigned to provide opinions, and may draw on them in order to craft a position likely to win approval in plenary, but is not required to incorporate them into its report. The enhanced Hughes procedure, introduced in 2002, was crafted with the expectation that committees would engage in 'enhanced co-operation' when a piece of legislation fell astride the substantive realms of two committees, or contained parts encompassing two distinct substantive policy areas. Among other things, enhanced Hughes calls upon the chairman of the responsible committee to accept the amendments of the co-operating committee relating to its field of jurisdiction.[8]

By extending to alternative committees augmented powers to introduce their amendments into the report on a piece of legislation, the enhanced Hughes procedure intensifies the lobbying focused on those committees, elevates the influence of interest associations in their policy network, renders their positions more distinctive and increases the threat that such committees will bring amendments directly to plenary. The lead committee must incorporate elements of the alternative committee's position because members of this committee acquire status as 'cue givers' on the legislation. In comparison with opinion-giving committees or groups of MEPs not operating under enhanced Hughes, committees granted enhanced status are, in the absence of a deal with the lead committee, more likely to persist with an effort to win plenary support for an alternative position.

The End-of-Life Vehicles Directive

In the late 1980s and early 90s, the Commission, Council and Parliament all heralded the concept of producer responsibility for several types of waste, including packaging waste, waste oils, batteries and polychlorinated biphenyls (PCBs). In November 1996, the European Parliament urged the Commission to propose legislation regulating waste streams. The EP's resolution specifically called upon the Commission to incorporate the principle of producer liability as the foundation of regulation governing end-of-life vehicles. In its 1996 Communication on waste management strategy, the Commission announced a departure from past waste management policy; rather than permitting producers to externalise the costs of disposal of products, producers would now bear responsibility for their products at the end of their useful lives (Commission of the European Communities 1997).

Approximately 9 million vehicles reach the end of their useful lives annually in EU countries. While the metallic portion of each vehicle—about 75 per cent—is fully recyclable, the remainder is shredded, generating about 2 million tons of landfill annually.[9] Moreover, the heavy metals and fluids in the automobile shredder residue constitute approximately 10 per cent of the hazardous waste in the EU (European Parliament 1999). A primary objective of producer responsibility for end-of-life vehicles is to give manufacturers an incentive to design vehicles that lend themselves to easier dismantling, re-use and recovery.

The European Commission's 1997 ELV proposal incorporated the producer responsibility principle for new as well as existing vehicles (Commission of the European Communities 1997). The proposal set a re-use and recycling rate of 85 per cent for new vehicles beginning in 2005, increasing to 95 per cent beginning in 2015 (Commission of the European Communities 1997, article 7). While manufacturers did not oppose the introduction of producer responsibility and an increase in re-use and recovery shares for newly designed autos, they attacked the retroactive nature of the proposed legislation. ACEA, the European Automobile Manufacturers' Association, estimated the cost of taking back each scrap auto at 370 Deutsche Marks, then approximately $195.[10] With 160 million vehicles already on the road, European auto manufacturers warned that the costs of the proposed regulation would harm their ability to compete with non-European producers—both recent entrants to the EU market with few vehicles on the road and those not facing a similar regulatory burden in their home markets.

Auto manufacturers pressed the Commission to address producer concerns in the draft proposal. Having failed at this stage in the legislative process, manufacturers resorted to well-worn channels of access at the national level, seeking to line up opposition to the regulation in the Council of Ministers (Coen 2004). German car manufacturers, who produce two fifths of Europe's autos, appealed to Chancellor Schroeder and the federal economics ministry, seeking to alter the proposed regu-

© 2008 The Author. Journal compilation © 2008 Political Studies Association
BJPIR, 2008, 10(1)

lation over the heads of national environment ministers.[11] The German government, occupying the rotating Council presidency, delayed the Council decision on a common position in March and again in June 1999.[12] However, the Environment Council in July 1999 agreed to a common position based on a compromise advanced by the Finnish presidency, which did not depart from the Commission proposal in principle, but pushed back the dates for obligatory manufacturer take-back of existing vehicles and for the higher recycling percentages.[13]

Auto producers still perceived an opportunity to amend the legislation in the European Parliament's second reading. German auto producers attempted to work through EP party delegations, including the European People's party, who furnished the Environment Committee rapporteur, German MEP Karl-Heinz Florenz; as well as Social Democrats tied to Germany's governing coalition. But the centrality of 'producer pays' presented by environmental interests retained its hold on other ENVI members, as did the view that cost sharing represented a repudiation of the Parliament's role as defender of the public interest. The cost-sharing amendments proposed by rapporteur Florenz were defeated in committee by a vote of 34 to 23. Auto producers faced a final chance to amend the Council position in the EP's plenary session.

Defending Collective Institutional Interests in the European Parliament

The commitment of ENVI members outside the EPP and German delegation to the PSE to the principle of 'producer pays', and the support of MEPs for collective institutional interests, were central to plenary defeat of amendments to the proposed end-of-life vehicles regulation that would share recycling costs for existing vehicles between manufacturers, dealers and car owners. The European Environmental Bureau (EEB) lobbied against the replacement of 'producer pays' with cost sharing, and cautioned that 'The reputation of the European Parliament [as] one of the driving forces of environmental protection in the EU is at stake'.[14] Members of the Environment Committee echoed this concern in defence of 'producer pays' in the plenary debate.

Having failed to secure support for cost sharing from the Environment Committee, Florenz and the EPP-DE reintroduced the amendment in plenary debate in the second reading of the proposed legislation. In addition to the EPP-ED, some German members of the European Socialists supported the cost-sharing amendment. Arguments included the claim that the proposal would preserve industrial competitiveness without diminishing the environmental protection secured by the regulation.[15] In the absence of cost sharing, the regulation would distort competition by imposing costs on vehicle manufacturers in direct proportion to their past production levels. Older producers would be disadvantaged relative to market newcomers, such as Korean auto manufacturers, and producers would likely challenge the legality of the law's retroactive aspect.

In plenary debate, Green MEPs appealed to collective institutional interests, echoing the EEB position that the issue had critical implications for the role and credibility of the EP as a defender of the public interest in environmental matters.

© 2008 The Author. Journal compilation © 2008 Political Studies Association
BJPIR, 2008, 10(1)

Swedish MEP Jonas Sjöstedt (European United Left (GUE)/Nordic Green Left (NGL)) asserted that 'If those amendments were adopted which would considerably weaken the directive, this would be very detrimental, not only from an environmental point of view but also for the European Parliament's credibility on environmental issues'.[16] Hiltrud Breyer, a German MEP from the Green Party Group, similarly argued that 'The credibility of Parliament as a champion of environmental protection is at stake'.[17] French Green MEP Marie-Anne Isler Béguin warned of the threat to the institutional reputation of the EP as a protector of the public interest on environmental matters if the body accepted the amendment on cost sharing supported by the EPP-ED: 'Parliament would, for the first time, not be acting as the defender of the rights of the consumers and citizens of Europe, it would be turning into [a] mere sounding box for different lobbies'. Such a step would represent a shift from the typical pattern of the EU seeking to improve upon Council positions on environmental protection to a weakening of the Council position by the EP.[18]

The collective value of defending 'producer pays' extended beyond auto recycling. As the ELV Directive entered conciliation, the European Commission was preparing to table another waste management regulation, this one covering electronic waste.[19] Ultimately, the effort to move from 'producer pays' to 'shared responsibility' in the name of competitiveness was rejected by plenary, where MEPs defeated the cost-sharing amendment by a vote of 335 to 180.[20] While the EPP had served as a conduit for producer interests, the Environment Committee as a whole embraced the interpretation of the connection between policy objectives and results presented by the EEB and other environmental interest associations. ENVI retained its commitment to 'producer pays', and plenary on balance took its cue from the committee.

Chemicals Regulation

In 1998, national environment ministers of several member state governments called upon the European Commission to develop a new regulatory framework for the chemicals sector. The Environment Council charged the Commission with incorporating several principles into a regulation governing the registration evaluation and authorisation of chemicals (REACH): (i) adoption of the precautionary principle, requiring that firms provide safety data before gaining authorisation to bring chemicals to market in cases where there is evidence or suspicion of a danger to health and environment; (ii) a single system for the review of all chemical substances; (iii) a shift in the burden of proof for demonstrating safety from public authorities to industry; and (iv) incentives for technical innovation (RAPID IP/03/1477, 29 October 2003; Shörling 2004, 59, 62). The initial approach to chemicals regulation incorporated in the European Commission's White Paper (Commission of the European Communities 2001) and endorsed by the European Parliament bore the imprimatur of the European environmental interests that had succeeded in placing the issue on the agenda. This approach involved registration of all chemicals produced in quantities above one metric ton, fixed terms for authorisations of hazardous chemicals and compulsory substitution of safer alternatives for all dangerous substances. However, by the time the European Parliament had completed its first reading and the Council of Ministers had reached a common position in late 2005, the text established far less rigorous environmental standards, reducing data and testing requirements for chemicals produced in smaller volumes and relaxing conditions for substitution. Ultimately, the contours of a piece of legislation originally focused on concerns for human health and environmental protection were moulded by the objective of industrial competitiveness.

How did REACH differ from the case of end-of-life vehicles? The initial battle over the REACH legislation in the Parliament was a struggle for jurisdiction—a struggle resulting from the legislation's quality as an environmental regulation with potentially significant implementation costs for industry. Accordingly, as for ELVs, the draft regulation invoked environmental and competitiveness concerns alike. The EP's Conference of Presidents (comprised of the President of the EP and the chairs of the political groups) initially assigned REACH to the Environment Committee. Asserting that the REACH regulation was about industrial policy as much as environmental policy, the Internal Market Committee[21] contested exclusive ENVI responsibility for REACH.[22] In response, the Conference of Presidents invoked the enhanced Hughes procedure, taking the unusual step of granting *both* the Internal Market and the Industry, Research and Energy committees enhanced status. This was a critical departure from the ELVs regulation. This step elevated the institutional position of additional EP committees on the issue, and thereby multiplied the number of cue givers for other MEPs.

The potential alternative to the Environment Committee position on REACH was represented by the Internal Market Committee. IMCO's position overlapped with that of the Competitiveness Council. Although IMCO, with a membership broadly representative of the full EP, retained a preference for slightly stronger environmental protection, its position contained the promise of faster agreement with the Council. In order to salvage more rigorous environmental protection without losing its majority in plenary, the ENVI rapporteur, Italian Socialist Guido Sacconi, had to incorporate concerns for industrial competitiveness up to the point at which the Sacconi Report on REACH overlapped with the position of the Internal Market Committee. Initially, this position involved a trade-off between acceptance of the IMCO position on chemicals registration (reducing information requirements for chemical substances produced in quantities up to 100 metric tons annually) and retention of the ENVI position on authorisation (which placed time limits on authorisations granted for especially dangerous substances), the latter being required to sustain support for the Sacconi Report *within* ENVI. Reflecting the influence of interpretations presented by the Internal Market Committee concerning the high cost burden of ENVI's preferred version of REACH and its impact on competitiveness of European chemicals producers, as well as the potential for IMCO to defeat the ENVI position, the compromise on registration supported by IMCO won plenary's overwhelming endorsement. In contrast, the authorisation package reflecting the ENVI position passed by only a narrow margin.[23] The latter result left the EP position on authorisation vulnerable to challenge by the Council. Further strengthening the Council's position in inter-institutional bargaining was the expressed desire of EP members to reach agreement and avoid conciliation.

© 2008 The Author. Journal compilation © 2008 Political Studies Association
BJPIR, 2008, 10(1)

Competitiveness Concerns Trump Collective Institutional Interests

The European chemicals industry federation (CEFIC) initially aimed its lobbying efforts across institutions as well as EP committees, including ENVI. However, with the Internal Market Committee and Industry and Research Committee being granted enhanced status, CEFIC could rely on established channels of access. This represents a significant contrast with the need for industry interests to rely on party groups and indirect access to the committee responsible for reporting to the full EP in the case of end-of-life vehicles. As a CEFIC official responsible for EU Government Affairs explained, 'During the process it became rapidly clear that in terms of getting our political messages across, we had to work more intensively with the Industry and Internal Market Committees, though you have to ensure that you keep all options open to get the winning compromise'.[24]

Further diminishing the Environment Committee's control over the policy outcome, environmental non-governmental organisations (NGOs), in contrast with chemical industry representatives, found their network links with Environment Committee MEPs substantially neutralised by ENVI's need to compromise with IMCO and ITRE. In sharp contrast with the instance of end-of-life vehicles, in which ENVI was solely responsible for the committee report, and therefore the principal cue for the full EP, environmentalists experienced an adverse asymmetry: while industry federations CEFIC and the Union of Industrial and Employers' Confederations (UNICE) enjoyed access to IMCO and ENVI alike, IMCO members expected environmental interests to present their arguments predominantly through ENVI.[25] Under these conditions, MEPs gave substantial weight to industry warnings about the high costs of REACH, the potential damage to industrial competitiveness and the need for more extensive impact assessment of the regulatory burden.

Reflecting the shift in the position of the Environment Committee required to prevent division of the plenary, ENVI incorporated many of IMCO's proposed amendments into the Sacconi Report.[26] Furthermore, IMCO used the enhanced status it garnered from the Hughes procedure to bring elements of its approach to the registration of chemicals directly to the plenary.[27] Indicating how the enhanced status of the Internal Market and Industry Committees exposed MEPs to competing interpretations of the link between policy choices and outcomes, and provided additional decision-making cues, a CEFIC official concludes that 'Undoubtedly, had the ENVI Committee been the only responsible committee, it would have been much more difficult to get industry's positions taken into consideration'.[28] In addition to the first reading triumph of producer interests on the issue of chemicals registration, weak plenary support for the Environment Committee's approach to chemicals authorisation and substitution left the EP position vulnerable to the demands of the Competitiveness Council. The ENVI position on authorisation of chemicals did not survive the EP's second reading, and the final legislation provided for compulsory research and development *plans* rather than compulsory substitution for the most hazardous chemicals.[29]

© 2008 The Author. Journal compilation © 2008 Political Studies Association
BJPIR, 2008, 10(1)

Competing Interpretations, Symmetrical Access and the Decline of Collective Institutional Interests: Nutrition Labelling as an Example

The legislative procedure within the EP in the case of REACH eroded asymmetry of access to the Environment Committee by environmentalists and created asymmetry in favour of industry in other committees. The enhanced Hughes procedure had the effect of multiplying cue givers and undermined deference to the Environment Committee by boosting the status of other committees. Furthermore, the institutional embedding of the competitiveness objective associated with the Lisbon process undermined the EP's collective commitment to institutional interests.

In this regard, REACH was not a unique instance. In a similar case, the European Commission in 2003 proposed a regulation that would restrict the use of health claims on food packaging. In particular, producers of foods having high levels of fat, sugar or salt would not be allowed to make claims about beneficial health effects. Such 'nutrition profiles' became the most contentious part of the proposal. The European Consumers' Organisation (BEUC) applauded the attempt to rein in the welter of false and misleading health claims, which threatened to encourage bad dietary habits among EU consumers (BEUC 2003). Meanwhile, representatives of food manufacturers such as the Confederation of Food and Drink Industries of the EU (CIAA) and Britain's Food and Drink Federation (FDF) criticised the Commission for categorising foods as 'good' or 'bad' rather than encouraging a focus on total dietary habits. The CIAA urged that there simply be a requirement of scientific substantiation for all health claims.[30]

As in the case of REACH, the European Parliament's Conference of Presidents responded to the intersection of health and competitiveness concerns by granting the Internal Market Committee enhanced status for the nutrition labelling proposal. Two provisions of the Commission proposal were especially contentious. The first (article 4) required that foods carrying health claims also carry nutrient profiles detailing the content of fats, sugars and sodium in the product. The second was a ban on implied health claims relating to general well-being or psychological and behavioural benefits (article 11).

The Environment Committee rapporteur, Adriana Poli Bortone, favoured nutrition profiles, as well as a procedure for authorising scientifically verifiable claims regarding psychological and behavioural effects such as reduction in the sense of hunger (European Parliament 2005b, 38–39). In contrast, the Internal Market Committee channelled into the debate producers' interpretations of the relationship between policy choices and outcomes. The Committee deleted article 4 in its opinion, justifying this step on competitiveness grounds. Arguments included the point that existing legislation on advertising and labelling already addresses the problem of misleading claims (European Parliament 2005b, 80). In addition, regulating packaging raises broader questions of applicability to advertising, threatening to create legal uncertainty in the food advertising industry, and the cumbersome nature of the proposed procedure for authorising behavioural claims threatens to create a barrier to innovation by food manufacturers (European Parliament 2005b, 81).

Industry lobbying focused on the impact of labelling restrictions on innovation and competitiveness. Furthermore, pressure from the Parliament's EPP-DE party group, both through the Internal Market Committee and its members in the Environment Committee, contributed to a divided Environment Committee. This division was reflected in the Environment Committee's April 2005 report to plenary for the first reading of the bill. The report, which dropped article 4 on the compulsory labelling of nutrient profiles, passed the committee on a 30 to 15 vote. Critics from within the committee attributed the outcome to lobbying by large industrial food companies from Germany and the UK.[31]

In the EP's first reading debate, the EPP-DE group, especially its German delegation, led the effort to frame the nutrition labelling regulation as an instance of excessive regulation, an infringement on consumer choice and a threat to the competitiveness of the European food industry. The Industry, Research and Energy Committee's draftsman, German EPP-ED MEP Angelika Niebler, invoked Lisbon as a basis for deleting articles 4 and 11: 'How this proposal for a regulation is supposed to be compatible with the Lisbon strategy, heaven knows'.[32] Similarly, PPE spokesperson Renate Sommer warned that the nutrition labelling regulation would undermine innovation in food manufacturing, destroy jobs and hurt small and medium-sized enterprises. MEP Avril Doyle invoked the promise that Commission President Barroso would 'Lisbon-proof' all Commission proposals, and called upon the Environment Commissioner to 'bring this particular piece of legislation to his attention and immediately "Lisbon-proof" it'.

The report of a divided Environment Committee gained tepid support in plenary, passing by 303 votes to 286, with 10 abstentions.[33] The commitment to collective institutional interests by MEPs had thoroughly dissipated. Ironically, the Council of EU Health Ministers restored article 4 to the nutrition labelling regulation in their common position of June 2005. It was the Council rather than the European Parliament that advanced the interests of diffuse health interests through EU regulation—the very outcome members of the Environment Committee had warned against in their appeal to collective institutional interests during the debate over ELVs.

Conclusion: The European Parliament's Emerging Competitive Logic

Intensified competition between committees in the European Parliament reflects the deeper infusion of broader European political debates into the EP. In particular, industry concerns about the impact of regulation on competitiveness have become firmly embedded not only in the EPP-DE party group, but also in the Internal Market and Industry, Research and Energy Committees. Whereas the EP long operated within the framework of a co-operative game to advance the collective interests of the institution—including deeper European integration and institutional aggrandisement—legislative politics in the EP increasingly conforms to a competitive logic in which parties and committees compete to harness the institution's influence to advance their policy visions. This accords with the findings of Simon Hix et al. that competition between the EPP and PES has increased, especially over environmental, agricultural and economic and social issues (Hix et al. 2003, 326–327). Charlotte Burns comes to a similar conclusion, arguing that competition between committees 'may ... be indicative of a normalization of the EP's internal organization as the parliament evolves into a mature legislature' (Burns 2006, 245).

Such an evolution has critical implications. The rising power of the European Parliament in the post-Maastricht era, and especially since Amsterdam, encouraged the mobilisation of diffuse interests that could find in the EP both a point of access and institutional advocacy for their environmental and health concerns. Two things facilitated this dynamic: (i) the deference accorded the Environment Committee on highly salient environmental issues, because of the Committee's embeddedness in a network with environmental interest associations that provided reliable information concerning threats to the environment and human health; and (ii) the coincidence of the European Parliament's advocacy of diffuse interests with the institutional objectives of the EP as a whole.

The ascent and institutional embedding of the competitiveness frame has altered this dynamic. Deference to the Environment Committee within the EP has been eroded significantly by closer attention to competitiveness implications of environmental regulations. Party and committee-based promotion of contending perspectives on Europe's economic model have transcended collective advancement of the institutional interests of the EP. Accordingly, incentives for interests seeking to reduce the regulatory burden on industry to lobby the European Parliament have increased dramatically. Whereas environmentalists could once claim privileged access to the Environment Committee within the EP and sometimes gain the Parliament as an institutional advocate, access is now less privileged and institutional advocacy more highly contested.

About the Author

Mitchell P. Smith, University of Oklahoma, Department of Political Science and School of International Area Studies, 455 West Lindsey, Room 205, Norman, OK 73019-2001, USA, email: *mps@ou.edu*

Notes

The author wishes to thank Andreas Bieler and Tony Zito for comments on an earlier version of this article presented at the Tenth Biennial International Conference of the European Union Studies Association, Montréal, Canada, 17–19 May 2007. In addition, the author thanks the issue editors and two anonymous referees for their comments.

1. In his investigation of political opportunity structures for environmental movements at the international level, Hein-Anton van der Heijden (2006) reviews literature that collectively identifies components of the capacity of interest associations to organise and gain access to the policy-making process, as well as the degree to which these efforts translate into policy outputs. Measured along the first dimension, the EU represents a favourable shift in opportunity structures; this is less so along the output dimension. I argue that only the latter is truly meaningful in that it is likely to stimulate further interest articulation at the European level, and therefore focus my analysis on legislative impact.

2. Rachel Cichowski (1998, 403) also identifies the significance of the European Court of Justice, whose expansive interpretations of environmental directives 'construct a legal

framework that opens the door to those who have been traditionally closed out of EU decision-making'.

3. As Marks and McAdam (1996, 250) assert, 'shifts in the structure and geographical locus of institutionalized power can be expected to be accompanied by simultaneous changes in the structure and locus of mass politics'. Fairbrass and Jordan (2001, 514) refer to the ability of 'previously marginalized environmental groups ... to use EU opportunities to outflank politically' their national government.

4. As Smith writes (1984, 51), 'The influence of an advocate over the decisions of members is ... both substantial and fragile'. See also Smith (1995, 99).

5. This is consistent with the finding of John Wright that congressional representatives 'respond and adjust to the balance of group pressures they experience'. See Wright (1990).

6. This commitment is reflected in data on co-decision outcomes: under the Maastricht provisions prevailing during the 1994–99 Parliament, 40 per cent of dossiers required conciliation. During 1999–2000, this dropped to 28 per cent; the proportion reached 15 per cent in 2003–04. Moreover, the fraction of files completed at first reading has trended upward, from 19 per cent in 1999–2000 to 39 per cent in 2003–04. See European Parliament (2004b, 13 and annex 4).

7. See, *inter alia*, 'REACH: the second half kicks off', *European Parliament News*, 13 July 2006; http://www.europarl.europa.eu/news

8. The rules state that 'the committee responsible shall accept without a vote amendments from the committee asked for an opinion where they concern matters which the chairman of the committee responsible considers, on the basis of Annex VI, after consulting the chairman of the committee asked for an opinion, to fall under the competence of the committee asked for an opinion, and which do not contradict other elements of the report'. Rules of Procedure of the European Parliament, 16th ed., July 2004, Article 47. Accessed at http://www.europarl.eu.int/omk/sipade3?SAME_LEVEL=1&LEVEL=2&NAV=X&DETAIL= &PUBREF=-//EP//TEXT+RULES-EP+20040720+TOC+DOC+XML+V0//EN

9. For additional information about the materials in end-of-life autos and their treatment, see N. Kanari, J.-L. Pineau and S. Shallari, 'End-of-Life Vehicle Recycling in the European Union', *Journal of Metallurgy*, August 2003, on-line version (http://www.tms.org/pubs/journals/JOM/ 0308/Kanari-0308.html).

10. Michael Mann, 'EU Car Recycling Law in Doubt as Industry Stalls', *Reuters News Service*, 17 June 1999.

11. See 'End-of-Life Vehicle Directive Blocked Again', *Automotive Environment Analyst*, 1 July 1999 (accessed via LexisNexis Academic database at http://web.lexis-nexis.com.ezproxy1.lib.ou.edu/ universe/form/academic/s_guidednews.html).

12. See 'Germany Postpones Discussion of End-of-Life Vehicle Directive', *Automotive Environment Analyst*, 1 April 1999; and 'Environment Council: Deal on Waste, Deadlock on Vehicle Recycling', European Information Service, *European Report* No. 2419, 26 June 1999 (both accessed via LexisNexis Academic database).

13. See 'Agreement on Recycling End-of-Life Vehicles', European Information Service, *European Report* No. 2427, 24 July 1999; and 'Germany Snubbed as Agreement Reached on Scrap Cars', *Automotive Environment Analyst*, 1 September 1999 (both accessed via LexisNexis Academic database).

14. Letter from the EEB to Members of the European Parliament, 2nd Reading of the End-of-Life Vehicles on 3rd February 2000, Brussels, 20 January 2000; http://www.eeb.org/activities/ waste/end_of_life/EEB-letter-to-Plenary-on-ELV-Feb2000.pdf

15. MEPs making this argument included German MEP Bernd Lange (PES) and Béatrice Patrie, a French PSE member. See European Parliament Debates, Thursday, 3 February 2000, Brussels; http://www.europarl.europa.eu

16. European Parliament debates, Thursday, 3 February 2000, Brussels; http://www.europarl. europa.eu

17. The argument about credibility was echoed by Torben Lund, Danish PSE member. See European Parliament debates, 3 February 2000.

18. European Parliament debates, Thursday, 3 February 2000, Brussels; http://www.europarl. europa.eu

19. Debate of the EP, Strasbourg, 6 September 2000, OJ edition. Also see 'Environment: Conciliation Committee Reaches Agreement on End-of-Life Vehicles Directive', European Information Service, *European Report* No. 2504, 27 May 2000.

20. 'Environment: Parliament Confirms Manufacturer Liability for End-of-Life Vehicles', European Information Service, *European Report* No. 2473, 9 February 2000 (LexisNexis Academic).

21. The Internal Market and Consumer Affairs Committee is the product of EP committee restructuring in 2004. IMCO's brief is the internal market, competitiveness and economic protection of consumers (protection of consumer health falling under the remit of ENVI).

22. See 'The New Chemicals Policy (REACH): an MEP's views on the upcoming Parliamentary debate', speech of MEP and Industry Committee Rapporteur for REACH Elly Plooij-van Gorsel to the Conference of the Industrial Minerals Association—Europe Conference, 13 May 2004; http://www.plooij.nl/engels/toespraken/096.htm

23. IMCO's position on registration of chemicals passed by a vote of 438 to 155, with 41 abstentions; ENVI's position on authorisation of dangerous chemicals passed by 324 to 263, with 13 abstentions. See Secretariat of the Committee on the Environment, Public Health and Food Safety, European Parliament, 'Background Note on the Results of the Vote on the Proposed New Chemicals Legislation (REACH)', Strasbourg, 17 November 2005; and 'REACH: MEPs strike a balance between health, the environment and industry', European Parliament news headlines, http://www.europarl.eu.int/news/public/story_page/008-2560-318-11-46-901-20051118STO02559-2005-14-11-2005/default_en.htm, accessed 20 February 2006.

24. E-mail correspondence, 16 January 2006.

25. Interview with EU Policy Officer, European Environmental Bureau, 3 April 2006; interview with Chemicals Campaigner, Friends of the Earth Europe, 5 April 2006.

26. ENVI adopted 89 of IMCO's 335 amendments. Calculated from European Parliament (2005a).

27. European Report No. 2995, 8 October 2005; http://web.lexis-nexis.com/universe.

28. E-mail correspondence, 17 January 2006.

29. See 'Parliament adopts REACH—new chemicals legislation and new chemicals agency', European Parliament press service, 13 December 2006; http://www.europarl.europa.eu/news

30. See 'Euro food and supplement industries balk at revised health claim proposal', Nutraceuticals International, 8:8 (August 2003); accessed via http://web.lexis-nexis.com

31. See 'MEPs drop compulsory labeling for "health" food', http://www.euractiv.com, 25 April 2005.

32. The quotations in this paragraph are taken from the European Parliament website, Debates, Wednesday 25 May 2005; http://www.europarl.europa.eu/omk/sipade3

33. 'Consumer Affairs: Parliament Waters Down Key Nutrition Claims Regulation', *European Report* No. 2965, 27 May 2005.

Bibliography

Beyers, J. (2002) 'Gaining and seeking access: The European adaptation of domestic interest associations', *European Journal of Political Research*, 41:5, 585–612.

Burns, C. (2006) 'Co-decision and inter-committee conflict in the European Parliament post-Amsterdam', *Government and Opposition*, 41:2, 230–248.

Cichowski, R. A. (1998) 'Integrating the environment: The European Court and the construction of supranational policy', *Journal of European Public Policy*, 5:3, 387–405.

Coen, D. (2004) 'Environmental and business lobbying alliances in Europe: Learning from Washington?', in D. Levy and P. Newell (eds), *Business in International Environmental Governance: A Political Economy Approach* (Cambridge MA: MIT Press), 197–221.

Collins, K., Burns, C. and Warleigh, A. (1998) 'Policy entrepreneurs: The role of European Parliament Committees in the making of EU policy', *Statute Law Review*, 19:1, 1–11.

Commission of the European Communities (1997) 'Proposal for a Council Directive on the end of life vehicles', COM(97) 358 final, 9 July.

Commission of the European Communities (2001) 'White Paper: Strategy for a future chemicals policy', COM(2001) 88 final, Brussels, 27 February.

Commission of the European Communities (2003) 'Proposal for a Regulation of the European Parliament and of the Council concerning the Registration, Evaluation, Authorisation and Registration of Chemicals (REACH), establishing a European Chemicals Agency and amending Directive 1999/45/EC and Regulation (EC) on Persistent Organic Pollutants', COM(2003) 644 final, 29 October 2003.

Corbett, R., Jacobs, F., and Shackleton, M. (2003) *The European Parliament* (5th edn) (London: John Harper Publishing).

European Consumers' Organisation (BEUC) (2003) 'BEUC Position Paper: Comments on the proposal for a Regulation of the European Parliament and the Council on nutrition and health claims', COM (2003) 424(01).

European Parliament (EP) (1999) 'Report on the proposal for a Council Directive on end of life vehicles', Committee on the Environment Public Health and Consumer Protection, COM(97)0358–C4-0639/ 97–97/0194(SYN)).

European Parliament (EP) (2004a) 'Activity Report of the Committee on the Environment, Public Health and Consumer Policy', 1999–2004 Parliament. DT\537810EN.doc.

European Parliament (EP) (2004b) 'Activity report of the delegations of the Conciliation Committee', 1 May 1999 to 30 April 2004 (5th parliamentary term), DV\530227EN.doc.

European Parliament (EP) (2005a) 'Report on the Proposal for a Regulation of the European Parliament and of the Council concerning the Registration, Evaluation, Authorisation and Registration of Chemicals (REACH), establishing a European Chemicals Agency and amending Directive 1999/45/EC and Regulation (EC) on Persistent Organic Pollutants', 2004–09 session document FINAL A6-0315/2005, 24 October 2005. Guido Sacconi, Rapporteur.

European Parliament (EP) (2005b) 'Report on the proposal for a regulation of the European Parliament and of the Council on nutrition and health claims made on foods', COM(2003 0424–C5-0329/2003– 2003/0165(COD)). Commission on the Environment, Public Health and Food Safety, Adriana Poli Bortone, Rapporteur. Final A6-0128/2005.

Evans, D. (1996) 'Before the roll call: Interest group lobbying and public policy outcomes in House committees', *Political Research Quarterly*, 49:2, 287–304.

Fairbrass, J. and Jordan, A. (2001) 'Protecting biodiversity in the European Union: National barriers and European opportunities?', *Journal of European Public Policy*, 8:4, 499–518.

Hix, S., Kreppel, A. and Noury, A. (2003) 'The party system in the European Parliament: Collusive or competitive?', *Journal of Common Market Studies*, 41:2, 309–331.

Hubschmid, C. and Moser, P. (1997) 'The co-operation procedure in the EU: Why was the European Parliament influential in the decision on car emission standards?', *Journal of Common Market Studies*, 35:2, 225–242.

Imig, D. and Tarrow, S. (2001) 'Mapping the Europeanization of Contention: Evidence from Quantitative Data Analysis', in D. Imig and S. Tarrow (eds), *Contentions Europeans: Protest and Politics in an Emerging Polity* (Boulder, CO, and Oxford, UK: Rowmann and Littlefield), 27–49.

Judge, D. and Earnshaw, D. (2003) *The European Parliament* (Basingstoke, UK, and New York: Palgrave).

Kaeding, M. (2004) 'Rapporteurship allocation in the European Parliament: Information or distribution', *European Union Politics*, 5:3, 353–371.

Marks, G. and McAdam, D. (1996) 'Social movements and the changing structure of political opportunity in the European Union', *West European Politics*, 19:2, 249–278.

McElroy, G. (2006) 'Committee representation in the European Parliament', *European Union Politics*, 7:1, 5–29.

Pedler, R. (2002) 'Clean air and car emissions: What industries and issue groups can and can't achieve', in R. Pedler (ed.), *European Union Lobbying: Changes in the Arena* (Basingstoke: Palgrave), 104–122.

Pollack, M. A. (1997) 'Representing diffuse interests in EC policy-making', *Journal of European Public Policy*, 4:4, 572–590.

Pollack, M. A. and Hafner-Burton, E. (2000) 'Mainstreaming Gender in the European Union', *Journal of European Public Policy*, 7:3, 432–456.

Schörling, I. (2004) *REACH—The Only Planet Guide to the Secrets of Chemicals Policy in the EU: What Happened and Why?* (Brussels: Inger Schörling, Greens/European Free Alliance in the European Parliament), available at http://www.mp.se.

Shepsle, K. A. and Weingast, B. R. (1987) 'The institutional foundations of committee power', *The American Political Science Review*, 81:1, 85–104.

Smith, R. A. (1984) 'Advocacy, interpretation, and influence in the US Congress', *The American Political Science Review*, 78:1, 44–63.

Smith, R. A. (1995) 'Interest group influence in the US Congress', *Legislative Studies Quarterly*, 20:1, 89–139.

Van der Heijden, H.-A. (2006) 'Globalization, environmental movements, and international political opportunity structures', *Organization & Environment*, 19:1, 28–45.

Warleigh, A. (2000) 'The hustle: Citizenship practice, NGOs and "policy coalitions" in the European Union—The cases of auto oil, drinking water and unit pricing', *Journal of European Public Policy*, 7:2, 229–243.

Wright, J. R. (1990) 'Contributions, Lobbying, and Committee Voting in the US House of Representatives', *The American Political Science Review*, 84:2, 417–438.

Würzel, R. K. W. (2002) *Environmental Policy-making in Britain, Germany and the European Union* (Manchester: Manchester University Press).

doi: 10.1111/j.1467-856x.2007.00319.x   *BJPIR: 2008 VOL 10, 84–104*

Labour and the Struggle over the Future European Model of Capitalism: British and Swedish Trade Unions and their Positions on EMU and European Co-operation

Andreas Bieler

Based on a critical International Political Economy (IPE) perspective including a strategic-relational approach to the state, this article analyses Swedish and British trade unions' position on Economic and Monetary Union (EMU) and European co-operation. Importantly, unions in both countries support EMU membership, but transnational British labour is much more in favour of co-operation at the regional level than Swedish transnational labour. While the latter still enjoys good access to policy-making within the Swedish form of state, the former is rather marginalised in Britain and looks to the European Union as an alternative arena for influence. It is further shown that on the one hand British unions continue to reject neo-liberalism. On the other, some trans-national sector unions in Sweden have, however, started to accept core neo-liberal concepts.

Keywords: Economic and Monetary Union; Sweden; trade unions; United Kingdom

Introduction

Economic and Monetary Union (EMU), part of the Treaty of Maastricht in 1991, was established within the European Union (EU) on 1 January 1999. Arguably, trade unions are one of the actors which have come under pressure most as a result of monetary integration. Firstly, due to the fixing of exchange rates and the introduction of the single currency it is easier to compare the different employment conditions within the European Union, while interest rates and exchange rates can no longer be used to counter economic differences between regions. The only adjustment mechanism left for less competitive regions is lowering wages and cuts in non-wage costs. 'This may happen even without asymmetric shocks, insofar as employers (and governments) seek price advantages, no longer attainable by currency depreciation, through wage and benefit cuts instead' (Martin and Ross 1999, 345). In short, there is a danger that the general deregulation and liberalisation within the Internal Market and EMU will result in a logic of competitive deregulation, leading to an undermining of national employment conditions and social standards (Schulten 2000, 232; Bieling 2001, 94). This does not mean that trade unions are necessarily excluded from decision-making. In fact, in what has been described as a shift from social to competitive corporatism, so-called social pacts between trade unions, employers' associations and the state have been established in many EU countries in the late 1990s (Rhodes 1998). The focus of these pacts was, however, on national competitiveness and included precisely cutbacks in line with the logic of competitive deregulation (Bieling and Schulten 2003).

Secondly, the pressures on the labour market are further intensified through the neo-liberal macroeconomic policy regime 'that could keep the growth of demand in Euroland as a whole too low to allow a significant reduction of unemployment to occur' (Martin 2000, 365). Within EMU, monetary policy for the single currency is set by the independent European Central Bank (ECB), which is solely committed to low inflation and price stability. Economic policy is tightly co-ordinated at the European level through the Stability and Growth Pact (SGP), committing members to stay within the neo-liberal convergence criteria and their emphasis on low budget deficits and national debt levels even after the start of EMU on 1 January 1999. Moreover, through the requirement to adhere to the Broad Economic Policy Guidelines including a general commitment to a balanced budget, the SGP further emphasises the overriding focus on low inflation (Jones 2002, 37–40).[1] The Lisbon strategy of the EU does include the goal of full employment. In the overall macro-economic policy matrix, however, this is clearly subordinated to the goal of price stability and, as a result, employment is mainly to be created through a deregulation of labour markets and comparatively small investment in training and education schemes (Bieler 2006, 13–14). Demand stimulation and job creation at the national level via lower interest rates and public investment in infrastructure projects have been made almost impossible. In sum, it is workers who pay the bill for EMU and this puts trade unions as their representatives under the most pressure (Carchedi 1997, 85–114).

In this special issue on 'economic interests' and European integration, this article focuses on the role of trade unions. Two specific questions are asked: first, what is the position of trade unions on EMU; and second, considering the common pressures of EMU, do unions shift their emphasis to the European, international level to defend the interests of their members? These questions are assessed here through a most-similar comparative analysis of British and Swedish trade unions. Both countries are outside EMU. In Sweden, EMU was rejected in a referendum on 14 September 2003 with 56 per cent of the votes against and 42 per cent in favour. In Britain, although committed to it in principle, a referendum on EMU is currently not on the agenda. Being outside, the positions on EMU are likely to be sharper than in those countries where unions have already had to adapt to the reality of EMU, whether they had initially supported it or not. Secondly, both the British and Swedish production structures are significantly transnationalised in several sectors, indicating a similar production structure.

Since the mid-1980s, the EU has participated in the general process of neo-liberal restructuring and has moved towards an Anglo-American, market-oriented model of capitalism embodied first and foremost within the specific set-up of EMU (Bieler 2006, 9–14). Importantly, the analysis of unions' positions on EMU and European co-operation is not a case study in itself. Rather, it is used to assess whether British and Swedish unions have accepted neo-liberal economics and, if not, to what extent they may be part of a future counter-neo-liberal alliance within the EU.

© 2008 The Author. Journal compilation © 2008 Political Studies Association
BJPIR, 2008, 10(1)

Before looking in detail at British and Swedish trade unions, the next section will first assess in what way labour can be conceptualised as an international/European-level actor in times of globalisation.

Globalisation and the Role of Trade Unions

Due to its state-centric conceptualisation of international relations including globalisation (e.g. Waltz 2000), neo-realist International Relations (IR) theory cannot understand trade unions as a potential international actor. From a liberal perspective, however, it is realised that against the background of the transnationalisation of finance expressed in the establishment of a globally integrated financial market (e.g. Helleiner 1994; Strange 1994, 90–118; Scholte 2000a, 116–120) and the transnationalisation of production characterised by production processes being organised across borders (e.g. Strange 1996, 44–65; Scholte 2000a, 51–52, 124–130), additional non-state actors such as transnational corporations (TNCs) (e.g. Stopford and Strange 1991) and non-governmental organisations also sometimes referred to as global social movements (e.g. O'Brien et al. 2000) have emerged. These new actors compete for authority with states in the global political economy (Higgott et al. 2000). Labour from a liberal perspective can, thus, be conceptualised as a transnational actor, next to a range of other actors in a pluralist understanding of policy-making (e.g. O'Brien et al. 2000, 67–108; Scholte 2000b; Smythe 2000). This neglects, however, the underlying social relations of production. As a result, liberal approaches are actor centred, conceptualising 'trans-national actors as autonomous entities rather than as embedded in, and indeed constituted by, transnational structures' (van Apeldoorn 2004, 148). By abstracting interest group interaction from the underlying power structure, however, it is overlooked that there are significant structural power asymmetries, placing especially trans-national capital in a privileged position (van Apeldoorn 2004, 163). Moreover, the fundamental role of labour and trade unions stemming from the capitalist social relations of production, and thus the very nature of the structural changes related to globalisation, is overlooked. As David Coates makes clear, this neglect is mainly the result of an undue focus on capital mobility as the core feature of globalisation. Capital is regarded in a fetishised form as a 'thing' instead of a 'social relationship'. Thereby, it is overlooked that capital can only realise itself on a global scale to the extent that real production processes are created on this scale. 'Capital is more geographically mobile than it was in the past because it now has more proletariats on which to land' (Coates 2000, 255). New strata of workers (e.g. women, rural workers and immigrants) have been employed in established capitalism and by spreading production processes to developing countries new proletariats have been additionally created, doubling the world proletariat to 3 billion people within a generation. Hence, through the transnationalisation of finance and production, capital 'actually alters the balance and character of social classes, and does so increasingly on a global scale' (Coates 2000, 256).

Comparative Political Economy (CPE) approaches provide alternatives of how to conceptualise the role of trade unions in the changing global economy. Rational choice CPE approaches, on the one hand, take into account the production structure as one possible explanatory variable next to other factors (e.g. Gourevitch

1986, 54–68; Frieden 1991, 438). The response of trade unions and employers' associations to opening up the economy to international competition and the related lobbying pressure on their government depends very much on the nature of the sector, it is argued. Unions and employers' associations in export sectors are understood to favour open borders, while unions and employers' associations in domestic production sectors generally prefer closed borders and state protectionism. In general, however, they overlook the importance of national institutional set-ups for the strategies trade unions and employers' associations may adopt. Trade unions, regardless of a country's production structure, may continue to focus on the national level, if they enjoy good access to domestic policy-making. On the other hand, historical institutionalist CPE approaches and here especially the varieties of capitalism literature emphasise national institutional diversity. Herbert Kitschelt et al., for example, focus on how the various different national institutional set-ups mediate these pressures, ensuring a continuation of divergence of national models of capitalism (Kitschelt et al. 1999, 440–441). In short, the varieties of capitalism literature point out that there are different national institutional set-ups due to a historically specific development of capitalism, mediating globalisation pressures in different ways. Some argue that countries are likely to converge around two optimal solutions, either a co-ordinated market economy or a liberal market economy (e.g. Hall and Soskice 2001); others speak of three models of capitalism, i.e. the market-led, Anglo-American model, the negotiated/consensual model and the state-led model (e.g. Schmidt 2002, 112–118). The main problem of this literature is, however, that in contrast to the rational choice CPE approaches, it overlooks the social relations of production underpinning particular national models of capitalism (Coates 2000, 176–177). Historical institutionalist approaches are, therefore, unable to explain why a particular set of institutions was established in the first place as well as to assess change emanating from alterations in the production structure.

Both sets of CPE approaches have the further problem of being implicitly based on a state-centric understanding of globalisation. Increasing levels of trade and capital mobility across borders are identified as the two core characteristics of globalisation. 'More liberal trade and financial regimes have inspired vast new flows of goods and capital across national borders, including a large increase in foreign direct investment' (Hall and Soskice 2001, 55; see also Iversen and Pontusson 2000, 23). As a result, trade unions as other actors are merely understood as domestic actors competing with each other over national adaptation policies to globalisation. Even where it is acknowledged that new actors have emerged at the international level in the form of pension funds and TNCs, they are understood as heavily connected to specific countries (Kitschelt et al. 1999, 446; Schmidt 2002, 16, 27). Daphné Josselin's analysis of the position of British, German and French trade unions on EMU demonstrates this. She also treats trade unions as domestic actors, which adjust to external pressures, be they EMU or globalisation (Josselin 2001, 55). They are not understood as being part of a wider restructuring changing the international state system. Nevertheless, globalisation as a new phenomenon is first and foremost characterised by the transnationalisation of production, not merely by increasing levels of economic interdependence (Bieler 2006, 47–54). TNCs clearly differ from export-oriented companies, the production facilities of which are still located at the national level and which, consequently, manoeuvre predominantly in one specific domestic context. Capital and labour related to TNCs are international actors, which potentially operate simultaneously within several different domestic arenas as well as at the international level.

A neo-Gramscian perspective can overcome the problems of liberal IR and CPE approaches by considering the social relations of production to be the starting point of an investigation (Bieler and Morton 2004). Thus, the relations which organise material production are considered to be crucial for the wider institutional repro-duction of social orders on both a national and an international level. By taking the social relations of production as a starting point, a neo-Gramscian perspective considers social class forces as engendered by the production process to be the most important collective actors. Class is defined as a relation and the various fractions of labour and capital can be identified by relating them to their place in the production system. Most importantly, capital is opposed by labour. There are, however, further differences within the capitalist mode of accumulation. While production was organised on a national basis in the post-war era, significant parts have been transnationalised since the early 1970s as part of the globalisation process. As a result of the partial transnationalisation of national production structures, a basic distinction can be drawn between transnational social forces of capital and labour, engendered by those production sectors which are organised on a transnational scale, and national social forces of capital and labour stemming from national production sectors (van Apeldoorn 2002, 26–34; Bieler 2006, 32–35).

A quantitative comparison with the Austrian, French and German production structures, taking into account absolute data of foreign direct investment (FDI) flows and FDI stocks, but also indicators such as FDI flows as a percentage of gross domestic fixed capital formation and FDI stocks as a percentage of gross domestic product (GDP), makes clear that both Britain and Sweden are highly transnationa-lised, while Austria is hardly transnationalised and France and Germany are somewhere in the middle (Bieler 2006, 55–67). In Britain, historically a strong international financial sector emerged independently from manufacturing early on. Hence, the latter had to rely on the stock market for large investments. In the 1960s, 'merger waves had led to a level of capital concentration which gave Britain the most highly concentrated large-firm sector in the world' (Lane 1995, 35). Sweden has fostered an impressive number of large TNCs and important parts of production were transnationalised as early as the turn from the 19th to the 20th century (Andersson et al. 1996, 27–47). The degree of transnationalisation in manufacturing with TNCs such as Volvo, Ericsson, Electrolux, etc., however, increased dramatically in the second half of the 1980s, when there was a drastic upturn in outward FDI. While inward FDI had only risen from US$ 396 million in 1985 to US$ 2,328 million in 1990, outward FDI increased from US$ 1,783 million to US$ 14,136 million during the same period (Luif 1996, 208). In short, in Britain transnational labour can be expected in manufacturing and finance, and in Sweden in manufacturing. National forces of labour are especially to be found in the public sectors of the two countries. These forces are located in the wider structure of the social relations of production, which do not *determine* but *shape* their interests and identity. Overall, the identification of the various fractions of labour and capital by relating them to their place in the production system makes structural changes such as globalisation accessible, since the emergence of new social forces engendered by the transnationalisation of production and finance can be incorporated. Globalisation, thus, is not only understood as an exogenous structural impact to which actors can merely respond. It is also regarded as enabling with transnational forces playing an active role, responding to and bringing about global structural change at the same time (Bieler and Morton 2001). In turn, if it is accepted that globalisation is brought about by identifiable agents, the possibility of resistance is suddenly clearer.

In addition to the changes in the social relations of production, neo-Gramscian perspectives identify a shift to neo-liberal economics at the ideological level as a key characteristic of globalisation. Neo-liberalism regained prominence in the 1970s as a political economy critique of Keynesianism, developed then into a programme of capitalist restructuring, first implemented in the USA and the UK during the 1980s, before it became associated with a positive interpretation of globalisation in the 1990s, developing into a hegemonic creed (Overbeek 1999; Gamble 2001). The exact neo-liberal policies including privatisation, central bank independence, liberalisation, flexibilisation of the labour market, public sector restructuring, cutting back of trade union rights, etc. and the extent of their implementation differ from country to country. Differences are also the result of the fact that there are two strands of neo-liberalism, the *laissez-faire* and the social market strand, which have a contrasting assessment of how the state can best ensure a fully functioning free market (Gamble 2006, 21–22). Nevertheless, all neo-liberal restructuring projects are based on two core assumptions: 'first is the belief that inflation is a greater threat to the general welfare than unemployment. Second is the belief that phenomena such as unemployment and inflation are due to the interventions of the state into an otherwise naturally self equilibrating economy' (Blyth 2002, 147). The fact that neo-liberalism became dominant is, however, not due to some kind of inert qualities. Rather, it was its material structure, the fact that it was pushed by the increasingly structurally powerful class fraction of transnational capital, supported by important forms of state such as the USA and Britain as well as international organisations such as the International Monetary Fund (IMF) and World Bank, which pushed it to the fore. Neo-liberalism, therefore, has to be understood as a project by capital to restore class power (Harvey 2006, 29).

The neo-Gramscian focus on class struggle in the explanation of structural change overcomes economic determinism (Cox and Sinclair 1996, 57–58). The essence of class struggle is exploitation and the resistance to it, and this confrontation of opposed social forces in concrete historical situations implies the potential for alternative forms of development. An analysis of production structures, however, only allows us to identify the specific social forces as core actors and the wider structural environment within which they operate as well as to formulate hypotheses. It does not imply that the identification of actors' location in the production process determines their actual behaviour and ideological outlook. In other words, the social relations of production are only determining in the first instance, indicating possible strategies (Rupert 2000, 13–14). To uncover the actual positions and activities of unions is the task of an empirical investigation.

In general, it can be conceptualised that trade unions' positions reflect to some extent the interests of employers in their sectors. Since trade unions represent these employers' workers and job security and better wages and working conditions are workers' main concerns, the economic well-being of employers is crucial. Arguably, a stable monetary environment and institutionalised free trade are highly important for TNCs' activities across borders. Unsurprisingly, European TNCs were actively involved in bringing about the EU Internal Market and they also pushed for setting up EMU (van Apeldoorn 2002). At the same time, it can be conceptualised that trade unions in transnational production sectors become aware that the national level is no longer sufficient to exert some level of control over employers in these sectors. TNCs frequently attempt to play off one national labour movement against another, while they themselves plan their strategies from a transnational perspective. Hence, the following hypothesis can be formulated in relation to EMU:

> that those trade unions, which represent workers in transnational production sectors, are likely to support EMU. They are also likely to engage in more extensive co-operation with other trade unions at the European level, to regain some of the control over capital lost at the national level. National production sector unions, on the other hand, are likely to oppose EMU, since it undermines national policy autonomy, on the support of which their economic sectors depend. Relying on the state, they may also be less concerned about European co-operation.

Nevertheless, although it has been accepted that social forces of labour are of a national and transnational nature and may operate at the national and international level, the structural environment of these actions has to be kept in mind. This is, first, the structure of the production system, which engenders social forces as core actors. It is, however, also the different national institutional set-ups that matter. In principle, a neo-Gramscian perspective accepts that social forces operate within and through different forms of state (Cox 1989, 41). What is missing, however, is a conceptualisation of the structural impact these institutions have on social forces. To overcome this shortcoming, it is here suggested to extend the above insights with Bob Jessop's 'strategic-relational' approach to the state. As an institutional ensemble the state is the framework within which various different strategies are possible. As such, however, the state 'can never be considered as neutral. It has a necessary structural selectivity' (Jessop 1990, 268), favouring certain social forces and strategies over others. Historically, capitalism emerged within already established states. As Hannes Lacher makes clear, 'the exclusive territoriality of capitalist political space derives not from the inner nature of capital, but from the way in which capitalism came to be born into a pre-existing system of territorial states' (Lacher 2006, 16). Hence, labour movements were formed in nationally distinctive ways and it was within states that trade unions developed their potential and became most effective in influencing concrete policy-making. This historical legacy implies that trade unions still look first at the domestic level when developing new strategies. Hence, the following second hypothesis can be formulated:

> that those trade unions, which continue to enjoy good access to policy-making at the national level, are reluctant to co-operate at the European level, even if they represent transnational labour. On the other hand, it is those trade unions, which have lost influence at home, which are most in favour of supranational initiatives.

© 2008 The Author. Journal compilation © 2008 Political Studies Association
BJPIR, 2008, 10(1)

At first sight, it could be argued that the first hypothesis is simply a reflection of rational choice CPE approaches on the positions of trade unions and employers' associations (see above). The second hypothesis then adds institutions as an additional, separate explanatory factor and it has to be empirically tested which variable is more decisive in which circumstances and for what reasons. Such a research strategy, however, overlooks that the apparent separation of state and market as well as other factors is only due to the historically specific way in which the social relations of production are organised around private property and wage labour within capitalism and the way the extraction of surplus value is organised not politically, but economically, since those who do not own the means of production are 'free', and thus economically compelled, to sell their labour power (Burnham 1995). Empirical pluralist approaches, in developing separate explanatory variables, reify this apparent separation into ahistorical categories. As a result, they cannot understand the historical specificity of capitalism, which in turn leads to an inability to question more fundamentally capitalist social relations. Nor is it possible to analyse the social purpose underlying unions' actions. For example, Josselin's analysis of EMU remains within the realm of the given and can only assess whether trade unions are in favour of European integration in general and EMU in particular (Josselin 2001, 71). The question of what kind of EU trade unions aspire to in relation to neo-liberal restructuring is not addressed. By contrast, here the focus is on the internal relations between the 'state' and 'market'—the way, for example, private property is legally ensured by the state—as well as other factors. They are regarded as the expression of the same social relations of production and while they and other forms of these relations may appear to be separate, they are internally linked precisely through the social relations of production (Bieler and Morton (forthcoming)). Hence, the two hypotheses do not imply that production structure and institutions are conceptualised as two separate, independent explanatory variables, the respective relevance of which can be systematically assessed. Rather, through a focus on class struggle and the agency of social forces, which operate within and through national institutional set-ups, both factors are internally linked in a holistic approach, which can then be applied to empirical situations. Similarly, as a post-positivist, critical theory, a neo-Gramscian perspective does not intend to test and verify or falsify these hypotheses in order to establish causal relationships in an assumed objective world. Rather, the hypotheses raised here need to be understood as questions, guiding the empirical research in these two particular case studies. The questions can be applied to other case studies, but the empirical results cannot be transferred. In this article, it is then possible to analyse the underlying rationale of trade unions' position on EMU and to ask whether they have started to accept neo-liberalism. Equally, it is possible in the Conclusion to reflect on possible challenges to neo-liberal restructuring in the EU. In short, thanks to the critical theory nature of neo-Gramscian perspectives (Cox 1981, 129), this analysis adds the additional focus on the social purpose of trade unions' activities. This is a separate concern in that trade unions' positions on EMU and European co-operation do not determine their acceptance or non-acceptance of neo-liberal economics. It is this additional focus, which makes a clear contribution to mainstream approaches and their analysis of 'economic interests' and European integration, which so often concentrates almost exclusively on the form of integration at the expense of its contents (van Apeldoorn 2002, 11–13; Bieler 2000, 8).

© 2008 The Author. Journal compilation © 2008 Political Studies Association
BJPIR, 2008, 10(1)

The next section will analyse British and Swedish unions' positions on EMU and European co-operation in order to determine whether the expectations as expressed in the two hypotheses are correct, while also paying attention to the underlying rationale of their positions.

EMU and European Co-operation: British and Swedish Trade Unions Compared[2]

Split over EMU Membership

The British Trades Union Congress (TUC) discussed EMU from the Delors appearance at the 1988 congress onwards (Interview No. 2) and swung fully behind it in 1996 (Josselin 2001, 61). This positive position was confirmed during the following years. EMU would imply that exchange rate uncertainty was overcome, helping especially export-oriented manufacturing, which was suffering from an overvalued pound (Interview No. 2). Remaining outside EMU, on the other hand, could imply that Britain drifted further apart from the rest of the EU. 'The TUC is particularly concerned at the statements attributed to a number of leading inward investors that the strong pound and the uncertainty about the Euro are threatening long-term investment in the UK' (TUC 2000, 7). There were also concerns about being squeezed with a relatively unimportant currency between the US dollar bloc and the Eurozone. The political implications of non-membership would be the relegation to a secondary place in the decision-making process, when the 12 finance ministers of the Euro-countries took their economic and monetary decisions (Interview No. 2). The Social Dimension was, however, regarded as an absolutely essential part of EMU. In its statement to the 2002 TUC Annual Congress, the TUC General Council emphasised the 'continuing balance between economic and social progress, enshrined within the European Social Model' (TUC 2002, 1). Thus, the TUC raised various elements it considered to be important including the Social Chapter, a flexible interpretation of the convergence criteria, more regional funds, a co-operative growth strategy and democratic accountability of the ECB (Verdun 2000, 142, 155). In contrast to some of its affiliated unions (see below), the TUC was less worried about the potential damaging effects of the convergence criteria on public investment levels. The criteria themselves were not regarded as unreasonable, as long as they were interpreted in a flexible way, and they would not be a problem for Britain, since the then Chancellor Gordon Brown applied even tougher targets aiming for national debt below 40 per cent of GDP (Interview No. 2).

This positive position on EMU was not shared by all affiliates. As expected in the first hypothesis, a split between unions representing workers in transnational production sectors and unions representing national social forces of labour can be identified. The Amalgamated Engineering and Electrical Union (AEEU) is taken as an example for transnational sector unions.[3] Considering that the vast majority of the AEEU's members are in export-oriented or transnational manufacturing, which have suffered from exchange rate fluctuations in recent years, EMU membership was deemed to be absolutely necessary. The AEEU linked job losses in manufacturing directly to the launch of EMU in 1999. As Maureen Rooney stated on behalf of AEEU, then already re-named as AMICUS, at the TUC Annual Congress in 2002,

> in the past 18 months we have lost 250,000 jobs in manufacturing, and when the Engineering Employers' Federation talk to us they are saying that the threat of job losses are not threats but they will become a reality before we have a referendum, if we put it off for much longer (TUC Annual Congress 2002).

Moreover, key investment decisions by foreign companies would be made on the basis of whether Britain participated in EMU or not. Finally, it was asked in what way Britain can continue to be a full EU member without actually being also a member of EMU. The convergence criteria were not feared, since public investment levels were at an all-time low anyway. There would also be some room for increased public investment within the criteria. The ECB was asked to consider employment levels more strongly in its monetary decisions, but one should not forget that unemployment was not necessarily due to EMU, but due to restructuring in times of globalisation. New jobs should be the result of a strong economy, not created by the government for the sake of creating jobs (Interview No. 4; see also Mulhearn 2004, 305).[4] Together with four other unions organising workers predominantly in transnational and export-oriented sectors, i.e. the print union GPMU, the community union ISTC, organising workers in the steel and metal industries, the general union GMB (see below) and the National Union of Knitwear, Footwear and Apparel Trades (KFAT), the AEEU formed the movement 'Trade Unionists for Europe' (TUfE). It is pointed out that even outside EMU 'Britain is already subject to the Growth and Stability Pact, the EU's common rules for government borrowing' (TUfE 2000, 11), while it would not have the same political input as other EU countries, which are also members of EMU.

On the other hand, unions in national production sectors fiercely oppose EMU. The public sector union UNISON is taken here as a representative example. UNISON's criticism was threefold. Firstly, the convergence criteria would limit what countries can spend on public services. On behalf of UNISON, Jane Carolan made this clear at the TUC Annual Congress in 2002: 'The fundamental part of the Growth and Stability Pact is that the only goal of European economic policy is price stability, a policy based on tight control of interest rates and public expenditure' (TUC Annual Congress 2002). Secondly, EMU would have a negative effect on employment and growth levels. Finally, EMU is rejected because of the ECB's lack of democratic accountability. In short, EMU is criticised for its underlying neo-liberal rationale and the concomitant restriction of an active employment policy. Rather than concentrating solely on low inflation, Britain would need strong investment in the public sector to create further employment (Interview No. 3; see also Strange 1997, 17).

This split between national and transnational forces of labour is also noticeable within the general unions. Being a part of the TUfE movement, the GMB executive supported by a majority of its members favours EMU membership at an early date. The main worries of the union were related to the job losses in manufacturing due to the overvalued pound (Interview No. 1). At its congress in June 2001, the

Central Executive Council of the union put forward a statement, which pointed to the problems of the current exchange rate for manufacturing, the potential loss of FDI in the future and lack of political influence on decision-making in the EU while remaining outside EMU (GMB 2001). Nevertheless, about a third of the GMB members are employed in the public sector and this wing of the union opposed EMU (Interview No. 1).

In Sweden, a similar split between transnational production sector unions and national sector unions can be observed. The Trade Union Confederation (LO), organising blue-collar workers, and several of its affiliates are taken as an example here. On the basis of an internal report on EMU (LO 1996), the LO executive board decided against membership in February 1997. It was concerned about the potentially deflationary implications of EMU (Bieler 2000, 103). At its congress in 2000, however, the position was reassessed and a conditional 'yes' formulated. Politically, the strongest concerns were voiced about the danger of remaining outside the inner decision-making circle of the EU as a non-EMU member (LO 2000, 3). Economically, membership would help the Swedish economy to retain competitiveness as it most likely implied slightly lower interest rates in the long term and even more room for a national fiscal policy (LO 2000, 4–5). The most important conditions put forward deal with the possibilities of how to counter asymmetric shocks within EMU, once adjustment via a free-floating currency is no longer possible. Membership should only be an option if a stable wage formation system was secured in Sweden and so-called buffer funds established, which could be used in times of economic recession to stimulate domestic demand (Interview No. 10).

Within LO, it was the Metal Workers' Union in 1997 which came out first in favour of Swedish EMU membership. The Metal Workers' Union represents workers in the transnationalised manufacturing sector, dominated by TNCs such as Ericsson, Electrolux and Volvo. It was argued that considering the union's sector depends on TNCs, which operate on the European and even global level, the union simply had to follow capital to the European level to re-establish a balance between capital and labour lost at the national level. The convergence criteria were not considered to be a problem. If anything, they had a positive impact on Sweden, forcing it to focus on low levels of inflation and a consolidated budget, putting it now with a budget surplus of 2 per cent in a position to employ more people in the public sector. The establishment of buffer funds as a safeguard against asymmetric shocks was rejected. It would make no sense to take money out of the economy in times of stable budgets (Interview No. 7).

On the other hand, the Transport Workers' Union and the Union of Commercial Employees, both affiliated to the LO, opposed Swedish EMU membership. Both have experienced some transnationalisation within their sectors—in the areas of transport and the security industry in the case of the former, and the appearance of some large chains in the retail and wholesale sectors in the case of the latter. Overall, however, the members of both unions still work for small domestic companies and shops, indicating a predominantly domestic production structure. The Union of Commercial Employees took its first view of expression on EMU in 1997. Politically, the union was concerned about the loss of influence on monetary policy *vis-à-vis* the democratically unaccountable ECB. Economically, higher Swedish wage increases due to near full employment would require a fluctuating exchange rate to counter asymmetric economic shocks. Moreover, the convergence criteria would cause mass unemployment and the ECB would stifle economic growth due to its unnecessarily high interest rates (Interview No. 5). This position was echoed by the Transport Workers' Union, the executive board of which decided to recommend to its members a 'no' in the referendum. It pointed to the 1992 Swedish currency crisis, when the rigid peg of the Swedish krona to the ecu had cost about 200,000 jobs in Sweden. Hence, the exchange rate was considered to be absolutely necessary for the stabilisation of the economy in times of crisis. The idea that buffer funds and/or a budget surplus would be enough was not regarded as realistic (Interview No. 11).

British and Swedish Unions and the Issue of European Co-operation

The division between British transnational and national sector unions on EMU was mirrored in a different emphasis placed on the importance of European-wide co-operation. UNISON considered both the national and European levels important for exerting influence and generally supported British EU membership (Strange 2002a, 348). Nevertheless, being in favour of an active employment programme in Britain, it had concentrated on the national level since Labour's return to power in 1997 (Interview No. 3). It was the transnational sector unions which were most in favour of European-wide co-operation. The AEEU was strongly involved with the European Metalworkers' Federation (EMF) and its attempts to co-ordinate national collective wage bargaining (Gollbach and Schulten 2000). In relation to European macroeconomic policy, the ECB was asked to consider employment levels more strongly in its monetary decisions (Interview No. 4). The GMB with its majority of members from transnational manufacturing went furthest in its direct involvement in Brussels. The EU level was considered to have become increasingly important and the union had maintained its own presence in Brussels for many years. It lobbied the Commission directly and had a close relationship with the Commissioner for Social Affairs (Interview No. 1). Moreover, support for EMU did not imply acceptance of neo-liberalism. The union was strongly in favour of employment-creating programmes at the national and European level, especially via European-wide infrastructure projects. It supported a larger budget for the EU to finance these projects and was in general in favour of a more expansive fiscal policy. If this implied going beyond the limits set by the convergence criteria, the GMB would not be worried (Interview No. 1). UNISON's rationale for rejecting EMU clearly indicates its opposition to neo-liberal economics. Nevertheless, transnational labour and the TUC too, despite their support for EMU and European co-operation, continued to question neo-liberal restructuring. They made the further development of the Social Dimension an absolute precondition for their support of EMU (Interview No. 2). The TUfE movement spelled this out most clearly by pointing out that 'without a strong framework of employment and social rights the EU will fail to gain the support of its citizens' (TUfE 2000, 6). This emphasis on the Social Dimension also included a commitment towards 'developing a European industrial relations system as part of this process' (TUfE 2000, 16).

© 2008 The Author. Journal compilation © 2008 Political Studies Association
BJPIR, 2008, 10(1)

While the positions on EMU taken by Swedish unions showed a similar split between national and transnational production sectors as in Britain, the attitudes towards co-operation at the European level by transnational sector unions were markedly different. National sector unions, as in Britain, were sceptical about the possibilities of European co-operation. The Union of Commercial Employees could not make out any substantial, concrete results of the Social Dimension. More international co-operation was necessary, it was argued, but only in order to strengthen trade unions at the local and national level, since change had always come from below. Due to the different national labour legislations, tax systems and social insurance systems, the co-ordination of bargaining at the European level would be impossible. The transfer of union competencies to the European level was rejected outright (Interview No. 5). From the perspective of the Transport Workers' Union, the EU social dialogue was valued too highly. The results would be simply too meagre and the fact that there was no right to take industrial action at the European level would significantly weaken the potential role of unions. Because there was no threat of transferring production abroad in the union's sectors, the co-ordination of wage bargaining was not deemed to be urgent (Interview No. 11).

Unlike transnational labour in Britain, however, the Metal Workers' Union, although arguing that a balance between capital and labour needed to be re-established at the European level, stated in contrast to the expectations of the first hypothesis that the lobbying of the Swedish government was still the most important way to influence policy-making. European-wide collective wage bargaining was rejected and the attempts of co-ordinating wage bargaining by the EMF would play no role in collective bargaining in Sweden. Rather, manufacturing unions and employers would still look at what happened in Germany and sometimes other EU countries (Interview No. 7). What is additionally striking in contrast to British unions is the fact that a further development of the Social Dimension was not put forward as a condition for support for EMU, nor was it mentioned in the context of EMU. In 1996, the LO team stated in its report on EMU that 'if a monetary union is to be discussed at all, in our opinion it must be balanced by an equally strong employment union' (LO 1996, 64). The conditional pro-EMU conference decision in 2000, however, neither referred to the idea of employment union, nor did it mention a further development of the Social Dimension (LO 2000). In general, the whole debate in Sweden about EMU oscillated around the question of how to stabilise the national economy as an EMU member in times of economic recession. Transnational sector unions argued that a budget surplus was enough, some argued in favour of additional buffer funds and those unions opposed to EMU argued that retaining the exchange rate was essential. The possibilities of how to generate economic growth and jobs at the European level were not explored in the discussion on EMU (Interview No. 9). Nor was there an outspoken criticism of neo-liberalism with the exception of the domestic production sector unions. In order to explain the reluctance of Swedish transnational labour to co-operate more extensively at the European level, the next section will compare the British and Swedish forms of state. The potential for trade unions to influence policy-making in each country is analysed, thereby turning to the second hypothesis of this article.

© 2008 The Author. Journal compilation © 2008 Political Studies Association
BJPIR, 2008, 10(1)

Unions' Position within the British and Swedish Forms of State

Historically, a cornerstone of unions' influence on British policy-making was their close link to the Labour party (Ludlam et al. 2002, 223–225). This ensured that unions had excellent access to government, when Labour was in power. Moreover, British unions had experienced a remarkable growth in strength from the mid-1960s to late 1970s as far as membership levels and political influence were concerned (Howell 1999, 28). Nevertheless, this was based on voluntarism and depended on full employment and state support. Unions did not seek the institutionalisation of their rights. This made it easy for both the state, then led by a Conservative government, and the employers to push back unions in the 1980s and 1990s. The Conservative government made industrial action more difficult for unions and employers moved towards a decentralisation of collective bargaining, opted for flexibility and some even de-recognised unions outright. As a result, 'collective bargaining between unions and employers is no longer the dominant system of industrial relations' (Howell 1999, 30). Looking at the British form of state during the 1980s and 1990s from a strategic-relational point of view indicates that whatever position unions adopted and whatever policies they wanted to influence within Britain, there was no contact point. It was during this time of Conservative government that the British unions changed their historically negative position on membership of the European Union (Rosamond 1998, 134). Since then, the TUC and its affiliated unions concentrated on the further expansion of the Social Dimension. First results of the social dialogue between the European Trade Union Confederation and the Union of Industrial and Employers' Confederations of Europe at the European level leading to a directive on parental leave in 1996, a directive on atypical work in 1997 and a directive on fixed-term work in 1999 transformed British unions into one of the strongest supporters of European integration in the UK. As demonstrated above, there is an internal union conflict over EMU, but none of the unions opposed to EMU would link this to a general rejection of British membership of the EU (Strange 2002a and 2002b).

Since Labour's return to power, trade unions have regained better access to government. New Labour introduced a minimum wage, established statutory union recognition and signed up to the EU social chapter, the latter going hand in hand with unions' own focus on EU-level developments. Those, however, who thought that with a Labour government the national form of state would provide better structural possibilities for influencing policy-making were disappointed. Already while the Labour party was still in opposition, the close party–union ties had been relaxed. Unions' share of the party conference vote was reduced to 49 per cent in 1995. The number of seats on party committees was cut back as was the union share of party funding (Ludlam et al. 2002, 228–230). Moreover, despite the Labour government's advances, actual policies did not fulfil unions' hopes. The minimum wage remained below union expectations, the statutory union recognition was watered down, Conservative employment legislation was not repealed and social partnership in the form of tripartism not institutionalised beyond the Low Pay Commission (McIlroy 2000a, 16–26). Privatisation in the public sector has continued through New Labour's attempt to attract private investment to the public sector via Private Finance Initiatives (PFIs) (McIlroy 2000b, 9–12). Finally, trade unionists were sidelined in the selection to advisory groups and taskforces established by New Labour. 'Only 31 places were occupied by trade unionists, and more than 350 by business people' (McIlroy 2000b, 5). In short, unions are still disadvantaged in their influence on policy-making within the structural selectivity of the British form of state. It is clear why in this situation unions, especially in the transnational production sectors, have been looking towards the EU level for improvements. They simply have no structural alternative than to move their emphasis abroad.

In Sweden, the developments at the form of state level were different. Traditionally, unions had close contacts with the Swedish Social Democratic party (SAP). Collective bargaining took place at the national, multi-sectoral level, with LO on the trade union side and the Confederation of Swedish Employers (SAF) on the employers' side setting a 'solidaristic' wage across the whole economy (Ryner 2002, 82–84). The SAP supported union–employer co-operation through a policy of full employment and an active labour market policy. At the beginning of the 1990s, this favourable position of the institutional set-up within the Swedish form of state changed drastically. First, the SAF withdrew from collective bargaining in the spring of 1990 (Pontusson 1995, 39). Then, the SAP government abandoned full employment as its main policy goal, replacing it with low inflation (Notermans 1993, 148). When in 1991 a coalition government led by the conservative Moderate party came to power, possibilities for trade unions to influence policy-making were at an all-time low. The SAP returned to power in 1994 but continued with its focus on low inflation and a consolidated budget as main priorities (Blyth 2002, 237). Some austerity measures were pushed through parliament against LO's will. Especially, the 1996 LO Congress was a congress of conflict with the government over changes in the labour law (Interview No. 10).

Collective bargaining, however, experienced a revival in 1997. The Engineering Employers' Association (VI), representing employers in the transnational manufacturing sector, would have preferred further decentralisation of wage bargaining towards cross-collar agreements at the firm or divisional level (Mahon 1999, 134). Nevertheless, VI was isolated within the Swedish Employers' Association in this respect, there was resistance within the VI by smaller companies and unions did not respond positively towards decentralisation of bargaining either. Finally, VI itself felt the disadvantages of decentralisation, when a higher wage settlement in the paper and pulp industry in 1995 forced VI to settle with the Metal Workers' Union at a similarly high level (Thelen 2001, 87). Hence, transnational employers retained a commitment to sectoral wage bargaining. However, not only transnational sector employers but also unions were in favour of a revival of sectoral bargaining. This can only be understood against the background of a favourable economic development reflected in economic growth in the second half of the 1990s with up to 4 per cent in 1999 and 2000 (OECD 2001, 23–24) and a resulting changed position by the unions on inflation. Once the Swedish government had decided to focus on low inflation as its main policy target and renounced the possibility to devalue the Swedish krona in order to restore competitiveness of the Swedish economy— policies which were also strictly adhered to by the SAP when returning to power in 1994—the pressure was put on wage formation not to lead to higher agreements than in neighbouring countries. Hence, nominal wage increases were much lower than in the 1970s and 1980s. Nevertheless, due to low inflation levels (consumer price index) of under 2 per cent between 1996 and 2000 (OECD 2001, 34), real wages actually increased, while large nominal wage increases in the past had often been crowded out by high inflation. Suddenly, low inflation levels were regarded as positive. This favourable assessment was further supported by the fact that Sweden, despite its policy of consolidated budgets, managed to halve unemployment from 8 per cent to 4 per cent between 1996 and 2000 (OECD 2001, 23, 88). Overall, as a result, trade unions no longer question the neo-liberal low-inflation policy and they have accepted that it has been and will be absolutely essential to keep wage formation under control to retain the international competitiveness of the Swedish economy and the related high levels of employment (Interview No. 6).

It is, therefore, no surprise that it was the transnational sector unions, white-collar as well as blue-collar, which signed in 1997 an industrial agreement, updated in 1999, with their counterparts of the employers covering all private sector industries. The agreement included the formulation of common assessments of the economic situation and an agreement on rules and procedures about collective wage bargaining at the sectoral national level, including the imposition of an impartial chair should negotiations stall. 'The purpose is to allow each party to conduct their union negotiations constructively, without industrial action, and to reach a new agreement with a balanced result before the old agreement expires' (Industrial Agreement 1999, 2). This Industrial Agreement was path breaking in the re-co-ordination of collective bargaining at the sectoral level, with one trade unionist hailing it as the new Saltsjöbaden agreement (Interview No. 8).[5] It was soon followed by similar agreements in other sectors. In 2000, the Swedish government established a new Mediation Authority to support further a smooth running of the wage formation system. By then, following the example of the Industrial Agreement of 1997, already '60% of the Swedish labour force [had been] covered by collective agreements that provide their own framework for mediation, and are thus excepted from the statutory rules' (Eironline 2001). In short, corporatist bargaining has been re-organised in Sweden, albeit at the sectoral level and with stronger government involvement.

It is this focus on co-operation with employers over wage bargaining at the national level against the background of a favourable economic development which explains Swedish unions' acceptance of a low inflation policy as well as their relaxed attitude towards the neo-liberal convergence criteria. This revived system gives unions clear structural possibilities of influence within the Swedish form of state, which makes a stronger focus on EU-level developments appear less urgent. To summarise, this confirms the second hypothesis that those unions, even if they represent transnational production sectors, are less likely to opt for European co-operation, if they enjoy a strong position within the structural selectivity of the national form of state.

Conclusion

This article introduced a neo-Gramscian, critical IPE perspective extended with a strategic-relational approach to the state, able to comprehend labour's role in the processes of transnational restructuring and, thus, able to conceptualise labour as a potential international actor without neglecting specific national institutional set-ups. Applied to a comparative analysis of British and Swedish trade unions and their positions on EMU and European co-operation, it was revealed that in line with the first hypothesis transnational forces of labour in both countries were in favour of EMU, pointing to the importance of gaining political say via membership. By contrast, national labour opposed EMU, referring to the deflationary implications of a monetary and economic policy which is mainly focused on price stability and low inflation. The views of transnational labour, however, diverged over the emphasis on European co-operation. While transnational British unions put stronger empha-sis on further developments at the European level, transnational labour in Sweden relies predominantly on its co-operation with transnational capital and the govern-ment at the national level. It concentrates on the question of how the national economy can adjust in times of economic recession once a free-floating currency is no longer available as a stabiliser within EMU. In contrast to Britain, where the form of state leaves labour hardly any space of structural impact, the Swedish form of state with labour's privileged access to the Social Democratic government and the strong bargaining structure with capital at the sectoral level allows labour much better influence on policy-making than the EU institutional set-up currently offers.

The different orientation has a potentially drastic impact on the formation of the future European model of capitalism. Concentrating on the social purpose under-lying British unions' positions, it has been shown that not only UNISON, which opposes EMU, but also those unions in support of British membership reject neo-liberal restructuring and demand a further development of the Social Dimen-sion and a stronger emphasis on employment instead. As Gerry Strange outlines, Euro-Keynesian macroeconomic management based on an ultimately centralised fiscal and monetary policy in a federal union combined with EU social partnership industrial relations is put forward by the British labour movement as a new project (Strange 2002b, 356–357). This framework could provide the basis for a challenge to the currently dominant neo-liberal development of the EU. In the mid-1990s, Swedish transnational labour indicated that it might become a pow-erful ally of such a project. While it had supported Swedish EU membership along with transnational capital, it had made clear that this should not lead to further neo-liberal restructuring of the Swedish form of state. Instead, it 'demanded addi-tional joint employment programmes and sometimes even a relaxation of the convergence criteria and the acceptance of a slightly higher rate of inflation in order to create more jobs' (Bieler 2000, 120). The Swedish debate over EMU membership, however, indicated a departure from this international outlook. The main debate was about how Sweden could adjust in times of economic recession, not about developments at the European level. This was based on the acceptance of a policy focusing on low inflation and the emphasis that wage formation was responsible for the maintenance of Swedish competitiveness, thereby adopting some core neo-liberal tenets. Whether unions can maintain this position in future economic recessions is an open question. What is relevant for the prospects of Euro-Keynesianism is that Swedish labour is currently unlikely to be a driving force in this project. Only a further development of unions' influence at the European level may convince Swedish unions to turn their focus to the EU again.

About the Author

Andreas Bieler, School of Politics and International Relations, University of Nottingham, Nottingham NG7 2RD, UK, email: *andreas.bieler@nottingham.ac.uk*

Notes

I am indebted to David Coates, Christel Lane, Madeleine O. Hosli and especially Donna Lee, David Howarth, Patrick Leblond and Adam David Morton for comments on earlier drafts. This article is part of a larger comparative project on European trade unions and EMU, including also an assessment of Austrian, French, German and European-level trade unions (Bieler 2006).

1. France's and Germany's repeated failure to fulfil their obligations within the SGP has led some commentators to argue that the Pact has been abandoned. Nevertheless, while the reform of the SGP in March and June 2005 made its implementation more flexible, member countries are still obliged to meet the criteria albeit in a slightly longer time frame. Additionally, it has to be noted that both France and Germany continue working towards meeting the criteria in the future. In short, the price stability policy as exemplified by the SGP continues within the EU (Howarth 2006, 84–85).

2. In this article a limited but representative sample of British and Swedish unions is analysed. For a more comprehensive study, which confirms the findings of this article, see Bieler (2006).

3. In January 2002, the new union AMICUS was formed as the result of a merger between the AEEU and the union Manufacturing Science Finance. In this research, the AEEU is considered as a separate actor, since its policy on EMU was formed prior to the merger.

4. UNIFI, representing around 150,000 workers in the highly transnationalised finance sector, also endorsed EMU membership as expected in the first hypothesis (Bieler 2006, 134).

5. In 1938, Saltsjöbaden was the place of a famous agreement between the central organisations of capital and labour, preparing the way for industrial peace and the establishment of the Swedish Model.

Interviews

Interview No. 1: General Secretary, General, Municipal and Boilermakers' Union (GMB); London, 28 March 2001.

Interview No. 2: Senior Economist, Trades Union Congress (TUC); London, 28 March 2001.

Interview No. 3: Head of Policy, UNISON; London, 2 May 2001.

Interview No. 4: International Officer, Amalgamated Engineering and Electrical Union (AEEU); Hayes (Kent), 23 May 2001.

Interview No. 5: Economist, Union of Commercial Employees/LO; Stockholm, 20 June 2002.

Interview No. 6: Head of Research Department/Researcher, Building Workers' Union (BYGGNADS); Stockholm, 20 June 2002.

Interview No. 7: EU co-ordinator, Research Department, Metal Workers' Union/LO; Stockholm, 20 June 2002.

Interview No. 8: Researcher/Researcher/Union Officer, Negotiator/International Secretary; Industrial Workers' Union/LO; Stockholm, 24 June 2002.

Interview No. 9: Head of Research, Paper Workers' Union/LO; Stockholm, 24 June 2002.

Interview No. 10: International Economist, LO; Stockholm, 25 June 2002.

Interview No. 11: International Secretary, Transport Workers' Union/LO; Stockholm, 26 June 2002.

Bibliography

Andersson, T., Fredriksson, T. and Svensson, R. (1996) *Multinational Restructuring, Internationalization and Small Economies: The Swedish Case* (London: Routledge).

Bieler, A. (2000) *Globalization and Enlargement of the European Union: Austrian and Swedish Social Forces in the Struggle over Membership* (London, New York: Routledge).

Bieler, A. (2006) *The Struggle for a Social Europe: Trade Unions and EMU in Times of Global Restructuring* (Manchester: Manchester University Press).

Bieler, A. and Morton, A. D. (2001) 'The Gordian knot of agency–structure in international relations: A neo-Gramscian perspective', *European Journal of International Relations*, 7:1, 5–35.

Bieler, A. and Morton, A. D. (2004) 'A critical theory route to hegemony, world order and historical change: Neo-Gramscian perspectives in international relations', *Capital and Class*, 82, 85–113.

Bieler, A. and Morton, A. D. (forthcoming) 'The deficits of discourse in IPE: Turning base metal into gold?' *International Studies Quarterly*.

Bieling, H.-J. (2001) 'European constitutionalism and industrial relations', in A. Bieler and A. D. Morton (eds), *Social Forces in the Making of the New Europe: The Restructuring of European Social Relations in the Global Political Economy* (Basingstoke: Palgrave), 93–114.

Bieling, H.-J. and Schulten, T. (2003) ' "Competitive restructuring" and industrial relations within the European Union: Corporatist involvement and beyond', in A. W. Cafruny and M. Ryner (eds), *A Ruined Fortress? Neoliberal Hegemony and Transformation in Europe* (Lanham MD: Rowman & Littlefield), 231–259.

Blyth, M. (2002) *Great Transformations: Economic Ideas and Institutional Change in the Twentieth Century* (Cambridge: Cambridge University Press).

Burnham, P. (1995) 'State and market in international political economy: Towards a Marxian alternative', *Studies in Marxism*, 2, 135–159.

Carchedi, G. (1997) 'The EMU, monetary crisis, and the single European currency', *Capital and Class*, 63, 85–114.

Coates, D. (2000) *Models of Capitalism: Growth and Stagnation in the Modern Era* (Cambridge: Polity Press).

Cox, R. W. (1981) 'Social forces, states and world orders: Beyond international relations theory', *Millennium: Journal of International Studies*, 10:2, 126–155.

Cox, R. W. (1989) 'Production, the state, and change in world order', in E.-O. Czempiel and J. N. Rosenau (eds), *Global Changes and Theoretical Challenges: Approaches to World Politics for the 1990s* (Lexington MA/Toronto: Lexington Books), 37–50.

Cox, R. W. and Sinclair, T. (1996) *Approaches to World Order* (Cambridge: Cambridge University Press).

Eironline (2001) 'Mediation authority seeks to improve wage-formation process (28/05/2001)', Available online at: http://www.eiro.eurofound.eu.int (accessed 17 June 2002).

Frieden, J. (1991) 'Invested interests: The politics of national economic policies in a world of global finance', *International Organization*, 45:4, 425–451.

Gamble, A. (2001) 'Neo-liberalism', *Capital and Class*, 75, 127–134.

Gamble, A. (2006) 'Two faces of neo-liberalism', in R. Robison (ed.), *The Neo-Liberal Revolution: Forging the Market State* (London, New York: Routledge), 20–35.

GMB (2001) *Statement on the European Union by the Central Executive Council of the GMB at the GMB Congress in June* (Brighton: GMB).

Gollbach, J. and Schulten, T. (2000) 'Cross-border collective bargaining networks in Europe', *European Journal of Industrial Relations*, 6:2, 161–179.

Gourevitch, P. (1986) *Politics in Hard Times: Comparative Responses to International Economic Crises* (Ithaca NY, London: Cornell University Press).

Hall, P. and Soskice, D. (eds) (2001) *Varieties of Capitalism* (Oxford: Oxford University Press).

Harvey, D. (2006) 'Neo-liberalism and the restoration of class power', in D. Harvey (ed.), *Spaces of Global Capitalism: Towards a Theory of Uneven Geographical Development* (London, New York: Verso), 7–68.

Helleiner, E. (1994) *States and the Re-emergence of Global Finance: From Bretton Woods to the 1990s* (Ithaca NY, London: Cornell University Press).

Higgott, R., Underhill, G. and Bieler, A. (eds) (2000) *Non-State Actors and Authority in the Global System* (London: Routledge).

Howarth, D. (2006) 'Internal economic and social policy developments', *Journal of Common Market Studies*, 44:Annual Review, 81–99.

Howell, C. (1999) 'Unforgiven: British trade unionism in crisis', in A. Martin and G. Ross (eds), *The Brave New World of European Labour: European Trade Unions at the Millennium* (New York, Oxford: Berghahn Books), 26–74.

Industrial Agreement (1999) *Agreement on Industrial Development and Wage Formation* (Stockholm: Industrial Agreement).

Iversen, T. and Pontusson, J. (2000) 'Comparative political economy: A Northern European perspective', in T. Iversen, J. Pontusson and D. Soskice (eds), *Unions, Employers, and Central Banks: Macroeconomic Coordination and Institutional Change in Social Market Economies* (Cambridge: Cambridge University Press), 1–37.

Jessop, B. (1990) *State Theory: Putting the Capitalist State in its Place* (Cambridge: Polity Press).

Jones, E. (2002) *The Politics of Economic and Monetary Union* (Lanham MD: Rowman & Littlefield).

Josselin, D. (2001) 'Trade unions for EMU: Sectoral preferences and political opportunities', *West European Politics*, 24:1, 55–74.

Kitschelt, H., Lange, P., Marks, G. and Stephens, J. D. (1999) 'Convergence and divergence in advanced capitalist democracies', in H. Kitschelt, P. Lange, G. Marks and J. D. Stephens (eds), *Continuity and Change in Contemporary Capitalism* (Cambridge: Cambridge University Press), 427–460.

Lacher, H. (2006) *Beyond Globalization: Capitalism, Territoriality and the International Relations of Modernity* (London: Routledge).

Lane, C. (1995) *Industry and Society in Europe: Stability and Change in Britain, Germany and France* (Aldershot: Edward Elgar).

LO (1996) *Wage Earners and EMU. A Report by the Economists of the Swedish Trade Union Confederation* (Stockholm: LO).

LO (2000) *This EMU. Summary of LO's View of the Economic and Monetary Union* (Stockholm: LO).

Ludlam, S., Bodah, M. and Coates, D. (2002) 'Trajectories of solidarity: Changing union–party linkages in the UK and the USA', *The British Journal of Politics & International Relations*, 4:2, 223–225.

Luif, P. (1996) *On the Road to Brussels: The Political Dimension of Austria's, Finland's and Sweden's Accession to the European Union* (Wien: Braumüller).

McIlroy, J. (2000a) 'New Labour, new unions, new Left', *Capital and Class*, 71, 11–45.

McIlroy, J. (2000b) 'The new politics of pressure—The Trades Union Congress and New Labour in government', *Industrial Relations Journal*, 31:1, 2–16.

Mahon, R. (1999) ' "Yesterday's modern times are no longer modern": Swedish unions confront the double shift', in A. Martin and G. Ross (eds), *The Brave New World of European Labour: European Trade Unions at the Millennium* (New York, Oxford: Berghahn Books), 125–166.

Martin, A. (2000) 'Social pacts, unemployment and EMU macroeconomic policy', in G. Fajertag and P. Pochet (eds), *Social Pacts in Europe—New Dynamics* (Brussels: ETUI), 365–400.

Martin, A. and Ross, G. (1999) 'In the line of fire: The Europeanization of labor representation', in A. Martin and G. Ross (eds), *The Brave New World of European Labor: European Trade Unions at the Millennium* (New York, Oxford: Berghahn Books), 312–367.

Mulhearn, C. (2004) 'Beyond "Euroland": British trade unions, the single currency and European integration', *Industrial Relations Journal*, 35:4, 296–310.

Notermans, T. (1993) 'The abdication from national policy autonomy: Why the macroeconomic policy regime has become so unfavorable to labour', *Politics and Society*, 21:2, 133–167.

O'Brien, R., Goetz, A. M., Scholte, J. A. and Williams, M. (2000) *Contesting Global Governance Multilateral Economic Institutions and Global Social Movements* (Cambridge: Cambridge University Press).

OECD (2001) *OECD Economic Survey: Sweden* (Paris: OECD).

Overbeek, H. (1999) 'Globalization and Britain's Decline', in R. English and M. Kenny (eds), *Rethinking British Decline* (London: Palgrave), 231–256.

Pontusson, J. (1995) 'Sweden: After the golden age', in P. Anderson and P. Camiller (eds), *Mapping the West European Left* (London, New York: Verso), 23–54.

Rhodes, M. (1998) 'Globalization, labour markets and welfare states: A future of "competitive corporatism"?', in M. Rhodes and Y. Mény (eds), *The Future of European Welfare: A New Social Contract?* (London: Palgrave), 178–203.

Rosamond, B. (1998) 'The integration of labour? British trade union attitudes to European integration', in D. Barker and D. Seawright (eds), *Britain For and Against Europe: British Politics and the Question of European Integration* (Oxford: Clarendon Press), 130–147.

Rupert, M. (2000) *Ideologies of Globalization: Contending visions of a New World Order* (London: Routledge).

Ryner, M. (2002) *Capitalist Restructuring, Globalisation and the Third Way: Lessons from the Swedish Model* (London, New York: Routledge).

Schmidt, V. A. (2002) *The Futures of European Capitalism* (Oxford: Oxford University Press).

Scholte, J. A. (2000a) *Globalization: A Critical Introduction* (Basingstoke: Macmillan).

Scholte, J. A. (2000b) ' "In the foothills": Relations between the IMF and civil society', in R. Higgott, G. Underhill and A. Bieler (eds), *Non-State Actors and Authority in the Global System* (London: Routledge), 256–273.

Schulten, T. (2000) 'Zwischen nationalem Wettbewerbskorporatismus und symbolischenm Euro-Korporatismus—zur Einbindung der Gewerkschaften in die neoliberale Restrukturierung Europas', in H.-J. Bieling and J. Steinhilber (eds), *Die Konfiguration Europas: Dimensionen einer kritischen Integrations-theorie* (Münster: Westfälisches Dampfboot), 222–242.

Smythe, E. (2000) 'State authority and investment security: Non-state actors and the negotiation of the Multilateral Agreement on Investment at the OECD', in R. Higgott, G. Underhill and A. Bieler (eds), *Non-State Actors and Authority in the Global System* (London: Routledge), 74–90.

Stopford, J. and Strange, S. (1991) *Rival States, Rival Firms: Competition for World Market Shares* (Cambridge: Cambridge University Press).

Strange, G. (1997) 'The British labour movement and Economic and Monetary Union in Europe', *Capital and Class*, 63, 13–24.

Strange, G. (2002a) 'British trade unions and European Union integration in the 1990s: Politics versus political economy', *Political Studies*, 50:2, 332–353.

Strange, G. (2002b) 'Globalisation, regionalism and labour interests in the new IPE', *New Political Economy*, 7:4, 343–365.

Strange, S. (1994) *States and Markets* (2nd edn) (New York, London: Pinters Publishers).

Strange, S. (1996) *The Retreat of the State: The Diffusion of Power in the World Economy* (Cambridge: Cambridge University Press).

Thelen, K. (2001) 'Varieties of labour politics in the developed democracies', in P. A. Hall and D. Soskice (eds), *Varieties of Capitalism: The Institutional Foundations of Comparative Advantage* (Oxford: Oxford University Press), 71–103.

TUC (2000) *Economic and Monetary Union: Memorandum to the House of Commons Treasury Committee (May)* (London: TUC).

TUC (2002) 'General Council Report 2002—Chapter 6: Europe', available online at: http://www.tuc.org.uk/congress/tuc-6413-f0.cfm (accessed 6 April 2005).

TUC Annual Congress (2002) 'Verbatim report Wednesday, 11 September', available online at: http://www.tuc.org.uk/congress/tuc-6858-f0.cfm (accessed 6 April 2005).

TUfE (2000) *A Trade Union Agenda for Europe. A Joint Report from AEEU, GMB, GPMU, ISTC and KFAT* (London: TUfE).

Van Apeldoorn, B. (2002) *Transnational Capitalism and the Struggle over European Integration* (London: Routledge).

Van Apeldoorn, B. (2004) 'Theorizing the transnational: A historical materialist approach', *Journal of International Relations and Development*, 7:2, 142–176.

Verdun, A. (2000) *European Responses to Globalization and Financial Market Integration* (London: Macmillan).

Waltz, K. N. (2000) 'Globalization and American power', *The National Interest*, 59, 46–56.

doi: 10.1111/j.1467-856x.2007.00320.x   *BJPIR: 2008 VOL 10, 105–128*

Economic Interests and the Construction of a European Single Pension Market

Alexandra Hennessy

This article asks why the EU member states were able to agree on an EU pension fund directive in 2003 whereas they had failed to do so in a previous attempt (1991). The main argument is that a single pension market was a desirable project before 2003, but bargaining inefficiencies prevented its realisation. This is because bargaining over integration in this sector requires credible signalling between Bismarckian and Beveridgean pension regimes. The co-ordination of divergent welfare and financial regimes depends on the ability of governments to send costly signals that only a limited range of outcomes are considered legitimate in their home state. In turn, the capacity to signal and the costs of bluffing hinge on international pressure for pension reform (Economic and Monetary Union) and the magnitude of changes governments have to make to their respective welfare finance arrangements.

Keywords: United Kingdom; Germany; corporate pensions; EU pension directive

1. Introduction

Although European Union (EU) regulations increasingly influence national welfare finance systems, the existing literature is only beginning to examine how EU decisions are affected by, and impact on, domestic institutions (Schmidt 2002; Marks and Steenbergen 2004; Callaghan and Höpner 2005; Ferrera 2005; Menz 2005). Is the Europeanisation of social and economic policies complementary or disruptive to national welfare states? When are EU-mandated reforms successful in domains where the member states have priority? This article attempts to shed light on these questions by analysing why the member states were able to agree on a European pension fund directive in 2003[1] (or 'IORP' directive) whereas they had failed to do so in a previous attempt (1991).[2]

Occupational pension regimes have not been sufficiently explored by the existing literature, mainly because of the limited comparability of second pillar pensions.[3] Yet, due to unfavourable demographic developments, stretched budgets and swelling non-wage labour costs it is impossible to deny the growing importance of employer-sponsored pensions. Given that cutbacks of social security pensions tend to be politically toxic, European governments feel mounting pressure to improve access to the second tier. However, affording more weight to the second pillar can be politically hazardous in countries where occupational pensions are viewed as an undesirable threat to pay as you go (PAYG) coverage. Labour unions in particular tend to disapprove of the inegalitarian properties of occupational plans (Esping-Andersen 1996, 328–329).

Another reason why occupational pensions increasingly move into the limelight is the mounting legislative activity by the European Union. European laws have influenced national pension systems for almost 40 years, ranging from the 1971 Council regulation that protects the social security rights of mobile persons to the 2005 directive proposal on pension portability. European institutions for occupational retirement provision (IORPs) cover about 25 per cent of Europe's labour force and manage assets worth 500 billion euros, or 29 per cent of the EU's gross domestic product (GDP).[4] Any transnational regulatory framework governing pension funds across borders requires a minimum harmonisation of investment, social and supervisory regulations. These, in turn, have a major domestic impact on economic interactions between governments, occupational pension plan sponsors and beneficiaries (Davis 1999; Ebbinghaus and Manow 2001; Estevez-Abe 2002).

Because European occupational pension regimes differ considerably in terms of institutional foundation, purpose and financial design, EU harmonisation efforts represent a classic co-operation problem: converging on common rules is desirable in principle, but deep divisions exist over both objective and means of harmonisation. EU pension policies may fit well with Beveridgean pension fund cultures, but not with Bismarckian insurance cultures. This makes any common policy hard to adopt.

In order to explain why IORP negotiations broke down in 1991, but succeeded in 2003, the article develops an analytical framework that captures the interaction of governments and national varieties of capitalism to explain the shift from negotiation failure to a politically efficient agreement. The main argument is that credible signalling between member states can promote co-operation in a policy area that is not 'truly European'. During the 1991 negotiations, member states were unable to distinguish between 'real' domestic constraints and cheap talk, leading to bargaining breakdown. The move to Economic and Monetary Union (EMU), however, changed the constraints of Bismarckian member states, making negotiation failure more costly to them. In this new macroeconomic environment, harmonisation offers made by Bismarckian nations were perceived as risky and therefore credible, paving the way for IORP compromise. The null hypothesis is that the Bismarckian countries did not face more adjustment difficulties than their Beveridgean counterparts. Thus, an empirical test showing that the Bismarckian states were bluffing and could have implemented an EU-wide pension framework with only marginal costs would undermine the argument advanced in this article.

The following part reviews existing approaches that have been applied to decision-making in the European Union. The subsequent section builds an account of government preferences, explicating why Bismarckian governments faced higher costs of bargaining breakdown after EMU was implemented. In the fourth part, the basic problem of pension market integration is captured by a dynamic game of incomplete information. The fifth part analyses who wins and who loses from the IORP directive. The final section concludes.

2. Formal and Informal Decision-Making in the European Union

In the majority of formal decision-making models, the reasons for negotiation breakdown are rarely explored. Proponents of procedural approaches, for example, have modelled the legal sequencing of EU decision-making processes. Their goal is to assess whether agenda setting, veto or gatekeeping rights empower an institutional actor, such as the European Parliament or the EU Commission (Majone 1994; Tsebelis and Garrett 1996; Kreppel 2002). The hidden assumption in those studies is that informal deliberations are unimportant compared to legal procedures. While not every legal rule is unequivocal, the clarity of legal procedures compares favourably to the obscure informality of pre-decision consultations. However, the outcomes of specific European decision processes are not only affected by formal institutional rules, but also by cognitive and normative orientations which define the game that is being played (Schmidt 2000; Risse 2001; Blyth 2003).

While acknowledging the importance of formal legislative institutions for bargaining outcomes, we contend that they are insufficient in explaining the actions of MEPs or Council members. Both in 1991 and in 2003 qualified majority voting was applicable. The introduction of the co-decision procedure with the Maastricht Treaty altered the decision-making process, although the direction of this change is contested in the literature. Some critics claim that the co-decision procedure only strengthens the EU Parliament on paper, but effectively tips the balance of power towards the Council (Curtin 1993). Others consider the Parliament a genuine co-legislator that is on a par with the Council (Crombez 1997). The latter position seems more plausible. The emergence of a sizeable coalition in the European Parliament advocating a certain course of action can indeed translate into strong political pressure, which the Commission may exploit to win over reluctant Council members. Before the inauguration of the co-decision rule, a blocking majority in the Council was sufficient to torpedo any integration effort. Does this mean formal decision-making procedures explain everything?

I disagree with this notion. As Christopher Achen pointed out, formal rules may set the boundaries within which action takes place, but they do not determine politicians' behaviour (Achen 2006, 124). It has been shown that informal deliberations prior to the legal steps are critical to political outcomes in the European Union (Wallace 2005). This implies that the deliberations preceding the formal decision-making process are more consequential than the narrow legalities. We do not wish to challenge the importance of legal structures in shaping policy outcomes since the passage of any EU directive is dependent on the formal ratification process. But an exclusive focus on legalities cannot explain why governments sometimes fail to reach an agreement despite tangible benefits from co-operation. Thus, understanding the nature of decision-making in the EU requires analysis of why informal negotiations sometimes result in deadlock, and sometimes in politically successful agreements.

Although bargaining approaches have been successfully applied to address this question (Arregui et al. 2004; Bueno de Mesquita 2004; Thomson et al. 2006), they are unsatisfactory for studying feedback effects between the EU and national levels.

Historical institutionalists have demonstrated that domestic modes of interest representation tend to be sticky. Therefore, we not only need to explore when and why politicians attempt to shift established policy patterns by brokering agreements at the European level, but also how EU directives might feed back on national elites and the public to sharpen certain cleavages and stifle others.

The article contends that a domestic constraints model, framed as a signalling game, is better suited for capturing the dynamics underlying the deliberations to the single pension market than standard procedural approaches, because the actor-centred perspective allows us to understand more precisely how EU integration is linked to domestic politics. The subsequent sections develop a testable argument about how functional necessities arising from integration in a particular policy field (Economic and Monetary Union) influence negotiation processes in another policy area (pension market integration).

3. Bismarck vs. Beveridge

At first glance, the governance of pension funds across borders may seem like a simple target for EU harmonisation efforts. The potential benefits seem sizeable: more integrated capital markets, fewer barriers to labour mobility and substantial savings in administrative costs for multinational businesses. However, a single European pension market required institutional changes that reflected the fact that co-operation was desired in issues over which preferences varied. Based on the insights of Thomas Schelling (1960) and Robert Putnam (1988), I hypothesise that the relative weight each government assigned to the costs and benefits of a single pensions market determined its bargaining type during EU-level negotiations.

Governments can be of two kinds: those representing a Beveridgean pension fund culture (Denmark, Britain, Ireland, the Netherlands) and a Bismarckian insurance culture (all other member states).[5] A European-wide framework for pension portability affects the two types differently because of their distinctive welfare-capitalism arrangements. Since the Bismarckian states harboured occupational pension sponsors and beneficiaries most likely to suffer from integration, they found the creation of a European single pensions market politically more costly than the Beveridgean countries.

Bismarckian insurance systems are aimed at status maintenance during old age (Esping-Andersen 1990; Schludi 2005). First pillar pensions constitute the primary retirement income for beneficiaries, whereas occupational and private pensions are underdeveloped. Beveridgean states, by contrast—where commercial and monetary interests have traditionally dominated pension policy—faced lower adjustment costs (Whiteside 2006). Aimed at poverty prevention, British social security pensions are ungenerous, providing either universal flat-rate or means-tested benefits. Most citizens do not expect their state pension to afford a comfortable transition from work to the retirement phase and therefore arrange for supplementary occupational or private pension plans.

Regarding the design of a common EU pension market, the most contested issues revolved around the issues of investment rules, biometric risk coverage and book reserve pensions. The basic problem was the trade-off each government faced between creating the collective good of a single pension market and maintaining national welfare finance regulations. Since an analysis of all member states' viewpoints on these issues would go beyond the scope of this article, the following discussion will be restricted to Germany and Britain. The former represents the ideal-type of a Bismarckian country, the latter a Beveridgean nation. We also exploit the fact that member states representing an insurance culture tended to side with the German position, while pension fund cultures were more likely to support the British stance.[6]

Investment Regulations

The most publicised clash between Bismarckian and Beveridgean systems centred on investment regulations for EU pension funds. Germany lobbied for restrictive ones, Britain coveted relaxed rules. Restrictive regulations are generally a reflection of a risk-averse society that lacks an equity culture. Until recently, German pension funds had to meet no fewer than six separate limits: they could not invest more than 30 per cent in EU equities; no more than 25 per cent in EU property; no more than 6 per cent in non-EU equity; no more than 6 per cent in non-EU bonds; and no more than 20 per cent in overall foreign assets. Such rules are routinely justified on the grounds that investors need protection against market risk (Nürk and Schrader 1995). In Germany, risk-averse attitudes are especially pronounced where pension providers are subject to co-determination. Joint control over pension assets essentially affects the composition of a company's executive board and implies that the investment behaviour reflects the attitude of the insured. This is mirrored in the small proportion of shares in the monetary assets of German households. Pension funds and their managers generally prefer steady profit development. Irregular development would result in an irregular distribution of profits to the insured over time and is perceived as unfair (Deutsch 2002).

The British financial system, by contrast, imposes a relatively short-term horizon on companies, but at the same time allows high risk taking. The UK has the highest exposure to equities in Europe, at 62 per cent.[7] Even after scandals like the Maxwell affair or the recent collapse of Allied Steel and Wire, when thousands of employees lost their future pension rights, British politicians and the Bank of England continue to defend liberal investment and supervisory regulations because the majority of occupational pension plans are provided as defined benefit schemes, where the employer bears all risk (Blake 2003). British politicians defend flexible rules on the grounds that employers' duty to honour defined benefit plans requires them to pursue a high-risk/high-return strategy. Even though many defined benefit schemes have been closed for new hires and defined contribution plans—wherein the employee bears all investment return and longevity risk—are becoming more popular, previous defined benefit commitments still strain the resources of many employers. Given that the EU Commission advocated the adoption of the relatively liberal prudent person rule, which is already used in Britain and therefore required no adjustment costs, the British financial industry stood to gain most from a single pension market. The City of London always held a clear competitive advantage in the business of pension management *vis-à-vis* continental financial centres (Talani 2000). Consequently, the British pension industry lobbied strongly for the creation of a single pension market.

Biometric Risk Coverage

The second controversy concerned the extent of biometric risk coverage, which denotes relatively expensive longevity, invalidity and dependent survivor insurance. The percentage of the population that has access to biometric risk benefits varies considerably across countries, and within the same country across different pension plans. In Germany, the generous earnings-related PAYG pensions provide extensive biometric risk coverage. Compared to Anglo-Saxon schemes, risk coverage in Germany tends to be more generous. Scholars of the German welfare state have demonstrated that important segments of the business community have on numerous occasions supported institutions of social risk insurance (Mares 2003). Emphasising the need for pension security, Germany strongly lobbied for making biometric risk insurance compulsory in a European regulatory framework.

In Britain, social policies enter the utility of employers with a negative sign because they do not fit with the high-return/high-risk strategy British companies pursue. Occupational pension plans often take the form of individual saving plans and are being paid out as a lump sum. In this case, the biometric risk of longevity is not covered. This implies that the pensioner might outlive the benefit. Coverage of other biometric risks, such as disability and benefits for dependent survivors, is also often lacking (Haverland 2004, 6). Biometric risk coverage raises the labour costs of companies, decreasing overall profitability. Social insurance is seen as an impediment to the ability of firms to deploy their labour market resources flexibly. The limited supply of biometric risk coverage demonstrates that the costs of social policies to the firm usually outweigh the benefits, indicating low solidarity with workers (Mares 2003).

British politicians vocally opposed German attempts to force EU pension funds to offer biometric risk insurance. Following Thatcher's reforms, British consumers are highly dependent on the second and third pillar for retirement income. In stark contrast to Bismarckian pension systems, occupational and private pension plans are more of a substitute, as opposed to supplement, to state-sponsored pensions. Consequently, the idea of coercing the pension industry to offer a certain product represented a taboo for British politicians.

Book Reserve Pensions

The third bone of contention between Bismarckian and Beveridgean countries constituted the regulation of unfunded book reserve pensions in Europe. Book reserve pensions only exist on firms' balance sheets. Employers' favourite pension vehicle in Germany, book reserve pensions function as a staff retention device and cheap capital to the firm.[8] They constitute golden handcuffs for the most cherished employees. Long waiting and vesting periods commit staff members to the firm for many years and tie up this capital in the sponsoring firm, underpinning Germany's long-term labour relations and capital flows (Hall and Soskice 2001). Ultimately, this money will have to be paid out as corporate pension. But until the employee reaches retirement age, the firm can do what it likes with the funds it keeps. Beveridgean governments have repeatedly called for the external funding of such pensions under a common EU framework because such unregulated capital constitutes an unfair advantage to German employers. Others have argued that unfunded pension liabilities might give rise to liquidity risks as future pension obligations might be inadequately reflected in company balance sheets. Given the centrality of book reserve pensions to Germany's co-ordinated market economy, the German government, the federal employer association BDA, as well as the occupational pension association aba, have all vocally lobbied for the exclusion of book reserve pensions from the scope of the IORP directive.

Variation in Adjustment Costs

In addition to these fundamental differences, there is also variation in adjustment costs across Bismarckian types. Differences in institutional structures, such as the size of the service sector (Iversen and Wren 1998), state capacity to 'impose' unpopular reform packages on social partners (Hassel and Ebbinghaus 2000), as well as government preferences over welfare spending on different age groups (Lynch 2006), all influence the precise costs of reform. While some Bismarckian states have successfully incurred short-term costs to introduce funded components to their PAYG pension systems, others have refrained from doing so in order to maintain a reputation as the guardian of the welfare state. Because the costliness of adjusting domestic pension systems to EU regulations is not directly observable from outside, governments have an informational advantage concerning their true cost types. Although EU negotiators meet in a variety of settings and swap information about each other, they may have an incentive not to disclose their information fully or accurately (Austen-Smith and Feddersen 2006, 209).

Even though the private information assumption regarding the true costs of reform also holds for the Beveridgean states, the congruence between the EU Commission proposals and Beveridgean pension systems attenuates differences in adjustment costs. Because variation in the benefits these states obtain from integration is sufficiently small, it is innocuous to assume that Beveridgean states are of one type.

Representation of Preferences

The nature of welfare finance arrangements in Bismarckian and Beveridgean states allows us to map their preferences over the IORP directive in a two-dimensional policy space (Figure 1). Germany's ideal point lies in the upper right corner of the 'high biometric risk coverage/high investment restriction' policy space. Such an outcome would impose restrictive investment rules on the European financial industry and force it to offer biometric risk coverage. Although such an outcome would have made cross-border pension funds legally possible, de facto it would have done little more than perpetuate the status quo. Most firms would have abstained from setting up European IORPs in other countries, because the costly absence of a single pension market would have been merely replaced with the costs of navigating an overly restrictive one.

© 2008 The Author. Journal compilation © 2008 Political Studies Association
BJPIR, 2008, 10(1)

Figure 1: Players' Indifference Curves

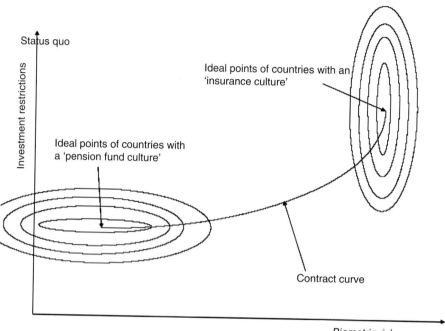

The British ideal point lies diametrically opposed to Germany's, in the lower left corner of the 'low biometric risk coverage/low investment restriction' policy space. This outcome would create the most flexible regulatory framework, enticing many firms to join the lucrative pensions market and creating the most cross-border activity. In this case, firms would apply the prudent man rule and leave biometric risk coverage to the employee or the state. The management of employees' pension claims in a single country would save multinational companies administrative costs. This version emphasises the financial aspects of the single pension market and tones down the social concerns.

The status quo is represented on the high end of the vertical axis and signifies the absence of a European regulatory framework. The shaded area is the intersection of Bismarckian and Beveridgean indifference curves and represents the set of all outcomes that are Pareto-superior to the status quo. Moving from outside the status quo inside the lens always leads to an improvement. The preferences of the two types on the issues of investment rules and biometric risk coverage are summarised by indifference contours centred about each one's respective ideal point (Figure 2).

The shape of the indifference curves—ellipses instead of concentric circles—reflects the assumption about countries' preference *intensity*, implying that Germany felt more intensely about the issue of biometric risk coverage than investment rules, while Britain felt more strongly about investment rules than biometric risk coverage. The contract curve in Figures 1 and 2 represents all Pareto-optimal outcomes,

Figure 2: Set of Pareto-Optimal Outcomes

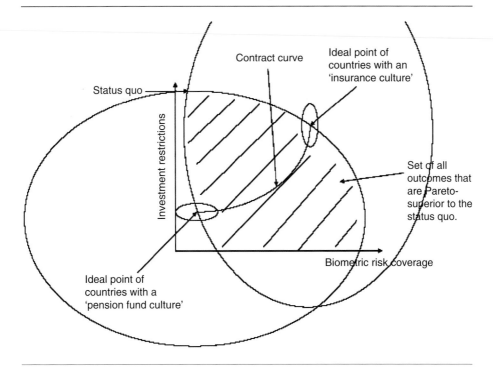

where no side can deviate from its position without making the other side worse off. Pareto-optimal outcomes on the contract curve include the two countries' ideal points as well as the universe of possible negotiated policy compromises between the two.

Failed First Attempt (1991)

Given the different pension cultures these governments represent, they envisaged radically different versions of a European-wide framework. While the Beveridgean states preferred to implement the single pensions market based on high harmonisation of investment regulations (the application of the so-called prudent man rule), high harmonisation of funding requirements and no harmonisation of biometric risk coverage, their Bismarckian counterparts envisioned the polar opposite: maintenance of quantitative investment limits, no harmonisation of funding requirements and high harmonisation of biometric risk coverage. In short, the two types had different political ideal points corresponding to divergent levels of integration.

However, the literature underscoring the significance of constrained domestic win-sets for international bargaining leverage is unsatisfactory for explaining the discrepancy between negotiation failure in 1991 and negotiation success in 2003. This body of research would have predicted a policy outcome more favourable to the ideal points of the Bismarckian states because the high costs of reform should have translated into a bargaining advantage. But this is contradicted by empirical evidence. The Commission's initiative in 1991 to tackle the restrictions inhibiting cross-border pension portability hit a brick wall of opposition from almost all EU countries (Rupprecht 2001; Deutsch 2002).

EU Commissioner Leon Brittan first presented his vision for pension market integration in 1991, after it emerged that pension funds had been forgotten in Jacques Delors' White Paper (1985) on the single market. To create pan-European pension funds, Brittan proposed reforms in three critical areas: freedom of investment, freedom of management and cross-border membership (EFRP 2001, 45). The member states' response to pension market integration was overwhelmingly negative. The Bismarckian member states not only opposed all of Brittan's suggestions, but even tried to turn the draft proposal on its head. Although the Commission's goal was to liberalise the movement of capital across borders, the Bismarckian states attempted to use the directive proposal to enshrine tough investment regulations, which ultimately made it unattractive to the countries that had sought its adoption, in particular Britain, the Netherlands and Ireland.

Although investment restrictions were frequently justified with the need to protect investors against market risk, a more important reason for opposing the delegation of control over investment regulations to Brussels was the Commission's plan to include unfunded book reserve pensions under the scope of the directive. As previously mentioned, employers in Bismarckian countries cherish book reserve pensions because they provide them with cheap company finance and an effective staff retention device (Esping-Andersen 1996; Estevez-Abe 2002). EU-mandated investment regulations, however, would have forced firms to *fund* these pensions, thereby obliterating firms' staff retention instrument. Because the Bismarckian governments realised that adoption of such sweeping regulatory change was politically hazardous, they offered to create a single pension market that corresponded more closely to their own national institutional frameworks. The counter-offer included the maintenance of quantitative investment restrictions, compulsory biometric risk coverage and the limitation of the directive to off-balance-sheet pensions.

Yet, despite ostensibly legitimate concerns over the impact of the directive on domestic employers, this counter-offer was quickly dismissed by the Beveridgean member states. The reason is that the proposal was not interpreted as a *costly* signal and therefore eroded the credibility of the domestic constraints argument. Given that population ageing, budgetary strain and concomitant reform pressures weighed more heavily on PAYG pension systems than on mature pension fund cultures, the Beveridgean states adopted a wait-and-see attitude, refusing to make any concessions to their Bismarckian counterparts. As a result of this deadlock, the Commission withdrew its proposal in 1994, a highly awkward move: 'This was the nuclear option, and it was embarrassing for everyone'.[9] Subsequent attempts to come to an agreement were made in 1999 when the original draft was amended, but these also failed and were shelved in the same year.

This episode demonstrates that, contrary to what the 'constrained win-set' literature would predict, each camp—insurance vs. pension fund countries—declined to reform its own welfare finance arrangements and instead urged the other side to adjust. Neither side was able to translate the domestic constraint logic into a bargaining advantage. Thus, what we seek to contribute to this debate is an argument about the conditions that make the constrained win-set strategy a credible choice of governments. As many scholars have demonstrated, it makes a difference whether domestic constraints are perceived as real or feigned (Schneider and Cederman 1994; Bräuninger et al. 2001; Hug and König 2002). In 1991, failure to distinguish between cheap talk and credible signals contributed to the breakdown of negotiations over the pension fund directive. Since both Beveridgean and Bismarckian states had the same preferences—designing the single pensions market without reforming their own social and economic institutions—their signals could not be informative. Bismarckian governments did not have to fear immediate audience costs resulting from negotiation breakdown, such as electoral punishment or loss of reputation. This is why each player tried to hold out for a better deal, and negotiations resembled a war of attrition.

Successful Attempt (2003)

In 2003, however, the single pension market was part of an overarching project—Economic and Monetary Union—and several steps towards further financial market integration had already been taken. These measures include banking and stock market regulation, as well as permission for banks, insurance and investment companies to operate EU-wide with a single licence. Realising their competitive disadvantage *vis-à-vis* insurance companies, pension funds, represented by the European Federation for Retirement Provision (EFRP), began to lobby for their own 'single passport' (EFRP 2001). Thus, European pension policies are not the result of attempts to build a 'social Europe', but the unintended consequence of policies aimed at solving problems stemming from internal market integration.

I hypothesise that, once Economic and Monetary Union was implemented, the economic and political costs of bargaining breakdown became much higher for the Bismarckian governments. This does not mean that the costs of complying with *any* European framework had diminished. While Bismarckian governments still faced high costs of implementing any European pension fund directive, the political costs of bargaining failure, however, had become even higher. This is because failure to establish a common framework threatened to do three things: (i) decrease sovereign credit ratings due to higher interest rates on government debt; (ii) diminish the legitimacy of cutting back on social security pensions at home; and (iii) confront governments with a highly unfavourable set of inter-temporal policy choices. Let us consider each in turn.

First, EMU changed the level of Bismarckian governments' implicit and explicit debt obligations and, as such, influenced the perception of their solvency (Fiess 2003, 4). By creating the European Central Bank, national governments lost the option of expanding the money supply to meet debt obligations, of which unfunded pension liabilities are the largest part (Eijffinger and de Haan 2000). Consequently, rating agencies may downgrade countries that fail to make their overstretched social security pension systems more sustainable for the future. As Rawi Abdelal has demonstrated, rating agencies provide international financial markets with a common language of risk and carry the 'force of law' in many countries around the world (Abdelal 2007, ch. 7). Lower ratings indicate a decrease in a country's readiness and willingness to meet debt obligations duly and therefore deter potential investors. This, in turn, may decrease the number of investment funds which will buy government bonds, and increase the interest rate on government debt.

Prior to EMU, the large credit-rating agencies focused on the debt obligations of national governments according to a complex set of quantitative and qualitative criteria, such as political risks, fiscal flexibility, monetary stability, external liquidity and economic structure (Hamilton and Flavin 1986). Since the implementation of EMU, however, rating agencies have proposed to use new criteria, similar to the ones applied to large corporations. Several studies have found that rating agencies do take unfunded pension liabilities of corporations into account when determining a firm's risk profile (Feldstein and Seligman 1981; Carroll and Niehaus 1998). According to this perspective, an underfunded pension plan represents a claim against future cash flows which decreases the security of other debt-holders' claims.

Other scholars (Truglia 2002) argue that unfunded pension claims of governments play only a minor role in assessing sovereign credit risk. Although calculations of future pension liabilities provide a projection of a given scenario, Vincent Truglia does not expect this projection to actually materialise:

> As a result ... large future pension claims have not greatly influenced our ratings of government debt in the industrialized world, even where net present value calculations would indicate very substantial claims on government resources over a 20–30 year time horizon. We simply expect that the government will 'default' in the future on its pension promises as currently written in law in a way that will favour creditors (Truglia 2002, 2–3).

This expectation implies, however, that the ratings of the affected countries could come under severe pressure unless appropriate reform steps are introduced. Lower ratings indicate a decrease in a country's readiness and willingness to meet debt obligations duly and may therefore deter potential investors. This, in turn, may decrease the number of investment funds which will buy government bonds, and increase the interest rate on government debt. While some insurance-based countries such as Germany, Austria and France consistently received the highest scores, rating agencies strongly emphasise the need for structural reform. Standard and Poor's country report in 2002 mentioned that 'the ratings on Germany will be supported by a consistent long-term approach in addressing the challenges of eliminating structural budget deficits, increasing employment growth and putting the increasingly overburdened health and pension systems on a more solid footing' (Standard and Poor's 2002). Other states such as Belgium, Italy and Portugal are rated lower.[10]

The increased costliness of negotiation failure in an EMU setting is furthermore connected to domestic perceptions of distributional and generational justice. Failure to strengthen pension portability at the European level imperilled the legitimacy of cutting back on social security pensions at home. As pension scholars never tire to point out, the trickiest question associated with reforming PAYG pension systems is how to avoid punishing one generation by requiring them to finance their parents' pensions and save for their own (Myles and Pierson 2001). Because young and highly educated employees are more likely to be mobile, they tend to benefit more from a single pension market than elderly employees with obsolete or firm-specific skills. This is because the prospect of owning occupational pension rights even in case of career changes or interruptions can be sold to domestic voters as a form of compensation: cuts in future social security pensions will be offset by better access to, and more efficient management of, existing occupational pension rights. Given that more than 60 per cent of young Europeans consider the possibility of being able to work anywhere in the European Union as an important right (Eurobarometer 1997, 113), this outlook is no small enticement.

Thirdly, and most importantly, all EMU countries are signatories to the Stability and Growth Pact (SGP), which limits the build-up of public sector deficits over time. Because governments face restrictions on the size of budget deficits and the overall build-up of public sector debt, their freedom of fiscal steering to offset these constraints is quite limited (Soskice and Iversen 1998). As a result, reforming pension schemes in the European Union has become even more urgent, especially in the member states with large PAYG pension systems. This new macroeconomic framework has altered the inter-temporal policy choice set governments are subject to. Without the SGP, governments had incentives to put off reforming their pension system into the future. Why incur costs in the present when the benefits will not accrue until the distant future and might benefit the other guy? However, the SGP altered political incumbents' time horizon: the longer European governments failed to reduce their future PAYG pension claims, the tougher the actual cuts required to live within the confines of the stability pact would have to be. Therefore, the longer the delay, the higher the likelihood that governments would need to cut entitlements of current beneficiaries (Truglia 2002, 4). The closer to the present the actual cuts in benefits are, the greater the risk that governments will suffer electoral punishment. In this respect, EMU-induced reform pressure may be seen as a way of overcoming the time inconsistency problem political incumbents invariably confront, namely incurring costs in the present to realise a collective good—in this case, better access to supplementary coverage and less pressure on social security pensions—in the future (Jacobs 2004). Critics have pointed to the failure of the European Union to enforce the SGP as evidence that it does not matter much, but recent research challenges the notion that rules have to be enforced to represent a credible commitment (Stone and Gent 2006).

For these reasons, it was perhaps not overly surprising that it was the Spanish and Italian presidencies of the EU (two Bismarckian states) which pressed forward with the pension fund directive. In 1993, newspapers had warned:

> if agreement on the directive is not reached by the end of the Belgian presidency [31 December 1993], the next five presidencies—Greece, Germany, France, Spain and Italy—are unlikely to give this particular piece of EU legislation any priority, because these countries do not at present have large and active private pensions industries.[11]

Yet, as the above discussion suggests, EMU substantially increased the political and economic costs of failing to realise the single pension market. As a result, Bismarckian states' requests for accommodation at the EU level to ease the pain of reforms were costly and therefore credible. This prompted the Beveridgean states to adopt an honest, accommodating position. The following section develops a formal model that captures the capacity of the European member states to send and receive signals, accounting for the discrepancy between bargaining inefficiencies in 1991 and informative exchanges in 2003.

4. Formal Model

Consider a simple game of incomplete information played between a single Bismarckian state (C) and a single Beveridgean state (L) in the European Union.[12] Both are concerned with the extent to which they have to reform their own social and economic institutions following any agreement at the EU level. They bargain over a convex policy space defined by the closed interval [0, 1]. C's ideal point lies at 0 and L's ideal point lies at 1. The players are assumed to have single peaked preferences. The utility functions are monotonically decreasing when moving away from their respective ideal points. The player with private information (C) can be of the high cost type (C_H) or of the low cost type (C_L). The two types differ with respect to their utility for an EU agreement, with the high cost type incurring more adjustment costs resulting from integration. Only C knows his true cost type, whereas L needs to make inferences about C based on C's actions. As illustrated in the game tree, nature moves first and determines whether Bismarckian state C is of the high cost or low cost type (Figure 3).

Figure 3: Sequence of Moves

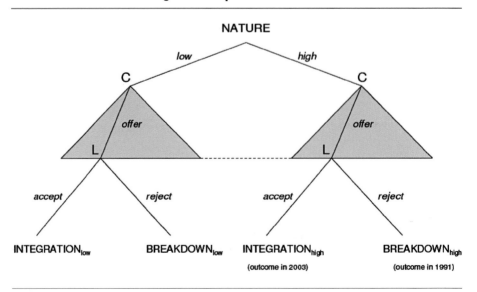

The Bismarckian state moves next and offers a level of integration x, with x in [0, 1]. The game is interesting because the liberal state does not know which type of C it is negotiating with. L prefers to deal with a low cost Bismarckian state to implement a single pension market that mirrors its own welfare finance institutions, but if L believes with certainty that C is of the high cost type, L prefers to move further away from its ideal point to accommodate C. This means L will accept a less favourable point in the policy space to avoid the worst possible outcome (no integration, or maintenance of status quo). However, L has a prior expectation q in [0, 1] about the distribution of types. Depending on the observed offer by C, the liberal state L updates its belief about C. The updated belief μ denotes the probability L attaches to C being of the low cost type. L takes the next step and decides whether to accept or reject C's proposed point in the policy space. If L accepts, the game ends, and the pay-offs resulting from an agreement are distributed. If L rejects, the negotiations collapse and the players receive the status quo utility minus a penalty, if any, for bargaining failure. The pay-offs for INTEGRATION and bargaining BREAKDOWN are determined by the costs involved in implementing any negotiated agreement. They are as follows:

BREAKDOWN:

$$U\left(C_H\right) = U\left(C_L\right) = 0,$$

$$U\left(L|H\right) = -k,$$

$$U\left(L|C\right) = 0.$$

INTEGRATION:

$$U\left(C_H\right) = -r_L x + I^c,$$

$$U\left(C_L\right) = -r_H x + I^c,$$

$$U\left(L\right) = -s + \left(1 - x\right) + I^L,$$

where $r_L < r_H$ and $r_L = 1$, $s = 1$, I^c, I^L in (0, 1) and x in [0, 1].

Notation: r_L and r_H denote the costs of reform C incurs to reach an agreement with L (r_L normalised to 1); [0, 1] is the policy space both parties bargain over; I^C and I^L signify the respective benefits the Bismarckian and Beveridgean states derive from integration; and s represents L's cost of accepting C's offer.

Recall that information about the true cost type is private information of the Bismarckian government. This means the Beveridgean state's decision about whether to accept or reject C's integration offer is shaped by its evolving assessment of C's true cost type. The appropriate solution concept in this game of incomplete information is Perfect Bayesian Equilibrium.[13] Note that no separating equilibrium exists. In other words, the Beveridgean government knows that a low cost Bismarckian government will always propose a point in the policy space that is more favourable to L and a high cost Bismarckian government will always propose a

© 2008 The Author. Journal compilation © 2008 Political Studies Association
BJPIR, 2008, 10(1)

point less favourable to L. However, such a course of action is not consistent with the incentives of a low cost Bismarckian government, which always prefers to pretend to be of the high cost type in the first phase, inducing its preferred outcome, 'low level of integration'.

An interesting equilibrium of the game is semi-pooling, in which both BREAK-DOWN and INTEGRATION can occur. Consider the first case: If L observes a low integration offer it might mistake a high cost Bismarckian government for a low cost government that is bluffing to get a more favourable deal. Although the Beveridgean state knows it might be making this mistake, the probability of dealing with a low cost C conveying cheap talk may be perceived to be sufficiently high that the Beveridgean state prefers to take its chances, reject the offer and find out C's true cost type. Under this outcome, L randomly challenges C, because claims about domestic constraints are cheap and thus cannot be informative. Since in this case L is trying to catch cheaters, bargaining breaks down.

In the second scenario, the outcome is INTEGRATION, because the Beveridgean state received a costly and therefore credible signal, enabling it to distinguish cheap talk from genuinely high costs of reform. This induces L to update its belief about C and accept a lower integration offer to avoid perpetuation of the status quo, a worse outcome for L. The key to a separating equilibrium is that L wants to get it right and make the correct inference about C. Mistakes occur when the negotiators choose an outcome that would not have been chosen had all private information been revealed prior to the vote (Austen-Smith and Banks 1996; Austen-Smith and Feddersen 2006).

Although the Beveridgean state prefers to deal with a low cost C to realise a European framework that is closer to its own ideal point, it clearly wants to avoid negotiation breakdown with a high cost type C. This is because bargaining collapse with a high cost Bismarckian state would signify a big victory for all risk-averse groups in Bismarckian states which are anxious to preserve the status quo, such as employers sponsoring book reserve pensions, risk-averse beneficiaries or pension funds balking at foreign competition. It would make L look like a loser and considerably diminish the prospect of reaching an agreement in the future. Thus, if L knows for sure it is dealing with a high cost C, it will always prefer to accommodate C and move further away from its ideal point to avoid bargaining breakdown, a worse outcome for L. Yet, as we have seen, errors can be made when member states' signals are costless. The following section examines the level of integration—or point on the contract curve—that was chosen when the member states eventually agreed on the 2003 pension fund directive, highlighting the extent to which the Beveridgean states accommodated their Bismarckian counterparts after credible signalling took place.

5. The IORP Directive: Winners and Losers

To understand how EU decisions translate into domestic policies, we apply Vivien Schmidt's (2002) analytical framework, which distinguishes between different EU adjustment pressures (decisions accompanied by more or less highly specified rules for compliance, suggested rules or no rules) and potential adjustment mechanisms

© 2008 The Author. Journal compilation © 2008 Political Studies Association
BJPIR, 2008, 10(1)

(coercion to a greater or lesser degree, mimesis or regulatory competition) to predict how EU regulations affect national policies (inertia, absorption or transformation) (Schmidt 2002).

Applied to the pension fund directive, the member states agreed on: coercion in the area of investment rules; the principle of home country control regarding quantitative investment limits and biometric risk coverage; and on the exclusion of book reserve pensions from the purview of the directive. Pension institutions will be able to select investment managers established anywhere in the EU. They will also need to comply with the newly established supervisory authorities in Brussels, Frankfurt and Paris.

Article 18 (5) represents a sacrifice on the part of the Beveridgean states by allowing member states to 'lay down more detailed rules, including quantitative rules', as long as they do not prevent institutions from investing 70 per cent of assets in equity, 30 per cent of assets in foreign currency and investing in risk capital markets.[14] The Beveridgean states were initially opposed to this stipulation, because it provides pension funds in Beveridgean countries with a disincentive to gain a foothold in those countries. The Bismarckian member states insisted on its inclusion to make clear to their domestic constituents that they cared about pension security. The general risk averseness and lack of an equity culture in Bismarckian member states demanded nothing less. As one Commission administrator put it, 'now they can at least protect their own nationals against unsound investments' (personal interview, 21 June 2006). Although the Beveridgean states conceded the article on quantitative investment limits to grant their Bismarckian counterparts a 'safety net', the overall investment policy put forward by the directive indicates the liberalisation of investment rules. In the spatial representation, this agreement denotes a point on the contract curve that is closer to the Beveridgean states' ideal point.

However, paragraph 5 qualifies this ostensible victory for the Beveridgean states by specifying that member states may apply more stringent investment rules in their respective home countries as long as they are prudentially justified.[15] The formulation 'prudentially justified' accommodates all member states uncomfortable with the prudent man rule, which they perceive as too relaxed. Since it is unclear even to Commission members involved in drafting the directive text what prudentially justified really means, it was relatively easy to agree on it (personal interviews with six Commission administrators, 20–23 June 2006).

While coercion was limited to investment regulations, the social aspects of the directive were defined by the principle of home country control. This is because the divergent welfare finance arrangements in the member states militated against a one-size-fits-all solution. Although a majority of MEPs originally wanted to force pension institutions to offer biometric risk coverage if desired by employers or employees, the Council opposed any framework that would compel pension institutions to offer a certain product. Council representatives reasoned that, aside from restricting competition, this provision would also violate the principle of subsidiarity (Karas 2003).

Yet, where insurance against biometrical risks is provided, the directive requires pension institutions to have sufficient provisions to cover these benefits.[16] Such pension schemes engaged in cross-border activity are also required to be fully funded at all times. This means that the Bismarckian states were able to maintain their ideal point on biometric risk coverage. At the same time, the principle of home country control allowed the Beveridgean states to retain their ideal point position on the same policy dimension, thus reflecting a Pareto improvement for both types of states.

Finally, the inclusion of article 2, section 2 (e) was very important to all Bismarckian states where book reserve pensions play a prominent role. Germany in particular insisted on removing unfunded book reserve pensions from the purview of the directive. This is because book reserve pensions would directly conflict with article 18 (e) ('assets shall be properly diversified'). Although the Beveridgean states countered that an exemption for book reserve pensions would give an unfair advantage to employers using them to finance current business activities, it soon became clear that no compromise would be reached if employers were forced to surrender their cherished source of cheap capital and staff retention device (interview, Commission administrator, 21 June 2006; interview, aba chairman Klaus Stiefermann, 29 June 2006). The Bismarckian states were able to signal credibly that such far-reaching regulatory change would never be accepted by domestic constituents. Consequently, only funded pension schemes will be defined as IORPs. This was acceptable to the Bismarckian states since externally funded pension schemes play only a minor role compared to book reserve pensions.

The Bismarckian states, on the other hand, reluctantly agreed to article 16, section 2, which specifies that member states may allow institutions 'for a limited period of time, to have insufficient assets to cover the technical provisions'. Given the chronically underfunded British pension plans, this provision reflects the position of the British government and pension industry, trumping concerns of the European insurance industry over adequate protection of consumers' pension rights.

The nature of the compromise the European member states reached in 2003 reveals two things: the Beveridgean states sacrificed more than their Bismarckian counterparts, and the Bismarckian states made concessions in areas they cared only marginally about. Although the overall regulatory approach to investment regulations was indeed 'coercion', the restrictions recorded in article 18(5) and paragraph 5 considerably softened the pain of liberalising investment regulations for the Bismarckian states. Furthermore, by agreeing on the principle of home country control regarding biometric risk coverage and permitting the exclusion of book reserve pensions from the purview of the directive, the Beveridgean states allowed the Bismarckian countries to maintain their ideal points in two crucial policy areas. This outcome supports our hypothesis that the 2003 directive is the result of credible signalling on the part of the Bismarckian states, while preferences over the design of the single pension market remained unchanged between 1991 and 2003.

Although the IORP directive constitutes a first step towards a single pension market, it is unlikely that there will be an upsurge in cross-border activity anytime soon. It remains to be seen whether individual member states will use the principle of home country control to increase or inhibit cross-border pension transfers. Furthermore, sensitive issue areas such as taxation of transferred pension claims have yet to be sorted out before we can speak of a truly integrated pension market. Nonetheless, given the manifold political and economic obstacles to integration, the 2003 compromise must be considered a bargaining success.

Conclusion

This article asked how the European member states with their divergent welfare finance regimes negotiate solutions to the problem of governing pension funds across borders. The central argument is that harmonisation success in such an 'un-European' policy area depends on the ability of governments to signal credibly that their domestic win-set is indeed constrained. We demonstrated that signals sent by Bismarckian governments in a non-transparent, pre-EMU setting were less credible than signals sent in a transparent, post-EMU environment. Furthermore, this article shows that the Beveridgean states, although more enthusiastic about a single pension market, would not create it at all costs. In 1991, failure to distinguish between sincere high cost Bismarckian governments and deceitful low cost ones led to negotiation breakdown.

Economic and Monetary Union, however, increased the costs of bargaining failure for the Bismarckian states. In this environment, requests for accommodation at the EU level were interpreted by the Beveridgean states as costly and were therefore met with an honest, separating response. As a result, the EU member states adopted a pension fund directive authorising high harmonisation of investment regulations, low harmonisation of funding requirements and no harmonisation of biometric risk coverage. Although sceptics have rightly criticised the directive as a deficient legislative bricolage, the fact that 15 member states with radically different occupational pension systems were able to adopt a pension fund directive makes it a negotiation success.

I do not, however, pretend that the model presented here is an accurate or exhaustive depiction of deliberations between member state representatives. The purpose of the signalling game is to provide a baseline model highlighting the role of information and informal signalling between the member states, an often overlooked aspect in the literature that has predominantly focused on formal decision-making processes. Scholars working on formal procedures may be guided by the baseline model, because it is important to understand the structure underlying information flows and the mechanisms that make signalling possible.

About the Author

Alexandra Hennessy is a postdoctoral researcher at the Skalny Center for Polish and Central European Studies, University of Rochester, Harkness Hall 101, Rochester, NY 14627, USA, email: *hennessy@bu.edu*.

Acknowledgments

For helpful comments on previous drafts, I wish to thank David Howarth, Patrick Leblond, Cathie Jo Martin, Sofia Perez, Tal Sadeh, Vivien Schmidt, Martin Steinwand, Randall Stone, Anthony Zito, and the anonymous reviewers.

Notes

1. Directive 2003/41/EC of 3 June 2003 on the activities and supervision of institutions for occupational retirement provision (IORPs).

2. Proposal for a Council Directive relating to the freedom of management and investment of funds held by institutions for retirement provision, COM (1991) 301 final, OJ C 312, 3 December 1991.

3. Corporate, occupational and employer-sponsored pensions all refer to second pillar retirement income. In contrast to state or private pensions, the second tier is provided by firms or sectoral umbrella organisations.

4. Commission of the European Communities RAPID: Preparation of Eurogroup and Council of Economics and Finance Ministers, Brussels, 12 May 2003.

5. For the sake of parsimony, we exclude other categories, such as mixed pension systems.

6. This is documented in the European Parliamentary Debates (1999–2004) and in the minutes of the European Parliamentary Financial Services Forum (2000–04).

7. Finfacts, 22 May 2006.

8. Sixty per cent of all occupational pensions are provided in the form of book reserves (Schoden 2003; more recent statistics show the same number: see http://aba-online.de).

9. Cabinet member of Internal Market Commissioner McCreevy, personal interview, 23 June 2006.

10. According to Standard and Poor's rating of 31 March 2006, Belgium is currently rated AA+, Italy AA− and Portugal AA− (http://www.standardandpoors.com).

11. European Savings Markets, 21 October 1993.

12. The formal model may be criticised for not including the role of the Council president or Commission as honest brokers who mediate between the member states (Sbragia 2002). Several analyses have detailed how the EU presidency can isolate or form alliances with certain member states to unlock incompatible negotiating positions (e.g. Tallberg 2004). While we do not wish to challenge these important contributions, we assume here that the Commission or Council president did *not* have privileged access to information in the IORP game. Without this assumption, we would not be able to explain bargaining failure in 1991. With superior knowledge of member states' true reform costs, presumably the Commission would not have put forward the 1991 proposal in the first place. Thus, we portray the Commission and Council presidency as focal points (Schelling 1960) around which member states co-operated after credible signalling took place.

13. See Appendix for existence conditions. For an overview of Perfect Bayesian Equilibria, see Gibbons (1992) or Ordeshook (1986).

14. Directive 2003/41/EC, article 18 (5).

15. Directive 2003/41/EC, paragraph 5.

16. Directive 2003/41/EC, paragraph 30; article 15 (2); article 17 (1).

Bibliography

Abdelal, R. (2007) *Capital Rules: The Construction of Global Finance* (Cambridge MA: Harvard University Press).

Achen, C. (2006) 'Institutional realism and bargaining models', in R. Thomson, F. N. Stokman, C. H. Achen and T. König (eds), *The European Union Decides* (Cambridge: Cambridge University Press), 86–123.

Arregui, J., Stokman, F. and Thomson, R. (2004) 'Bargaining in the European Union and shifts in actors' policy positions', *European Union Politics*, 5:1, 47–72.

Austen-Smith, D. and Banks, J. S. (1996) 'Information aggregation, Rationality, and the Condorcet Jury Theorem', *American Political Science Review*, 90:1, 34–45.

Austen-Smith, D. and Feddersen, T. J. (2006) 'Deliberation, preference uncertainty, and voting rules', *American Political Science Review*, 100:2, 209–217.

Blake, D. (2003) *Pension Schemes and Pension Funds in the United Kingdom* (2nd edn) (Oxford, New York: Oxford University Press).

Blyth, M. (2003) 'Structures do not come with an instruction sheet: Interests, ideas, and progress in political science', *Perspectives on Politics*, 1:4, 695–706.

Bräuninger, T., Cornelius, T., König, T. and Schuster, T. (2001) 'The dynamics of European integration. A constitutional analysis of the Amsterdam intergovernmental conference', in G. Schneider and M. D. Aspinwall (eds), *The Rules of Integration. Institutionalist Approaches to the Study of Europe* (Manchester: Manchester University Press), 46–68.

Bueno de Mesquita, B. (2004) 'Decision-making models, rigor and new puzzles', *European Union Politics*, 5:1, 125–138.

Callaghan, H. and Höpner, M. (2005) 'European integration and the clash of capitalisms: Political cleavages over takeover liberalization', *Comparative European Politics*, 3:3, 307–332.

Carroll, T. J. and Niehaus, G. (1998) 'Pension plan funding and corporate debt ratings', *The Journal of Risk and Insurance*, 65:3, 427–441.

Crombez, C. (1997) 'The co-decision procedure in the European Union', *Legislative Studies Quarterly*, 22:1, 97–119.

Curtin, D. (1993) 'The constitutional structure of the Union: A Europe of bits and pieces', *Common Market Law Review*, 30:1, 17–69.

Davis, E. P. (1999) 'Institutionalisation and EMU: Implications for European financial markets', *International Finance*, 2:1, 33–61.

Delors, J. (1985) 'Completing the Internal Market: White Paper from the Commission to the European Council (Milan, 28–29 June)', *COM(85)310*, June 1985 (Brussels: Commission of the European Communities), available at http://www.europa.eu/documents/comm/white_papers/pdf/com1985_0310_f_en.pdf.

Deutsch, K. G. (2002) 'A single Market for Occupational Pensions', *Deutsche Bank Research, Frankfurt Voice: EU Financial Market Special* (Frankfurt am Main).

Ebbinghaus, B. and Manow, P. (2001) *Comparing Welfare Capitalism: Social Policy and Political Economy in Europe, Japan and the USA* (London, New York: Routledge).

EFRP (2001) *The European Federation for Retirement Provision at 20 years* (London: IPE International Publishers Ltd).

Eijffinger, S. C. W. and de Haan, J. (2000) *European Monetary and Fiscal Policy* (Oxford: Oxford University Press).

Esping-Andersen, G. (1990) *The Three Worlds of Welfare Capitalism* (Cambridge: Polity Press).

Esping-Andersen, G. (1996) 'Conclusion: Occupational welfare in the social policy nexus', in M. Shalev (ed.), *The Privatization of Social Policy?: Occupational Welfare and the Welfare State in America, Scandinavia, and Japan* (Houndmills, Basingstoke, New York: Macmillan Press, St Martin's Press), 327–338.

Estevez-Abe, M. (2002) 'Reforms of German and Japanese pension systems in comparative perspective', Paper presented at the annual meeting of the American Political Science Association, 31 August–2 September 2002, Boston.

Eurobarometer (1997) *The Young Europeans* (47.2) (Brussels: The European Commission).

Feldstein, M. and Seligman, S. (1981) 'Pension funding, share prices, and national savings', *Journal of Finance*, 36:4, 801–824.

Ferrera, M. (2005) *The Boundaries of Welfare: European Integration and the New Spatial Politics of Social Protection* (Oxford: Oxford University Press).

Fiess, N. M. (2003) 'Pension reform or pension default?: A note on pension reform and country risk'. Background paper for regional study on social security reform, the World Bank.

Gibbons, R. (1992) *Game Theory for Applied Economists* (Princeton NJ: Princeton University Press).

Hall, P. A. and Soskice, D. W. (2001) *Varieties of Capitalism: The Institutional Foundations of Comparative Advantage* (Oxford, New York: Oxford University Press).

Hamilton, J. and Flavin, M. (1986) 'On the limitations of government borrowing: A framework for empirical testing', *American Economic Review*, 76:4, 808–819.

Hassel, A. and Ebbinghaus, B. (2000) 'Striking deals: Concertation in the reform of continental European welfare states', *Journal of European Public Policy*, 7:1, 44–62.

Haverland, M. (2004) 'European single market vs. national social policy. The crucial case of occupational pensions', Paper presented at the annual conference of the Dutch and Flemish Political Science Associations, Antwerp, 27–28 May 2004.

Hug, S. and König, T. (2002) 'In view of ratification, governmental preferences and domestic constraints at the Amsterdam intergovernmental conference', *International Organization*, 56:2, 447–476.

Iversen, T. and Wren, A. (1998) 'Equality, employment, and budgetary restraint: The trilemma of the service economy', *World Politics*, 50:4, 507–546.

Jacobs, A. M. (2004) *Governing for the Long-Term: Democratic Politics and Policy Investment* (Department of Government, Harvard University, Boston, unpublished dissertation).

Karas, O. (2003) *Die Richtlinie über die Tätigkeiten und die Beaufsichtigung der Einrichtungen zur betrieblichen Altersvorsorge*. Broschüre zur Pensionsfondsrichtlinie. Available online at: http://www.othmar-karas.at

Kreppel, A. (2002) *The European Parliament and Supranational Party System* (Cambridge: Cambridge University Press).

Lynch, J. (2006) *Age in the Welfare State: The Origins of Social Spending on Pensioners, Workers, and Children* (Cambridge, New York: Cambridge University Press).

Majone, G. (1994) 'The rise of the regulatory state in Europe', *West European Politics*, 17:3, 77–101.

Mares, I. (2003) *The Politics of Social Risk: Business and Welfare State Development* (Cambridge, New York: Cambridge University Press).

Marks, G. and Steenbergen, M. (2004) *European Integration and Political Conflict* (Cambridge: Cambridge University Press).

Menz, G. (2005) *Varieties of Capitalism and Europeanization: National Response Strategies to the Single European Market* (Oxford: Oxford University Press).

Myles, J. and Pierson, P. (2001) 'The comparative political economy of pension reform', in P. Pierson (ed.), *The New Politics of the Welfare State* (Oxford: Oxford University Press), 305–333.

Nürk, B. and Schrader, A. (1995) 'Von der Pensionsrückstellung zum Pensionsfonds: Eine Chance für den deutschen Finanzmarkt', *Deutsche Bank Research* (Frankfurt am Main).

Ordeshook, P. C. (1986) *Game Theory and Political Theory: An Introduction* (Cambridge, New York: Cambridge University Press).

Putnam, R. D. (1988) 'Diplomacy and domestic politics: The logic of two-level games', *International Organization*, 42:3, 427–460.

Risse, T. (2001) 'A European Identity? Europeanization and the Evolution of Nation State Identities', in M. G. Cowles, J. Caporaso and T. Risse (eds), *Europeanization and Domestic Change* (Ithaca NY: Cornell University Press), 198–216.

Rupprecht, G. (2001) 'Die Auswirkungen der neuen EU-Richtlinie auf die betriebliche Altersversorgung in Deutschland', in B.-J. Andresen, N. Rößler and J. Rühmann (eds), *Betriebliche Altersversorgung im 21. Jahrhundert. Rechtliche, personalpolitische und finanztechnische Herausforderungen* (Köln: Verlag Dr Otto Schmidt), 471–486.

Sbragia, A. (2002) 'Conclusion to the special issue on the institutional balance and the future of EU governance: The Treaty of Nice, institutional balance, and uncertainty', *Governance: An International Journal of Policy, Administration, and Institutions*, 15:3, 393–411.

Schelling, T. C. (1960) *The Strategy of Conflict* (Cambridge: Harvard University Press).

Schludi, M. (2005) *The Reform of Bismarckian Pension Systems: A Comparison of Pension Politics in Austria, France, Germany, Italy and Sweden* (Amsterdam: Amsterdam University Press).

Schmidt, V. A. (2000) 'Values and discourse in the politics of adjustment', in F. W. Scharpf and V. A. Schmidt (eds), *Welfare and Work in the Open Economy* (Oxford, New York: Oxford University Press), 229–309.

Schmidt, V. A. (2002) *The Futures of European Capitalism* (Oxford, New York: Oxford University Press).

Schneider, G. and Cederman, L. E. (1994) 'The change of tide in political co-operation: A limited information model of European integration', *International Organization*, 48:4, 633–662.

Schoden, M. (2003) *BetrAVG, Betriebliche Altersversorgung: Kommentar für die Praxis mit arbeitsrechtlicher Einführung* (Frankfurt am Main: Bund-Verlag).

Soskice, D. and Iversen, T. (1998) 'Multiple wage bargaining systems in the single European currency area', *Oxford Review of Economic Policy*, 14:3, 110–124.

Standard and Poor's (2002) 'Fiscal slippage in Germany: A co-ordination problem?', Tech. rep., Standard and Poor's.

Stone, R. and Gent, S. (2006) 'Formalizing informal co-operation: Norm-based co-operation and the European Stability and Growth Pact', Working Paper, University of Rochester.

Talani, L. (2000) 'Who wins and who loses in the City of London from the establishment of European Monetary Union?', in C. Crouch (ed.), *After the Euro* (Oxford: Oxford University Press), 109–139.

Tallberg, J. (2004) 'The power of the presidency: Brokerage, efficiency, and distribution in EU negotiations', *Journal of Common Market Studies*, 42:5, 999–1022.

Thomson, R., Stokman, F. N., Achen, C. and König, T. (2006) *The European Union Decides* (Cambridge: Cambridge University Press).

Truglia, V. J. (2002) 'Sovereign ratings and aging societies', Paper presented at Financing Global Aging Conference, Brandeis University, Rosenberg Institute of Global Finance.

Tsebelis, G. and Garrett, G. (1996) 'Agenda Setting Power, Power Indices, and Decision Making in the European Union', *International Review of Law and Economics*, 16:3, 345–361.

Wallace, H. (2005) 'An Institutional Anatomy and Five Policy Modes', in H. Wallace and W. Wallace (eds), *Policy-Making in the European Union* (Oxford: Oxford University Press), 49–92.

Whiteside, N. (2006) 'Adapting private pensions to public purposes: Historical perspectives on the politics of reform', *Journal of European Social Policy*, 16:1, 43–54.

Appendix

Equilibrium Characterisation

A Perfect Bayesian Equilibrium consists of the players' optimal actions, given the other players' equilibrium actions and beliefs about types. To simplify construction of the equilibrium, assume C_H has a dominant strategy of always offering $x = 0$.

Let x^* be the offer for which L is indifferent between accepting and rejecting, i.e. x^* satisfies

$$-(1-x) + I^L \geq 0 \Rightarrow x^* = 1 - I^L.$$

Next, we define off-equilibrium path beliefs. For any $x \in (0, 1]$, let L believe it faces C_L, i.e. it sets its posterior belief to $\mu = 1$. This assumption has intuitive appeal, since C_H has a dominant strategy of always offering $x = 0$, and thus does not stand to gain from deviating to $x > 0$.

With these off-equilibrium path beliefs (and with beliefs on the equilibrium path obtained by Bayesian updating), optimal strategies in a mixing equilibrium (corresponding to BREAKDOWN) are given by the probability that C_L offers $x_0 = 0$,

$$p = \frac{(\pi - 1)(I^L + k - 1)}{\pi(I^L - 1)},$$

where π is L's prior belief about C's type, and the probability that L rejects an offer x_0,

$$q = \frac{x^*}{I^c} = \frac{1 - I^L}{I^c},$$

such that (existence conditions)

$$k > \frac{I^L - 1}{\pi - 1} \quad \text{and} \quad I^L + I^c > 1.$$

Proof of existence (omitted) follows directly from the construction of the equilibrium.

How do changes in the valuation of agreement affect the probability of bargaining breakdown?

The probability of bargaining breakdown is given by

$$q((1-\pi)+\pi p).$$

Substituting in for q and p, and taking the first derivative with respect to I^C gives

$$-x^*\left(1-\pi+\frac{(\pi-1)(I^L+k-1)}{I^L-1}\right)\leq 0.$$

In order to ensure that higher valuations of agreement lead to a lower probability of bargaining breakdown, this expression must be less or equal to 0. Rearranging and simplifying gives

$$\frac{(\pi-1)k}{I^L-1}>0.$$

Since π, $I^L < 1$, this condition is always met.

doi: 10.1111/j.1467-856x.2007.00321.x   *BJPIR: 2008 VOL 10, 129–137*

Policy-Making and Integration in the European Union: Do Economic Interest Groups Matter?

Amy Verdun

What lessons can be learnt about the role of economic interests in European integration? This article seeks to answer this question by looking at four themes: (1) the role of economic interest groups on national preference formation; (2) the role of economic interest groups on EU policy-making; (3) the effect of the EU on the economic interest groups; and (4) the role of economic interest groups on the process of European integration. This article finds that economic interests groups do not 'a priori' act in favour of European integration. Also we can conclude that economic interest groups seek to influence both national and EU level actors and institutions. Finally, the process of European integration affects the overall environment in which economic interest groups operate. Overall, economic interest groups appear to play a more prominent role in EU governance and policy-making than the literature on European integration theories typically has emphasised.

Keywords: economic interests; interest groups; political science; European Integration

Economic interests have been of great importance in pluralist or neo-pluralist[1] understandings of governance (Dahl 1961; Moe 1998; McFarland 2004) which in turn have formed an important sub-field of the study of US politics. Applying pluralist and neo-pluralist understandings to the European Union (EU) has been more problematic. Whereas US politics is often characterised as (neo-) pluralist per se—including a crucial role for lobbying and economic interest group pressure—the setting in the European Union and its member states is less obviously pluralist.

The EU setting is different from that of the US in a number of ways. For example, Jan Zielonka (2006) recently conceptualised the EU as being not Westphalian but rather neo-medieval. In his view this characterisation is important as it allows us to understand why an overly state-centric and centralist view of the EU might not be helpful. Where a Westphalian state model stresses concentration of power, hierarchy and sovereignty, the neo-medieval model assumes overlapping authorities, divided sovereignty and diversified institutional arrangements (Zielonka 2006). Already in 1996 James A. Caporaso made a similar assessment of the nature of the EU when he analysed whether the EU fits a 'Westphalian', a 'regulatory' or a 'post-modern' form of state. Although he did not seek to assess which of the three models fits the best, his analysis did stress that the EU corresponds to all three in one way or another, depending on which dimension of EU governance one is seeking to understand (Caporaso 1996, 48). Beate Kohler-Koch is another author who identified the process of governance in the EU as being different from the national setting. She identified a process of 'network governance' to be at the heart of EU governance and policy-making (Kohler-Koch 1999 and 2005). Network governance implies that there is a multitude of actors at play without there being a central hierarchy. Furthermore, she identifies both public and private actors as playing an important role. Finally, in a large recent study, Ingeborg Tömmel and Amy Verdun (2008) seek to capture the nature of governance and policy-making in the EU in a large range of policy-making sectors. They also conceptualise governance in the EU as having four ideal-typical modes of governance, only one of which can be characterised as being hierarchical. The others are softer modes of governance that are based on negotiation, competition and co-operation. In each of these three non-hierarchical modes of governance it is clear that a mix of actors play a role and that in the EU the 'state' does not play the same centralist, hierarchical steering roles as it more typically plays in the national setting. In this context the EU state would be the Commission, both the college and the bureaucracy, in combination with the Council and Parliament.

Thus, following these views on the nature of EU governance, one should expect actors to access the EU polity on various levels, with multiple centres and regarding a variety of processes. Others have identified the institutional structure of member states in which interest groups operate as corporatist (or a variation on corporatist, with preferential access points for some specific economic interest groups). In this view there are special institutional structures that give trade unions, employers' organisations and representatives of business a role at the bargaining table for many important socio-political decisions. Yet others stress the fact that member states in Europe have a rich set of political parties. Economic interest groups do not quite have the same access to them as their counterparts have in the US (Olson 1965; Schmitter and Lehmbruch 1979; Katzenstein 1985). That said, for many years trade unions in Europe typically had better access to the Labour party (or social democratic equivalents in other western European countries) than business groups have had to more market-oriented political parties such as those that are liberal or conservative. Yet, this preferential access of unions to the left-wing parties has been waning over the past decades. Thus, in light of the above, it should come as no surprise that economic interest groups have typically not been regarded to be quite as important in EU member states and the EU as they have been in the US.

Having said that, in the maturing EU, an increasing share of all legislation is initiated and passed at the EU level. The entire *acquis communautaire* is seriously impacting the EU member states. Especially, given its small bureaucracy, the policy-making process has been influenced considerably by economic interest groups. These major changes in the EU have led a number of authors to try out a more US-style pluralist approach on the EU to see if there is a fit between it and the developments of policy at the EU level. It is no surprise that scholars like Jeffry Frieden (1991) and Andrew Moravcsik (1993; 1998) seek to apply those insights (see also Smith 2008, this issue). Frieden's seminal article looked at the role of national economic interests in the distributional impact of capital mobility (Frieden 1991) and suggested that economic interests are crucial for analysing the politics of capital mobility. The main question of course remains: are the two jurisdictions sufficiently alike that one can learn from the insights on the one (the US) in studying the other (the EU).

This focus on economic interest groups is important from the point of view of European integration theory. The early theorising of the process of European integration has not focused much on the role of economic interest groups in influencing national politics or national preferences. Intergovernmentalism focused on the role of the state and state leaders in determining the outcome of integration. Neo-functionalism did conceptualise a role for interest groups, for example the role of trade unions. However, neo-functionalism had a particular view on how trade unions would facilitate the process of integration. The role of economic interest groups was *not* to influence the policy-making process involving either domestic politicians or those at the EU level, but rather to transcend it and focus on the supranational level as the one at which problems could be solved that no longer could be addressed adequately at the national level. Thus, the idea was that unions would seek to collaborate at the 'European level' (Haas 1964). Many years later, liberal intergovernmentalism has moved beyond the original intergovernmentalism of Stanley Hoffmann (1966) and includes a better understanding of state prefer- ences by emphasising the role of national preferences (Moravcsik 1998). At the same time, liberal intergovernmentalism does not theorise exactly how economic interest groups operate or influence the policy-making process. Neither the exact setting nor the groups are made clear in this view of integration. The understanding is that these interests somehow influence what member states' government leaders perceive to be in their national interest.

When looking at the literature that examines the EU policy-making process, we do of course find studies that look at interest intermediation (Grant 1992; Kohler- Koch 1994; Greenwood 2007). These and many other analyses show how inter- est groups have an influence in the EU policy-making process. They emphasise the focus on 'networks' and the way in which they operate and access the 'multi- levelled' nature of governance in the EU, and also what mechanisms are adopted to influence the process. Special attention has been given to how lobbying takes place in the EU (Mazey and Richardson 1993; Coen 2007). The lobbying literature shows the sophistication with which interest groups operate to seek to ensure their preferred policy outcome (such as venue shopping, using an advo- cacy coalition, offering expertise in networks, etc.). However this literature does not necessarily concentrate on seeking to understand what role interest groups play in furthering (or obstructing) the process of European integration in a more general sense.

Let us turn to the various contributions of the authors of this special issue and assess what lessons can be learned from their studies for our general understanding of the role of economic interests in the broader process of European integration. Rather than treating them one by one, the articles in this special issue will be discussed according to the following four themes:[2] (i) the role of economic interest groups in national preference formation; (ii) the role of economic interest groups in EU policy-making; (iii) the effect of the EU on the economic interest groups; and (iv) the role of economic interest groups on the process of European integration.

© *2008 The Author. Journal compilation © 2008 Political Studies Association*
BJPIR, 2008, 10(1)

1. Role of Economic Interest Groups on National Preference Formation

The articles of this special issue offer us new insights on how economic interests influence national preferences. The article by Alexandra Hennessy examines the role of economic interests and developments in creating a single market for pension funds in 2003. Although her study focuses on national preference formation, it leaves aside the mechanisms that involve the pressure by economic interest groups. Hennessy looks at structural factors, i.e. the difference between the types of pension systems. Her article suggests that national governments can use the domestic scene to signal to others their room for manoeuvre. The role and influence of domestic economic interests is thus related to how well national governments can communicate to each other these pressures from the domestic arena. Thus, we see an interesting insight into how domestic preferences, domestic structural factors and the European outcome (European pension fund) interact.

Lucia Quaglia sheds important light on the question of how domestic economic interest groups influence national preference formation. In her case studies of Germany and the UK, she finds that the access of these groups to the national policy-making process determines importantly the way and extent to which these actors have an influence. Interest groups are more inclined to be involved in the policy-making process if the issues at stake are more short term and if they immediately speak to their interests. They are less likely to be involved when larger matters are at stake and it is unclear how exactly they will affect the interests of the economic interest group.

In the work of Andreas Bieler we learn that trade unions seek to influence national policies on Economic and Monetary Union (EMU). The study shows that trade unions in Britain and Sweden that have a predominantly domestic focus are sceptical about EMU whereas those trade unions that are transnational in nature are in favour of EMU. Furthermore Bieler's study suggests that trade unions have had greater access to government when there was a Labour (left-wing) government. Thus we find a confirmation of the more traditional view that links the unions to a Labour government.

Similarly Patrick Leblond stresses that economic interest groups get involved when there are clear matters on the table. They are less likely to be involved (or at least are not as vocal) when they are confronted with big institutional design matters; their turn comes when there are specific policy-making choices to be made which they can more clearly identify as being in their favour or not.

Although mostly focusing his analysis at the level of the EU, the study by Andreas Dür suggests that economic interests played an important role in determining national state preferences in France and Germany on an EU trade policy: exporters, importers and farmers alike sought to influence national trade policies.

In other words, we find that economic interest groups have a role to play at the national level in determining national preference formation. However this role is to be played rather when the general matters have already been settled (the nature of the policy, the institutional set-up of the EU, etc.), at which point they seek to influence the domestic politics orientation. Such an orientation could be, for instance, support or opposition to the next step of European integration (European pension fund or Economic and Monetary Union) which is being discussed or prepared at the EU level.

2. Role of Economic Interest Groups in EU Policy-Making

Although a number of the articles of this special issue focus attention on how economic interest groups seek to work on national preferences, some of them point to the way in which economic interest groups directly seek to affect EU policy-making.

Mitchell Smith's contribution looks at how economic interest groups directly affect EU policies by targeting the European Parliament committees. One reason that interest groups move to the EU level is due to the fragmented EU political system. If domestic groups are not embedded in the domestic policy networks and domestic institutional structure, they are better off focusing their attention immediately at the EU level. Likewise, the EU institutions themselves may find it useful to receive feedback immediately through interest intermediation at the EU level. Furthermore, with the increase in salience of EU institutions in the legislative process, such as the European Parliament, more interest group activity is effective when targeted at the EU level.

Likewise Patrick Leblond examines a few cases of policy failure, and focuses in particular on how business interests lobby against certain proposals. Leblond assumes that the firm (group) that lobbies the most should in principle win. He finds firms willing to wait until the process has moved up to the level of the EU and then lobby the EU institutions should the draft legislation not be in their interest. He also differentiates between interests that can be identified as lining up as national interests—in which case the lobbying will be done by interest groups at the national level, in order for governments to bargain at the EU level on the preferred legislation. If national preferences are split (for example when small and large firms want different legislation), then the economic interest groups will lobby EU institutions so as to persuade them to adopt their preferred legislation.

Finally, Andreas Dür looks at how economic interest groups affect EU trade policy. Besides concentrating on the national level, he also focuses on how European business interests have supported EU policies. He examines the role of UNICE (European employers' association) as well as for example the European Roundtable of Industrialists. Furthermore, national associations target the EU level directly. They had excellent access to decision-makers at the EU level (as well as at the national level). The Commission actively sought out the advice and opinion of market leaders, to know what their opinion was in advance of having to set its formal proposal. The result of this all is that the EU stance is in line with national and European-level business associations.

In other words, these articles find an influence of certain economic interest groups on the process of EU policy-making that resembles the mechanisms identified by the literature on lobbying. These groups know what the venue is at which they should seek to make their views known, they identify clear access points, they benefit from their expertise and seek to offer it to those contemplating various policy options and so on. We also learn that these groups do not shy away from lobbying at the national level even if the ultimate decision will be taken at the EU level.

3. The Effect of the EU on Economic Interest Groups

None of the articles of this special issue really addresses head on the effect of the EU on economic interest groups. A number of them treat the issue in passing—when they observe that an increasing number of legislative acts are clearly determined at the EU level. When they observe this fact, they increasingly reorient their attention away from the national level in favour of the EU level. Another effect of the EU on economic interest groups is through the very mechanism of European integration. The more the EU is active in setting common rules, standards, legislation and the further integrated that area of policy-making is, the more likely that economic interest groups are active at the European level (or active at the national level with a specific aim of mobilising government representatives to work towards a favourable policy-making outcome at the EU level). Various articles in this special issue point out that even though particular economic interests may be in favour of European integration in principle, they may not be necessarily in favour of the details of the proposed legislation (even if that legislation would enhance European integration). But seeing that no single article is primarily concerned with this question of how European integration affects economic interest groups, further discussion of this topic is left for the Conclusion.

4. The Role of Economic Interest Groups in the Process of European Integration

From the articles in this special issue we learn that economic interest groups have a multitude of effects on European integration. On the one hand they operate at the national level, by influencing what national governments might see as 'national state preferences'. They also directly lobby the national government in order to inform them of their interests. Economic interest groups assume national governments will negotiate at the EU level so as to create legislation that is favourable to national economic interests. On the other hand, economic interest groups may target EU institutions directly. They will do so when national interests are diverging, or when individual economic interest groups find that the draft legislation that is being negotiated at the EU level is contrary to their interests. The upshot is that these economic interest groups do have an effect on the process of European integration.

It is not true that economic interest groups always enhance the process of integration. In particular, the contribution by Leblond suggests the circumstances under which European integration is obstructed by economic interests. He suggests that when the idea of European integration is still rather vague, economic interest groups might favour the idea of enhanced European integration in a particular area (for instance software legislation or takeovers) and seek to influence the exact law that is being prepared. However, as the legislative act is made more specific, economic interest groups may more easily be able to assess the cost and benefits of that particular draft legislation and conclude it might not be in their immediate interests.

Bieler's article also sheds some light on how economic interest groups can reduce the speed with which integration may proceed. In his article we learn that national and transnational labour may have different views on the desirability of integration (in this case European monetary integration in Britain and Sweden). Domestic labour was either more cautious or against and managed to influence the perception of integration even if transnational labour was in favour of EMU. The article by Dür suggests that economic interests were fully in line with the EU negotiating positions on trade issues. His work suggests that one should be more on the lookout regarding overlaps between economic interests and progress in EU policy-making in a particular sector. Furthermore, his analysis suggests that moving trade policies from the national to the European level implied isolating the mechanisms that could have led to a more protectionist trade policy. His analysis of European trade policy is that it was in line with the demands of economic interests. He dares to suggest that they were an important push behind the development of a common trade policy, the EU position in the Kennedy and the Doha round, and thus the more liberalised policy (even if agricultural policies are not fully liberalised).

Conclusions

Based on these six articles that focus on the role of economic interests in EU policy-making, either directly (by pressuring EU-level institutions), or indirectly (putting pressure on national-level actors), one can draw some preliminary conclusions about the following core questions: (i) how do economic interest groups further the process of European integration; and (ii) what role do economic interest groups play at the national and the EU level and how do they directly influence the policy-making process? In response to the first question, we can conclude that economic interest groups do not *a priori* act in favour of European integration. Even if economic interest groups have an interest in the general process of integration and may be 'euro-enthusiasts' they need not necessarily act in favour of integration. Furthermore, there are a number of cases discussed in this special issue that show that economic interests may be at odds with one another, either within one member state (for example small vs. large firms), or across member states (different 'nationalities' have different interests; or nationally oriented groups have different interests from transnationally oriented groups). If these differences cannot be settled, the EU legislative process may be stalled and need to await better times when a larger number of economic interests can be lined up to favour the same kind of legislation.

With regard to the second question—what role do economic interest groups play at the national and at the EU level and how do they directly influence the policy-making process—we can conclude that economic interest groups seek to influence both national and EU-level actors and institutions depending on a number of factors. These factors include the assessment of the likelihood that national state preferences will be uniform (not conflicting) and hence whether the national governments will be bargaining in their favour. Some economic interest groups will target EU-level institutions if they observe that draft legislation has moved too far away from their preferences. They will also engage with EU-level institutions if the EU (in particular the Commission) is seeking to obtain information about suitable legislation in so far as technical standards are concerned.

Finally, the process of European integration affects the overall environment in which economic interest groups operate. They are no longer able to rely exclusively on the national domain for putting pressure on to secure certain legislative acts that will be in their favour. As European integration progresses, an increasing amount of legislation is made at the EU level and this legislation has a clear impact on the national level. Furthermore, economic interest groups may find that their national government may not be favourable to their needs, but that the EU level offers another policy-making arena to which they can turn to seek to secure their interests.

Almost two decades after Frieden (1991) kick-started a debate on the importance of economic interests through their distributional implications of international capital mobility, we find that in European integration economic interests indeed play an important role. However, we find that economic interest groups are not the only ones, nor even the most important ones to influence national state interests; economic interest groups are not always those which determine the outcome of the policy-making process. Governments can act in isolation from interest groups, or be influenced by others (other governments, their own political party platform, etc.). Also national governments may at times be at odds with economic interest groups. Nevertheless, we do see governments to the best of their ability actively pursuing the interests of economic interest groups. Economic interest groups seek to operate in the arena in which they deem they can be most influential or at least most successful (given the circumstances) to secure the legislation they prefer—which can be both the national and the European arenas.

Reflecting on all the articles of this special issue, economic interest groups appear to play a more prominent role in EU governance and policy-making than that which the literature on European integration theories typically has emphasised. It suggests to me that the time has come to look at EU governance more carefully from a comparative perspective in order to highlight the roles of actors in the policy-making process. Economic interest groups surely play their role in this process.

About the Author

Amy Verdun, Department of Political Science, University of Victoria, PO Box 3050, Victoria BC, Canada V8W 3P5, email: *averdun@uvic.ca*

Notes

The author wishes to thank the editors of this special issue for useful comments on an earlier draft of this article.

1. The original pluralist thought of the 1960s was criticised for insufficiently taking into consideration class and different access to power. A revised pluralist view, referred to as neo-pluralism, acknowledges these differences (see Smith 1990).

2. See the introduction to this special issue for a brief description of the articles.

Bibliography

Caporaso, J. A. (1996) 'The European Union and forms of state: Westphalian, regulatory or post-modern?', *Journal of Common Market Studies*, 34:1, 29–52.

Coen, D. (2007) 'Empirical and theoretical studies in EU lobbying', *Journal of European Public Policy*, 14:3, 333–345.

Dahl, R. A. (1961) *Who Governs: Democracy and Power in an American City* (New Haven CT: Yale University Press).

Frieden, J. (1991) 'Invested interests: The politics of national economic policies in a world of global finance', *International Organization*, 45:4, 425–451.

Grant, W. (1992) 'Models of interest intermediation and policy formation applied to an internationally comparative study of the dairy industry', *European Journal of Political Research*, 21:1–2, 53–68.

Greenwood, J. (2007) *Interest Intermediation in the European Union* (2nd edn) (Houndmills, Basingstoke: Palgrave).

Haas, E. B. (1964) *Beyond the Nation State: Functionalism and International Organization* (Stanford CA: Stanford University Press).

Hoffmann, S. (1966) 'Obstinate or obsolete? The fate of the nation-state and the case of Western-Europe', *Daedalus*, 85, 872–877.

Katzenstein, P. (1985) *Small States in World Markets* (Ithaca NY: Cornell University Press).

Kohler-Koch, B. (1994) 'Changing patterns of interest intermediation in the European Union', *Government and Opposition*, 29:2, 166–180.

Kohler-Koch, B. (1999) 'The evolution and transformation of governance in the European Union', in B. Kohler-Koch and R. Eising (eds), *The Transformation of Governance in the European Union* (London: Routledge), 14–35.

Kohler-Koch, B. (2005) 'Network governance within and beyond an enlarged European Union', in A. Verdun and O. Croci (eds), *The European Union in the Wake of Eastern Enlargement* (Manchester: Manchester University Press), 35–53.

McFarland, A. S. (2004) *Neopluralism: The Evolution of Political Process Theory* (Lawrence, KS: University of Kansas Press).

Mazey, S. and Richardson, J. J. (eds) (1993) *Lobbying in the European Community* (Oxford: Oxford University Press).

Moe, T. (1998) *The Organization of Interests: Incentives and the Internal Dynamics of Political Interest Groups* (Chicago IL: University of Chicago Press).

Moravcsik, A. (1993) 'Preferences and power in the European Community: A liberal intergovernmentalist approach', *Journal of Common Market Studies*, 31:4, 473–523.

Moravcsik, A. (1998) *The Choice for Europe: Social Purpose and State Power from Messina to Maastricht* (Ithaca NY: Cornell University Press).

Olson, M. (1965) *Logic of Collective Action: Public Goods and the Theory of Groups* (Cambridge MA: Harvard Economic Studies).

Schmitter, P. C. and Lehmbruch, G. (eds) (1979) *Trends toward Corporatist Intermediation* (London and Beverly Hills CA: Sage).

Smith, M. (1990) 'Pluralism, Reformed Pluralism and Neopluralism', *Political Studies*, 38:2, 302–322.

Smith, M. P. (2008) 'All access points are not created equal: Explaining the fate of diffuse interests in the EU', *The British Journal of Politics & International Relations*, 10:1, 65–84.

Tömmel, I. and Verdun, A. (eds) (2008) *Governance and Policy-Making in the European Union* (Boulder, CO: Lynne Rienner).

Zielonka, J. (2006) *Europe as Empire. The Nature of the Enlarged European Union* (Oxford: Oxford University Press).

© 2008 The Author. Journal compilation © 2008 Political Studies Association
BJPIR, 2008, 10(1)

Textbooks from **CQ Press**

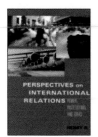

Perspectives on International Relations
Power, Institutions, and Ideas
Henry R. Nau

Provides a framework to help students recognise and evaluate the different perspectives used to make sense of international politics. Comprehensive, engagingly-written, and packed with student-friendly tools, a companion website gives students a range of opportunities to assess and improve their understanding.

978-1-933116-46-4 paperback £22.99

Spectrum of Terror
R. Hrair Dekmejian

Places terrorism within a spectrum of political violence, creating a typology of terror based on scale and intent as well as by type of actor. Informed by game theory, and with coverage of terrorist groups from around the world, the book discusses typical tactics, patterns of violence, and possible solutions for stopping the cycle of violence.

978-1-933116-90-7 paperback £20.99

Contemporary Cases in U.S. Foreign Policy
From Terrorism to Trade
Third Edition
Edited by Ralph G. Carter

15 recent real-world case studies highlight the pluralistic process and range of actors that compete to influence the way U.S. foreign policy is shaped. With introductory and background sections, timelines and a descriptive list of key actors, students are encouraged to question motives, consider alternatives, and analyse outcomes.

978-0-87289-472-3 paperback £20.99

Politics in Europe
An Introduction to the Politics of the United Kingdom, France, Germany, Italy, Sweden, Russia, Poland, and the European Union
Fourth Edition
M. Donald Hancock et al.

'...an excellent introductory textbook that combines a common analytical framework with enough room for exploring country specific topics'.
Andreas Busch, Hertford College, Oxford

978-1-933116-45-7 paperback £24.99

To receive an inspection copy or for more information, please email: smiller@cqpress.com

CQ Press
P.O. Box 317, Oxford OX2 9RU

www.cqpress.com

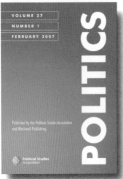

Political Studies Association

58th ANNUAL CONFERENCE
Democracy, Governance and Conflict:
Dilemmas of Theory and Practice

1-3 April 2008
Swansea University, UK

About the Conference

The 58th Annual Conference of the Political
Studies Association will be hosted by the
Department of Politics and International Relations
at Swansea University. The conference is the
largest UK gathering of researchers in politics and
international relations.

Proposals for Panels and Papers
Proposals are invited on any aspect of politics.
For details of how to submit a proposal see the
Conference website: **www.psa.ac.uk/2008**.

Inquiries should be sent to the academic convenor,
Dr Jonathan Bradbury:
j.p.bradbury@swansea.ac.uk.

The final date for the submission of proposals is
28 September 2007, but earlier submission is
strongly encouraged.

www.psa.ac.uk/2008

Political Studies Association

President
Professor Wyn Grant

Honorary Vice-Presidents
Rt. Hon Alan Beith MP
Austin Mitchell MP

Vice-Presidents
Professor Brian Barry
Professor Samuel Beer
Professor Hugh Berrington
Professor A. H. Birch
Professor Sir Bernard Crick
Professor Ian Forbes
Professor Michael Goldsmith
Professor M. M. Goldsmith
Professor J. E. S. Hayward
Professor Elizabeth Meehan
Professor Lord Norton
Professor Geraint Parry
Professor Lord Plant
Professor R. A. W. Rhodes
Professor Richard Rose
Professor Sir Maurice Shock
Professor Lord Smith

Executive Committee

Chair
Professor Jonathan Tonge
j.tonge@liv.ac.uk

Hon. Secretary
Professor Paul Carmichael
p.carmichael@ulster.ac.uk

Hon. Treasurer
Professor John Benyon
johnbenyon@scarman.freeserve.co.uk

Annual and Heads of Department Conferences
Dr Lisa Harrison
lisa.harrison@uwe.ac.uk

Awards and Prizes
Dr Thom Brooks
t.brooks@ncl.ac.uk

Awards Ceremony
Dr Sarah Childs
s.childs@bristol.ac.uk

Education and Teaching
Dr Jacqui Briggs
jbriggs@lincoln.ac.uk

External Relations
Professor Terrell Carver
t.carver@bristol.ac.uk

Graduate Network
Dr Lyndsey Harris
l.harris@ulster.ac.uk

IT and Media
Dr Lawrence Saez
l.saez@lse.ac.uk

Publications
Professor David Denver
d.denver@lancaster.ac.uk

Research and RAE
Dr Andrew Russell
andrew.russell@manchester.ac.uk

Specialist Groups and Conference Grants
Dr Joanna McKay
joanna.mckay@ntu.ac.uk

Executive Committee Member
Dr Katherine Adeney
k.adeney@sheffield.ac.uk

Editors, *Political Studies*
Professor Matthew Festenstein
mf517@york.ac.uk
Professor Martin Smith
m.j.smith@sheffield.ac.uk

Co-Editor, *Politics*
Dr Paul Graham
p.graham@socsci.gla.ac.uk

Editor, *British Journal of Politics and International Relations*
Professor Chris Pierson
chris.pierson@nottingham.ac.uk

Editor, electronic publications
Professor Richard Topf
topf@psa.ac.uk

Editor, *PSA News*
Professor Neil Collins
n.collins@ucc.ie

BISA Representative
Professor Colin McInnes
cjm@aber.ac.uk

2008 Conference Academic Convenor
Professor Jonathan Bradbury
j.p.bradbury@swansea.ac.uk

2008 Conference Local Organiser
Professor Roland Axtmann
r.axtmann@swansea.ac.uk

National Office

Executive Director
Jack Arthurs

Membership Secretary
Sandra McDonagh

Political Studies Association
Department of Politics
University of Newcastle
Newcastle upon Tyne
NE1 7RU
UK

Tel: 0191 222 8021
Fax: 0191 222 3499
e-mail: psa@ncl.ac.uk

www.psa.ac.uk

The Political Studies Association is a Registered Charity no. 1071825 and a Company limited by guarantee in England and Wales no. 3628986